PANIC-PROOF INVESTING

PANIC-PROOF INVESTING
How to Profit from the Crash of '87

Gray Emerson Cardiff

PRENTICE HALL PRESS
NEW YORK LONDON TORONTO SYDNEY TOKYO

Prentice Hall Press
Gulf+Western Building
One Gulf+Western Plaza
New York, NY 10023

Published by the Prentice Hall Trade Division

PRENTICE HALL PRESS and colophon are registered trademarks of Simon & Schuster, Inc.

Library of Congress Cataloging-in-Publication Data

Cardiff, Gray Emerson.
Panic-proof investing.

Includes index.
1. Investments—United States—Handbooks, manuals, etc. 2. Stocks—United States—Handbooks, manuals, etc. I. Title.
HG4921.C32 1987 332.6'78 87-43149
ISBN 0-13-429390-8

Manufactured in the United States of America

10 9 8 7 6 5 4 3 2 1

First Edition

For Linda with love,
admiration, and gratitude

With love to
Myles, Lindsay, and Heather

Acknowledgments

Linda Pasche-Cardiff had a lot to do with creating this book. She provided the historical research and ideas necessary to compile the historical perspective of the stock market. She also rewrote many parts and her critical review of the manuscript at various stages proved to be invaluable.

The readability of these pages can be attributed to the talents of John Raeside. This book would not be the same without John's dedication and editorial input.

I also appreciate the assistance given by the U.S. Department of Commerce; the Bureau of Mines, the U.S. Department of the Interior; the International Monetary Fund; the World Bank; the Bureau of Public Affairs, the U.S. Department of State; the U.S. Department of Agriculture; the National Association of Realtors; the National Association of Home Builders; and various librarians at the University of California at Berkeley and in the San Francisco and Contra Costa County public library systems.

Contents

Introduction

On October 29, 1929, the Dow Jones Industrial Average plunged more than thirty points during a day of feverish trading. As it did, word flashed across the country from Wall Street to Main Street—something very unusual was happening. Over the next few weeks that feeling of uneasiness persisted despite a flood of reassuring statements from the nation's newspapers and newly created radio networks. "There's nothing to worry about," the experts said. "This is just a momentary correction in a strong bull market. Prices will go up again soon." They were, of course, quite wrong.

Fifty-eight years later, almost to the day, the Dow plunged an unimaginable 508 points, lashed by a trading volume that would boggle the imagination of even the most determined doomsayers. In a matter of hours the market witnessed losses that in percentage terms far exceeded the Great Crash of 1929. Five hundred billion dollars were lost in one day—an amount larger than the gross national products of many nations. After six and a half agonizing hours the longest and most fabulous of all bull markets came to an end. Suddenly Wall Street—the avenue of dreams that for years sizzled with rumors of junk bonds, takeover attempts, and arbitrage killings as it watched the creation of millionaire traders by the hundreds—was a very subdued place.

They said it could never happen again, but it had. For more than half a century, investors had been haunted by the memory of the Crash of 1929, but they trusted their advisers when they were told that the market was immune to disaster, was operating rationally, and was grounded in rock-solid economic foundations. These investors thought their fortunes were being made the sensible way but, like their ancestors, they awoke on a cold October morning to discover that they had been riding a whirlwind.

The stock market crashes of 1929 and 1987 were harsh tonics indeed, but they each served to open the eyes of large and small investors to the fact that investing is an absorbing, exhilarating, and frequently risky game that must be played with both courage and caution. Today's investors have experienced a typhoon. And it may not be the last. They now know they are sailing through the hurricane latitudes; the eyes scanning the horizon are cautious.

And that is as it should be.

The Crash of 1987 does not need to mark the end of any individual's search for financial security. The promise of the nation's markets—whether in stocks, real estate, or precious metals—is as strong as ever. But investing does require an increased measure of character.

Today's investor must be constantly alert to the fact that a market's complexion can change dramatically, and with scant advance notice. Like the mariner who has been forced to learn all the vagaries of the weather, today's investor must know the historical forces that are always at work on markets. He must never forget that market prices always fall much more rapidly than they rise, that prices tend to break in the face of the most optimistic of circumstances, and that markets tend to operate in cycles. Sharp advances always are followed eventually by even sharper declines.

This book has been written for today's investor—sober, chastened, cautious, but determined to continue the search for financial security and independence. In the pages that follow, we will take a close look at the stock market, and at the other markets that compete with it for investment capital. We will look at many of the previous cycles of fortune and collapse that have rolled through our economic history. We will come to see that highly visible and well-remembered cycles of hope and despair, such as the stock market boom of the 1980s and the crash that so recently brought it to an end, are not rare and isolated phenomena that come to call once or twice in a century but are just unusually extreme and bald examples of forces that are at work in every market, every day. We will watch and exploit the delicate financial minuet that markets dance with one another, and we will obtain a new and sophisticated set of tools with which to chart our investment destiny.

And finally we will come to understand that no market, even in today's fully mature, interrelated, and globally responsive economy, is immune from the heady brew of human greed and fear that always drives prices too high and too low. Despite the Crash of 1987, there are big profits to be made in the stock market as well as in precious metals and real estate. This book will give you the tools you'll need to find out when these markets are about to boom and, more important, when they are about to crash. That's what panic-proof investing is all about.

STOCK MARKET CYCLES

1

The Sleepers, the Traders, and the High-techers

What if I were to tell you that in the pages of this book you can find a set of tools that would have signaled the Crash of 1987, and that would have signaled the beginning of every crash and bear market since 1950 (and every bull market)—every one, totally, reliably, without fail. Would you believe me?

If you're like most investors, the answer is no. Most investors believe they know only one thing about the stock market for sure: that it's unpredictable. And if they had any doubts on that score, the clamorous arrival of Black Monday erased them. Just look at the stock market crash, they'll say. Didn't prices break in the face of generally positive economic news? Hasn't the presence of computerized program trading produced a market that is now moving too fast to be comprehended totally? Didn't the pictures of panic-stricken traders prove that even the best and brightest of stock market experts were flummoxed totally by the Monday massacre? Clearly the market, and the economy whose pulse it tries to monitor, is too insanely complicated and is moving too fast for any formula to work reliably. Isn't it?

Absolutely not. When you finish this book you will have in your possession the tools you need to pursue secure profits in the stock market and to avoid devastating spasms like the October crash. These tools are quite different from the aphorisms and jingles that so often pass for stock market advice. Like all precision tools, they require some training to use, and must be attended to and kept in good repair. But this effort, if you make it, will separate you from most investors forever and will bring you great rewards.

If the Crash of 1987 proved anything unambiguously, it was that most investors do not arrive at financial independence through their participation in the stock market. It is not surprising that the most venerable of all pieces of advice to investors is the same as that offered to neophyte gamblers: "Don't invest more than you can afford to lose." For the fact is that most investors have about as much chance of making consistent long-term profits in the stock market as they have of winning consistently at the roulette wheels in Las Vegas or Atlantic City.

How do we know this? By looking at the market itself. American financial markets are the daily record of what most investors do. All the information is there. And while events like those that began on Black Monday strike each new generation of investors as unique and terrifying, in fact they are not unique. Even a casual look over the charts that traced the pulse of the market over the decades will show a consistent pattern in which most investors are herded into the market at its peaks and blown out at its bottoms. Not that most investors think alike. They don't. But they do fall into one of three broad categories. Let's call them "sleepers," "traders," and "high-techers."

Sleepers are in for the long term. They refuse to get excited when boom-time profits flood into their portfolios, and they refuse to panic when sharp downturns bleed those profits away. These investors are usually heavily invested in blue chip stocks and they take great comfort in the long-term upward progress over the years of the Dow Jones Industrial Average. They are not lazy; they are just firm in their belief in the long-term health of the American economy—a healthiness they are convinced will be reflected always in the prices of blue chip stocks.

Traders are the opposite of sleepers. Traders turn to the business section of their daily paper before they do anything else. They subscribe to the *Wall Street Journal* or *Investors Daily,* several business weeklies, and they never miss an episode of "Wall Street Week." They listen to the news with finely tuned ears. "Does fish oil result in longer life? Let's see who makes it and buy in." "Is there labor trouble at General Motors? Maybe it is time to short-sell or buy some puts." Traders never turn down an opportunity to pontificate on the significance of the balance of trade. They can be found in the corners at parties discussing the internal politics of the Federal Reserve Board. And most of all, they are convinced that they can keep up with the blizzard of information that the market digests each day and keep ahead of the flow. They spend hours pouring over charts to find support and resistance levels so that they can scalp the short-term swings.

High-techers have no such illusions. They have long since concluded that in the information age it is madness to rely on one individual's instincts to survive in the market—no matter how savvy that individual may be. They are convinced that the market is being taken over by computers, and they want to be sure that their portfolios are tucked away safely inside a well-programmed mainframe. These investors have put their money into mutual funds. They are comforted by the fact that their life savings are in the hands of high-tech professionals.

You probably have many friends who belong to one of these three families of investors. You are quite aware of the vast quantities of anecdotal evidence they can call on confidently to support their respective sets of judgments; however, you probably haven't heard such talk in the last few months.

The most obvious truth of investing is that a strong bull market makes everyone look good, and the bull market that came to a crashing halt during the early fall days of 1987 was one of the most magnificent ever seen by the stock market. During the five-year-long advance of the market, blue chip portfolios piled up enormous profits. So did most mutual funds. And, of course, the bull market was a trader's dream. With advancing issues outnumbering decliners by two-to-one ratios day after day, it actually required a superhuman effort to fail.

But anyone who stepped back and looked at the bull market of the 1980s in historical context could have arrived at one inescapable conclusion: It was not going to last forever. Sooner or later it was going to peak and fall. And history was clear on another point: When the crash came it was going to take most investors with it.

The bald fact is that all of the lofty rationalizations issued by sleepers, traders, and high-techers are, when looked at historically, just so much whistling in the wind. These three broad categories that include most investors are just three different approaches that add up to the same thing: blind faith.

Take the sleepers, for instance. Let's say that in 1950 an investor bought a portfolio consisting of all the blue chip stocks that make up the Dow. In November 1987, these stocks would have a value ten times higher than in 1950. But, unfortunately, in order to determine the actual value of these stocks it is necessary to take the relative value of dollars into consideration. When adjusted for inflation, the figures that emerge are not so pretty. Since 1900, even though the stock market has spent less than 20 percent of the time in severe downturns, those crashes were sufficient to reclaim most of the profits that the upward climbs had deposited. Even if the world's most dedicated sleeper bought a broadly diversified portfolio of stocks in 1900 and held onto them, at the peak of the boom in August 1987, his holdings would have increased only 4.7 percent per year. That gain is not much greater than the rate of inflation, which rose an average of 3.6 percent a year over that same period.

Did the high-techers fare better? No. It is a rare mutual fund that does as well as the market averages. (Even during the bull market from August 1982 through the end of 1986 the average fund rose 170 percent while Standard and Poor's 500 Index rose 224 percent.) What most investors fail to ascertain in the midst of all this talk about the computerized market is that most of the computerized activity is centered on the nearest of terms. Computers may help brokers deal with the quick and violent fluctuations that can occur within a market on any given day, although the huge volumes generated by the Crash of 1987 rendered them almost useless. As predictive instruments they are no better than the people who program them.

The truth is that despite the computer capacity at their fingertips, most of the managers of large pension and mutual funds are basically conservative men and women who are following their most sober judgments. These are not the kind of people who tend to defy the crowd—even though that is precisely how money is made in the stock market over the long term. And as sober and conservative as these technicians are, the programs that they write for their computers are even more sober and conservative. The programs are never subject to that rare instinct that might strike a professional money manager; that nagging feeling that this time the crowd might be wrong; that rogue hunch that despite widespread euphoria, prices may be on the verge of collapse; or that despite widespread despair, the market may have bottomed and started up again.

As we will see countless times in this book, the zone where profits are made in the stock market is the zone that lies just ahead of popular perception. Without being able to stay ahead of the crowd, the high-techers, and the computers to which they have entrusted their fortunes, never will be in the right place when the market presents its greatest opportunity for profit.

How about the traders? As a broker and investment adviser for many years, I have to say they support me and my colleagues. And we have done our best for them, too. We have looked at the same statistics, we have read the same newspapers and magazines, and we have given them the benefits of our sophisticated access to industry information and stock analysis. With our help they have won more often than they have lost. But by any long-term measure, it must be admitted that they haven't won much.

In all my years in the business, I have never met an investor who became wealthy solely through his or her efforts as a trader. Stock market traders have taken on a very absorbing and demanding hobby. Sometimes it is a profitable hobby, more often it is an expensive one. That's because in the short term the market is not predictable. As we will see, and eventually be able to measure, the market is quite reliably predictable in the long term, but anything can happen in the immediate day-to-day context that is the realm of the trader.

It doesn't require a very close look at the history of the stock market to determine that investors who make real money in the market do so by knowing when to get into the action—and when to get out. The market offers us many opportunities to make impressive profits, but what it gives, it always takes away from all but the most wary and well-prepared investor.

What would have happened if, since 1900, an investor had been able to avoid the major downturns in the market? The results are astonishing. Even if his money was earning just 4 percent annually during the days it was in the bank avoiding downturns in the market, he would have made twenty-four times more than the money made by the sleeper over the same period. Obviously the avoidance of bear markets is of paramount importance to any investor.

And that's why the tools you will soon learn to use are significant. These tools stem from a fundamental observation about the physics of the market: that it moves in broad cycles of fortune and failure. These cycles are so large, and take so long to play themselves out, that they become almost invisible to the untrained eye. They are the forest that is being hidden by the trees. I am going to call these massive market undulations "supercycles" because they operate above and beyond the more observable economic cycles that fill the pages of our newspapers and business magazines.

There have been five of these supercycles in stocks during the twentieth century. Each of them began during days of widespread economic despair as a few perceptive investors discovered that stock prices simply had been driven too low by a crashing market. As they began to buy their way back in, and as the market began to adjust to this early buying, other investors began to take notice. As the braver souls among them climbed on board, the market picked up steam. Finally the day arrived when the market was understood to be, and was formally labeled as, a bull market. At this point the herd moved in, driving prices higher and higher, and attracting more and more attention. Soon the price increases themselves began to furnish the reason for continued optimism. At this point, the market began to take leave of its underlying foundations and became ever more vulnerable to exposure. Sooner or later that exposure happened, prices collapsed, and the supercycle ended where it began in the dismal climate of dashed hopes and shattered fortunes.

Small investors were not the only ones to be affected by these collapses. Professionals have always been just as likely to underestimate the threat of imminent collapse, as the Crash of 1987 clearly demonstrated. I have been in this business long enough to know quite well the wonderful exuberance that stock market professionals feel during a bull market as strong as the one we just saw. They all knew that it would come to an end some time. They are more aware of past stock market crashes than most. Still, in their hearts they nourished an irrational confidence that somehow they would sense when the turn was about to come. In the case of many of the market's most sagacious observers this might have happened except that their hunches always will be influenced by the sheer delight of being at work during a raging bull market. They may have wondered in a quiet moment how long it would all last—they knew it couldn't last forever—but in the morning when they arrived at work to the symphony of ringing phones and excited conversation, those thoughts inevitably began to fade until it was too late. Irrational confidence turned to full-blown panic.

That's why it is so important to look beneath the noisy surface of the market, to study where history repeats itself again and again. The great bull market of the late eighties was not an unprecedented economic phenomenon. In fact, it was no different from any of the last four supercycles that rolled through the stock market since the beginning of this century. These supercycles differ only in degree, and they function in ways that are easily accessible to those investors who know where to look. Because these supercycles function so similarly, it is possible to develop reliable tools to predict their movements. These tools will serve as the barometer we will need in order to chart safely the stormy seas of today's stock market.

The tools we will use have never failed. But they are demanding. They require you to have the courage to go against the grain, to be able to buy when times are scary and all of your friends and colleagues are selling, or to sell when they are all counting their profits happily. The emotions that must be overcome in order to profit consistently from the stock market are very compelling, but with the help of the tools you will soon acquire, you should be able to chart a steady course.

This book is about how to profit from being in the stock market and how to know when to get out of it. It is also about most investors and how they are condemned to live in an informational sandstorm, bombarded by more data than they can possibly absorb—data with no context. No wonder they are finally ready to accept the same spoon-fed answers that are being given to everyone. To keep from joining them we will have to look deeper than they would ever think necessary, not into the ephemera of the economic short term, but into that wonderful and fabulously perverse machine that is the stock market of the twentieth century.

2

A Historical Perspective

Though the origin of securities trading can be traced back at least as far as ancient Greece, the American stock exchange as we know it today basically had its origins in the late 1890s. During that period, America saw most of its first modern corporations being born in a flood of mergers and acquisitions. In 1899 alone, more than twelve hundred companies were involved in consolidations, and the result of these frenzied mergers was the modern industrial conglomerate whose emergence was to be the hallmark of twentieth-century American business. Within a five-year period, Union Carbide, General Electric, United States Rubber, Westinghouse Air Brake, Borden's Condensed Milk, Electric Boat (which was to become General Dynamics), National Distillers, Standard Oil of New Jersey, Allis Chalmers, DuPont Chemical, Eastman Kodak, U.S. Gypsum, American Tobacco, and U.S. Steel came into being.[1]

On January 2, 1897, Dow Jones and Company began publishing a market measure that was made up of the prices of twelve of these active industrial stocks. Dow, along with other financial services, also began to publish financial data and analysis on a number of major U.S. corporations. The dissemination of this financial information made it possible to open up Wall Street to broad popular participation for the first time.

Charles H. Dow, one of the founders of the company and the editor of the *Wall Street Journal,* published his predictions for the twentieth century during the last years of the nineteenth:

> It is as certain as anything in the future that industrial securities will form the principal medium for speculation in this country. The field for the formation of industrial corporations is vast, and varying degrees of skill in management, coupled with the succession of good times and bad times, will make constant changes in values that will be discounted by movements in the prices of stocks.[2]

Of all the predictions that were made about life in the twentieth century, few would be as accurate as Dow's forecast. The country was entering an era of vast technological innovation and change. Each of these innovations—the automobile, the airplane, the computer, electric and then nuclear power—would result in enormous changes in the American economy, and the nation's stock exchanges were indeed to become the places where that change could be plotted. And the added factor of speculation, which Dow so correctly foresaw, was to etch the path permanently of that change into a series of bell-shaped curves that charted both the success of numerous generations of American investors and their ruin. As the century began to turn, Mr. Dow's patented industrial average began to record the first of the powerful price cycles that have dominated the stock market throughout all of this century. In 1897, as William McKinley took over the presidency, the United States saw the beginnings of what was to become its first twentieth-century supercycle.

Supercycle One

Supercycles are not created in a vacuum. Even though they are born in the gloomiest of times, they always have their roots in strong economic fundamentals. Supercycle one was no exception. In fact, those fundamentals could hardly have been stronger. McKinley's election signaled Wall Street that it could expect a continuation of the laissez-faire political atmosphere that had done so much to nourish business during the Gilded Age of the 1890s. For several years there had been only one small cloud marring a completely bright economic forecast—a shortage in the money supply necessary to continue America's unparalleled economic expansion. Since U.S. currency was entirely gold-backed, a decline in the quantity of gold in the country per capita was causing widespread worry, until news came of new gold discoveries in the Klondike and the Yukon.

With the currency question settled, almost all of the economic news was good. American industrial capacity continued to expand, exports climbed over $1 billion for the first time, topping imports by more than $286 million. Even after buying the Philippines for $20 million, and after paying all of the expenses of the Spanish-American War, the U.S. Treasury still was showing a surplus.

The bull market that all of this good news sponsored was as majestic as any that has been experienced by the market in this century. By the end of 1900, all of the market measures, including the Dow, had increased more than 40 percent over their levels in 1897. A prominent broker described the spirit of the times:

> The business of commission houses swelled beyond all precedent, and weary clerks toiled to midnight adjusting the accounts of lawyers, grocers, physicians, waiters, clergymen, and chorus singers who were learning to acquire wealth without labor. From every lip dropped stories of fortunes gained in a week by this or that lucky strike. Florists, jewelers, perfumers, restaurateurs, and modistes rejoiced in the collateral prosperity secured to them by the boom in stocks.[3]

The market roared upward without significant pause for two more years; by the end of 1902 the market averages were another 30 percent higher. And although a gradual accumulation of worried sentiment—particularly on the part of small investors—that stock prices were simply becoming too high was sufficient to cause a brief panic and skidding prices in 1903, by 1904 the market was again at new heights. This rapid recovery virtually eliminated any skepticism that had remained about the strength of the market, and the boom was on again.

The huge jump in stock prices between 1904 and 1907 was unprecedented. By the middle of 1906 the Dow had nearly doubled, reflecting not only the superheated market but the amazing performance of the American economy as well. The money supply expanded as a result of increased gold production, and while this pushed up consumer prices, no one was worried. Workers were sharing in the general prosperity, and the purchases that came from their increased wages helped keep the factories humming. Financial pages were becoming the nation's most compelling reading, with stories like the one that appeared during the summer of 1906 about how a hike in dividends on the stock of the Union Pacific Railroad from $6 to $10 had been sufficient to boost the price of the stock by a full 40 points. The boom was infectious. By the autumn of 1906 booms also were underway in markets from Berlin to Japan.

By the end of 1906, the boom had continued in force for ten years, and the effect on the prices of individual stocks was stunning: American Tobacco stood at $363, up from $51; General Electric closed the year at $159.87, (up from $10) in 1896; Union Pacific had shot up from $4 to $179.

Although it wasn't foreseen by many at the time, this first documented stock market supercycle peaked at the end of that wild ten-year ride. It didn't peak because of any strong changes in underlying economic fundamentals—in fact, American industrial production was to hit an all-time high in 1907—but because the boom had begun to fuel itself. Stock prices had come loose from those fundamentals and were adrift at far higher levels than even the rosiest economic forecasts justified. A small but growing number of cautious investors began to worry that price rises had become their own reason for further price increases and they began to hedge their bets. Some of them also may have noticed that under the blowtorch of a superheated economy, interest rates had begun a steady increase in 1906, an increase that might well interfere eventually with a booming stock market. And when they began to look at other competing markets, stock investors began to notice some interesting new investment options. The real estate market, for instance, was at the very beginning of a boom of its own.

In the first quarter of 1907, the Dow slid from 71.4 to 61.3. There was a brief rally in April and May, but it lacked the conviction that investors were used to seeing, and that was sufficient to spread doubt still further. By October, worry about the future of the bull market was widespread. At that time most of the broad market indexes, like the Standard and Poor's 500 Stock Index, had fallen by 30 percent or more. Finally, on October 21, the other shoe dropped, and a strong selling wave drove prices down further. Newspaper financial pages began to carry stories about stocks like Westinghouse, which fell from 103 to 35 in a matter of days. During the course of 1907, American Tobacco saw its stock price drop more than 45 percent, General Electric dropped 31 percent, U.S. Steel by 50 percent, American Woolen by 80 percent, and U.S. Rubber by a full 70 percent.

Stock market analysts labeled the entire catastrophe the "panic of 1907." What the long dark year of 1907 had been was not a panic but the overture to the long decline of supercycle one. After a brief recovery to peak levels at the end of 1909, prices zigzagged ruthlessly downward for more than eleven years. The only reason that this long decline was not even more precipitous was because it was countered by the boost given to many of the nation's largest industrial corporations by our entry into World War I. The Dow Jones Industrial Average showed a new peak in 1916—an indication of how much the war benefited the twelve large industrial corporations that the Dow was measuring at that time—and after the number of stocks the Dow tracked was expanded to twenty, the adjusted measure showed another new record in 1919. Significantly, however, broader measures like the Standard and Poor's 500 showed no such gain and, in fact, continued to meander downward despite the boost given to the economy by the war.

By the end of 1919, not even the Dow Jones industrial stocks could resist the general downtrend in the stock market. In 1920, stock prices were in a virtual free-fall, signaling the approaching end of the supercycle. The Dow, which had peaked at 118 in late 1919, had plunged to 64 by the middle of 1921. The S&P 500, which in 1919 already had fallen from its peak by 23 percent, had dropped another 18 percent by the middle of 1921. U.S. Steel and Union Pacific both watched their stock prices fall by 30 percent, and they were lucky. General Motors was down more than 70 percent, Crucible Steel by 75 percent, and American Woolen by 66 percent.

Exacerbating the crash in its final stages were the actions of the fledgling Federal Reserve Bank that had been created in 1914. Frightened by the rapid escalation in wholesale prices that the nation had seen in the years following the war (wholesale prices doubled between 1915 and 1920), the Federal Reserve decided to raise the discount rate (the interest rate at which banks borrow money from the government). This raise in the discount rate had a much stronger effect than the board expected, and inflation reversed into deflation. When the discount rate was lowered in 1921, the action was sufficient to end the crash in the stock market.

So ended the first supercycle. It was a classic specimen. It had started in a burst of justified optimism, peaked in the face of news that seemed equally positive, continued its crash despite the stimulating intrusion of the war in Europe, and ended when millions of investors had convinced themselves justifiably that the market would never recover. As measured by broad market indicators like the S&P 500, stock prices plunged more than 40 percent from their peak (chart 2.1A), but even this underestimated the extent of the loss. Though the supercycle had begun during those calm, gold standard days when inflation was not a factor, wholesale price increases had entered the picture in a very big way before the supercycle ended. When the value of money itself was factored into the equation, the damage was multiplied further. In real terms, an investor who remained in the stock market after its peak in 1906 would have seen his investment decline in value by more than 65 percent (chart 2.1B).

When supercycle one ended, it would have been difficult to imagine another boom in stock prices. The long decline in stocks meant that a whole generation had come of age since the last boom swept through the stock market. This generation was not looking to make money in stocks. But that was exactly what they were about to be offered the chance to do. Supercycle two was about to begin, and it was due to become a boom/bust cycle that no one would ever forget.

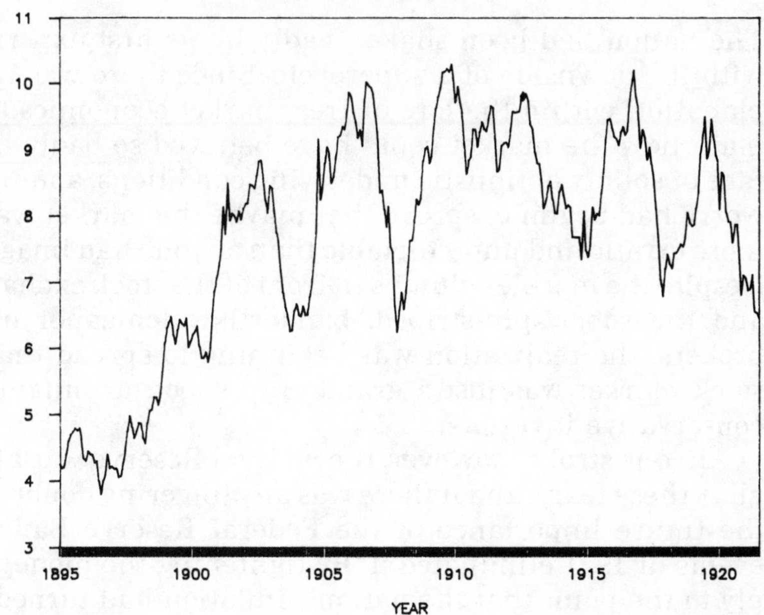

Chart 2.1A. Supercycle One

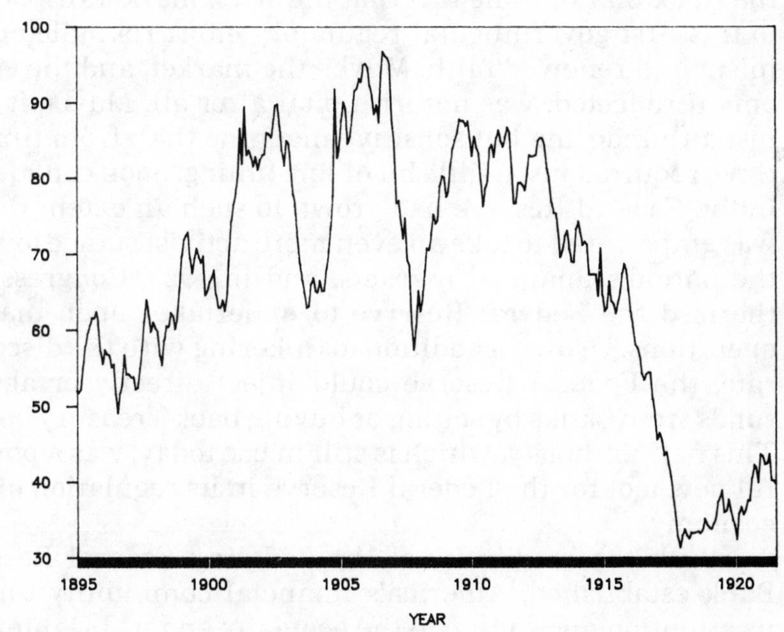

Chart 2.1B. Supercycle One Adjusted for Inflation

Supercycle Two

The nation had been shaken badly by its first experience with the downside of a supercycle. Since there was no explanation within the lore of free market economics to explain how the market could have behaved so badly in the face of solidly optimistic underlying conditions, a numbing worry had begun to spread that maybe the market was far more erratic and unpredictable than anyone had imagined. Despite the marble columns in front of the stock exchanges, and the sober, pin-striped, bankerlike demeanor of the brokers, the realization was beginning to spread that the stock market was just a grand crap shoot, unsuitable for conservative investors.

In one stroke, however, the Federal Reserve was able to allay these fears, and if there was any lingering doubt about the future importance of the Federal Reserve Bank, the events of 1921 eliminated it. By tightening the money supply to the point that the nation's inflation had turned into deflation, and then loosening it, the Federal Reserve's Board of Governors immediately reversed the downward skid of the stock market. The fact that the stock market responded to this first governmental regulatory effort rekindled optimism and renewed faith. Maybe the market, and the economy it reflected, was not irrational after all. Maybe it was just a thundering but sensitive machine that, from time to time, required just a little bit of fine tuning. Soon confidence in the Federal Reserve had grown to such an extent that it was empowered to take an even more activist stance toward the nation's financial markets, and in 1923, Congress authorized the Federal Reserve to undertake "open market operations." Now, in addition to tinkering with the discount rate, the Federal Reserve could inject directly or absorb funds from banks by selling or buying back Treasury bonds. This new authority, which is still in use today, was a powerful new tool for the Federal Reserve in its regulation of the economy.

With the credibility of the fledgling Federal Reserve Bank established, America's financial community turned its attention once again to the economy and its brightening prospects. The recently concluded depression had cleared out inventories, and factories were booming to make up lost ground. By 1923, industrial production was up more than 50 percent, personal income was up 20 percent, and inflation was dormant at less than 1 percent. At the same time, the war-ravaged European continent, its industrial base largely destroyed, had become a huge new market for American goods. The United States quickly established a strong, positive balance of trade that was to last through the whole decade.

As new demands were placed on American industrial capacity, it responded with forays into the development of new technologies. Factory after factory was electrified and automated, resulting in huge leaps in productivity even in the absence of massive capital outlays. Another merger wave, although much more modest than the one that had swept through the nation at the turn of the century, was sufficient to bring about increased industrial efficiency and higher corporate profits. In 1924, Henry Ford produced his ten-millionth automobile, and that Model T was heralded widely as the emblem of the new age of prosperity. The election of another laissez-faire Republican, Calvin Coolidge, was expected to favor economic progress. American business had never had it so good.

The effect of all this concentrated good fortune on the stock market was dramatic. Even the most pessimistic of investors had to admit that the nation clearly was entering a new era of prosperity. Soon the great pools of capital that had been lying since the depression in more conservative investment niches like the bond market were lured back into stocks. By the end of 1924, the Dow had reached the region of all-time highs, having advanced 86 percent since the low that had been registered in mid-1921. Even the broader Standard and Poor's 500 Stock Index was up more than 60 percent; it began to hit record highs in January of 1925. Supercycle two was underway with a vengeance.

Meanwhile, market managers were finding new ways to accommodate the multitude of small investors that was eager to crowd into the action. The newest invention was something called a "financial trust." These trusts were later to evolve into what we know today as mutual funds, and like today's version, they allowed small investors to buy into a professionally managed stock fund at a fairly low fee. As a result of all of these developments, trading volumes on the nation's stock exchanges began to skyrocket. In 1925, the volume of daily trading on the New York Stock Exchange averaged 1.7 million shares—more than double the volume that had been seen only two years before. For the remainder of the decade, there would never be a trading day when the volume would not reach at least 1 million shares. As the volume continued to grow, so did the profits made by investors.

When the course of supercycle two is charted, 1926 represents a sort of base camp before the towering peak that lay ahead. Although the S&P 500 was to eventually score a modest gain of 8 percent by the end of the year, it was not without some turbulence. Stocks fell in March and April, recovered over the course of the summer, but declined again in October. The October dip was largely the result of events that were taking place far from Wall Street. For several years, Florida had been involved in a sizzling land boom. Largely based on razor-thin credit margins, the boom already was in the early stages of collapse when a substantial part of the state was hit with a devastating hurricane. The Florida real estate market collapsed, huge fortunes disappeared overnight, and ripples of worry swept through the economy.

As it turned out, however, Wall Streeters had no reason to be concerned. Real estate and stocks compete with each other for available capital, and, although it was seen as just another sign of the general good fortune that was embracing the nation, the Florida land boom had, in fact, been draining money from the stock market. With the Florida land boom at an end, and with investor confidence in real estate momentarily shaken, investment capital continued to shift toward Wall Street.

It was a well-fed bull market that trotted into 1927; the Coolidge administration's loose monetary policy was forcing interest rates down and the money supply up. Meanwhile, optimism throughout the country was as high as the daring new hemlines of the flapper era. Nowhere would that optimism be better symbolized than by Charles Lindbergh's historic solo flight across the Atlantic. The strong reaction to Lindbergh's success affected not only the price of the stock of Wright Aeronautical—the builder of the Spirit of St. Louis, which soared from $25 to $245—but stocks across the ticker. By year's end the Dow had closed at 194, up a solid 25 percent.

When Herbert Hoover won the election of 1928, a euphoric market reacted strongly. By the end of the year, the

Dow jumped yet another 50 percent, topping 300. The S&P 500 followed suit, climbing 30 percent. By now, trading volumes routinely were topping 6 million shares a day, exceeding the capacity of the ticker to such an extent that it was not at all unusual to find the tape running more than two hours behind the action on the floor.

As the Dow pushed on further and further into uncharted territory, some market professionals began to get a bit nervous. Both Joseph Kennedy and Bernard Baruch, for instance, were beginning to pull out of the stock market. They may have been frightened when the Federal Reserve made its first real attempt to cool things off by hiking the discount rate—an action the Fed took three times in 1928—or maybe they had noticed that while all eyes were on Wall Street, the American economy at large was softening appreciably. But most probably they were simply worried about the extent to which speculation was running rampant in the market. To Baruch, gold mines in Alaska had become a much less risky investment than stocks.

In 1929, it seemed as if the boom would go on forever; in the frenzy a shortage of stocks had surfaced. The June issue of *American* stated: "The economic condition of the world seems on the verge of a great leap forward."[4] On Tuesday, September 3, 1929, the Dow closed at 381.17. Adjusted for stock splits and dividends, Radio Corporation of America had risen from $26 a share to $505 since 1923, U.S. Steel from $85 to $366, General Electric from $168 to $1,612, General Motors from $51 to $1,075, and DuPont from $106 to $1,617. The average price/earnings ratio of stocks was more than 20, which was high in relation to the early twenties, but it still seemed modest in view of the surge in corporate earnings that "the great leap forward" could be expected to produce.

As the ticker tape stopped that day, an introspective trader could have mused contentedly about the spiral of fortune that seemed firmly in place. As stocks went up they provided more and more profits to invest in stocks, forcing prices up further. More stocks were owned by more people than ever before, and there was every reason to be enthusiastic. There were few investors who had even the slightest glimpse of the dark future that lay ahead, but as the trading floor quieted that early September afternoon, Wall Street had seen the end of the stock market boom of the roaring twenties.

For the next two months a series of air pockets sent the market noticeably lower. On Tuesday morning, October 29, 1929, the *New York Times* observed blithely that "the investor who purchases securities at this time with the discrimination that, as always, is a condition of prudent investing may do so with utmost confidence."[5] This day would become known as Black Tuesday. The volume that day soared to over 16.4 million shares and the Dow plunged 30.5 points —the equivalent of a drop of 216 points from a Dow level of 2700.

The next day the market rallied and the rise enticed bottom guessers. John D. Rockefeller announced that "my son and I have for some days been purchasing sound common stocks." In early November the *Wall Street Journal* wrote "The sun is shining again, and we will go on record as saying some good stocks are cheap. We say (this) because John D. Rockefeller said it first. Only the foolish will combat John D.'s judgment." On November 3, the Rockefellers bought 1 million shares of their key holding, Standard Oil of New Jersey. But by the end of 1930 this stock declined from its high of 83 down to 3.[6]

The stock market continued to crash through the middle of 1932. The Dow Jones Average collapsed from its peak of 381.17 and finally bottomed July 8, 1932, at 41.22. The S&P 500 dropped 85 percent (chart 2.2A). U.S. Steel dropped from its peak of $262 a share to $22, Radio from $505 to $18, General Electric from $396 to $28, General Motors from $182 to $8, Westinghouse from $313 to $16, and Montgomery Ward from $467 to $4 a share.[7]

The deflation that accompanied the crash made the dollar more valuable and that softened the blow somewhat, but the decline was so steep that it made little difference. Adjusted for deflation, the S&P 500 still fell 75 percent (chart 2.2B).

Supercycle Three

From our modern perspective the years between the Great Crash of 1929 and the beginning of World War II seem like one long panorama of hardship and unemployment—and

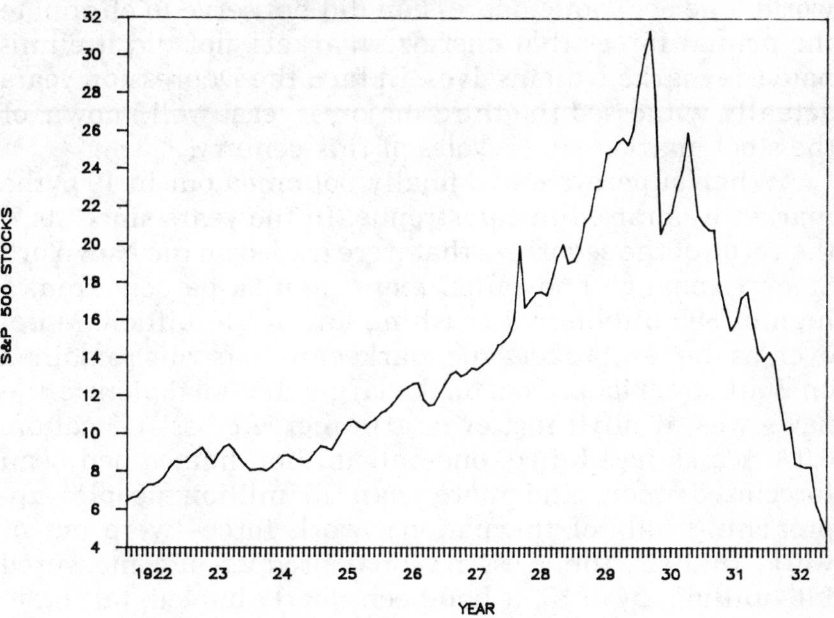
Chart 2.2A. Supercycle Two
S&P 500 STOCKS
32
30
28
26
24
22
20
18
16
14
12
10
8
6
4
1922
23
24
25
26
27
28
29
30
31
32
YEAR

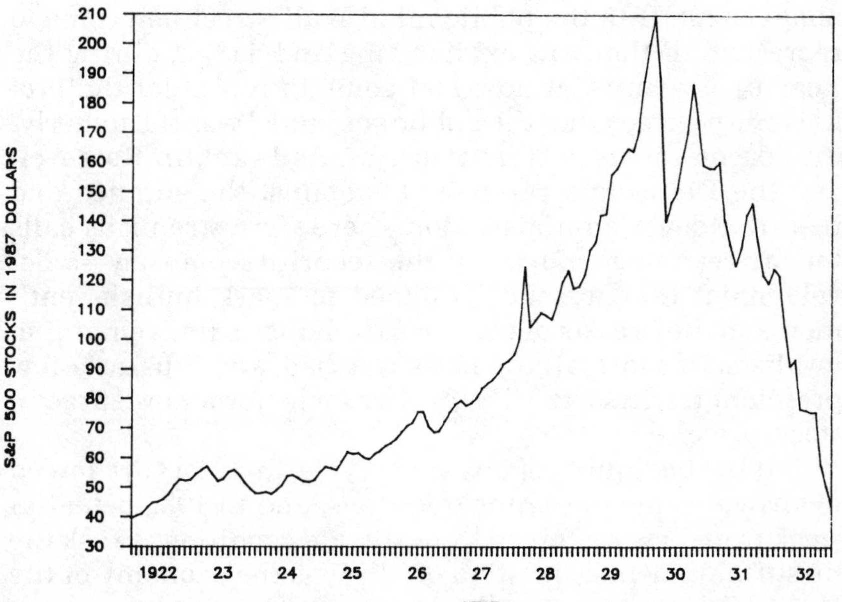
Chart 2.2B. Supercycle Two Adjusted for Inflation
S&P 500 STOCKS IN 1987 DOLLARS
210
200
190
180
170
160
150
140
130
120
110
100
90
80
70
60
50
40
30
1922
23
24
25
26
27
28
29
30
31
32
YEAR

for most Americans it was. But the existence of a brutal worldwide economic depression did not serve to eliminate the primal forces that energize markets, nor did it eliminate the markets themselves. In fact, the Depression years actually witnessed the third major, if least well known, of the stock market supercycles of this century.

When supercycle two finally bottomed out in 1932 the market was mired in catastrophe. In the years since 1929, the value of the securities that were traded on the New York Stock Exchange had fallen more than 84 percent from a high of $90 billion to a crushing low of $16 billion. Moreover, as the few brokers and market analysts who remained on Wall Street looked out on the larger financial picture, the news was, if anything, even grimmer. Across the nation, 6,000 banks had failed, one-half million homes had been foreclosed upon, and more than 15 million people—approaching half of the nation's work force—were out of work. In 1929, the gross national product had measured $104 billion; by 1933, it had been nearly halved, falling to $56 billion.

Also contributing to the gloomy picture was the fact that investor confidence in the stock market virtually was nonexistent. If in the public mind Wall Street had come to represent all that was exhilarating and daring during the Roaring Twenties, it now had come to represent the profligacy and greed that the public suspected was the underlying reason for its current miseries. As Franklin Roosevelt and the Democrats campaigned against the stunned and reeling Hoover administration, there were strenuous calls for far-reaching reforms of the securities industry—a development that was not designed to spark bullish sentiments in the breasts of the stock exchange's few remaining loyalists. In short, all the news was bad, and thus, as a few prescient traders saw, the time was ripe for a new surge in stock prices.

At the beginning of any supercycle, investors are forced to answer some searching questions, and in 1932 potential stock traders were forced by desperate conditions to ask the most fundamental question of all: Was the economy of the United States about to collapse entirely? If it was, then even the current prices of severely battered stocks were obviously still too high. But if the economy was strong enough to survive, then the value of America's industrial securities had fallen far below their intrinsic value and had become bargains.

The most important balm for soothing the nerves of America's economists and investors was more social and political than strictly economic: the landslide election of Franklin Roosevelt. Despite the good measure of fear and distaste felt by Wall Streeters for some of the New Deal's more far-reaching economic theories, everyone had to admit that the White House once again was assuming an aggressive leadership role in the economy, and its actions finally were introducing hope back onto the national scene. This was enough to convince those few far-sighted investors, who are the vanguard of every supercycle, that the economy of the United States was not going to collapse and that stocks were at price levels that represented a definite bargain. As they bought into it, the market began a rally that coincided with the early days of the New Deal, which in turn seemed to ratify the effectiveness of the whirlwind of economic interventions that Roosevelt's brain trusters were throwing at the economy.

And indeed, the New Deal's economic stimulations did seem to be working. Almost miraculously after years of deflation, the gross national product stopped its downward drift and, in 1933, actually scored a modest gain while corporate profits began what was to become a meteoric rise—from $200 million in 1933 to $5.7 billion in 1936. By the middle of 1933, the bull market on Wall Street had lifted prices more than 135 percent from their bottom in 1932.

Despite rising stock prices and skyrocketing corporate profits, the Depression was proving to be very intractable and unemployment was still at record levels. This, coupled with uneasiness over the effect of the new federal regulations, led to a brief stagnation of the market. By the autumn of 1934, prices had settled back nearly 22 percent, but the supercycle was underway, and the fundamental conditions that were fueling it were far too strong to be diverted.

By the end of 1934, the market had again turned strongly bullish, and the trend continued into 1935. By the end of that year most stocks were reporting sizable gains: American Express had gone from $114 to $175; AT&T from $50 to $155; General Motors from $22 to $56; U.S. Steel from

$9 to $49; and RCA from $6 to $12. The Standard and Poor's 500 Index hit 13.04 in December of 1935, up a healthy 47 percent since the 1934 respite.

Although there was a slight pause in the market's momentum as Wall Streeters joined the rest of the nation in watching the outcome of the 1936 presidential election, the mood in the offices that surrounded the exchanges remained buoyant. For the first time since 1929, firms actually were beginning to train new brokers as demand for stocks grew.

With Roosevelt's reelection, the New Deal brain trust began to evaluate the state of the economy. Determining that there was a good deal of latent strength there, the government cautiously lifted some of the restrictions that had been placed on industrial production. The economy responded sharply, and by year's end, the GNP had reached $482 billion—up 46 percent in just three years. This new industrial vitality was immediately echoed on Wall Street. At the end of 1936, the S&P 500 had grown another 30 percent, while the Dow topped 184—way up from its low of 41 in 1932. Although the memory of the Great Crash had not faded from minds of small investors, these gains were difficult for even the most cynical to ignore, and as they bought back into the action the result was a more broadly based market than had been seen since the twenties.

The peak came in a fury of trading that again saw daily volumes topping the 1-million share level. The S&P 500 peaked at 18.11 and the Dow hit 194.40. Ironically the peak came just as *Fortune* came out with an article announcing that the market valuation of all of the stocks listed on the New York Stock Exchange had risen from $19.7 billion to $62.5 billion. It would be years before these figures would be reached again.

By the middle of 1937, the stock market had begun to plunge, and by October 1937, vanguard investors obviously were convinced that stock prices had gone too high. As they pulled back, the worst stock market panic of the Roosevelt years began. Before it was over, General Motors was to fall from $70 to $30, U.S. Steel from $126 to $48, AT&T from $187 to $144. On Monday, October 18, the trading volume topped 7 million shares.

Declines continued through the end of the year as the Dow fell to 113.64, and the skirmishes between Wall Street and Washington intensified. Investors blamed the New Dealers for sparking the crash by overrestrictive regulation. Federal regulators were having none of it and charged that the decline was just another instance of the securities industry failing to police itself adequately, particularly in terms of overly liberal margin requirements that they felt had allowed speculation to superheat the market. The government reacted by raising the margin requirement and forcing investors to put 50 percent down on their securities purchases. This might have been a wise move earlier in the supercycle, but in the face of plunging prices, the new regulations had the obvious effect of driving potential investors out of the market and accelerating the decline further.

Faced with a plunging stock market and signs of distress elsewhere in the economy, Roosevelt backed away from his flirtation with budget balancing and returned to using deficit spending to try to restimulate things. But it was far too late for Wall Street. The market was now deeply into a skid that would last for the remainder of the decade. The investor confidence that had been restored by the upside of the supercycle was quickly vanishing.

The market continued to drift downward throughout 1938 and 1939, ignoring factors that should have been optimistic. In 1939, for instance, the city of New York unveiled its long-anticipated World's Fair, celebrating substantial new technological achievements and such milestones as the beginning of scheduled transatlantic passenger air service. What the new air travelers found when they arrived in Europe, of course, was a continent that was rapidly gearing up for war. In the United States war industries rose in expectation of all-out war, and corporate profits began to increase.

Upon news of the German invasion of Poland, the stock market was flooded with buy orders, but the uptick was very brief. The downtrending supercycle was proving immune to almost any outside data, even data that seemed to indicate that the economy finally was recovering from what always would be remembered as the Great Depression. In April 1942, the Standard and Poor's Index finally bottomed at 7.84 (charts 2.3A and 2.4B), and the Dow sank to 92.92—both measures down more than 50 percent from their respective 1937 peaks. Again a supercycle had swept through the market, leaving a wake of confusion and destruction in its wake.

Chart 2.3A. Supercycle Three

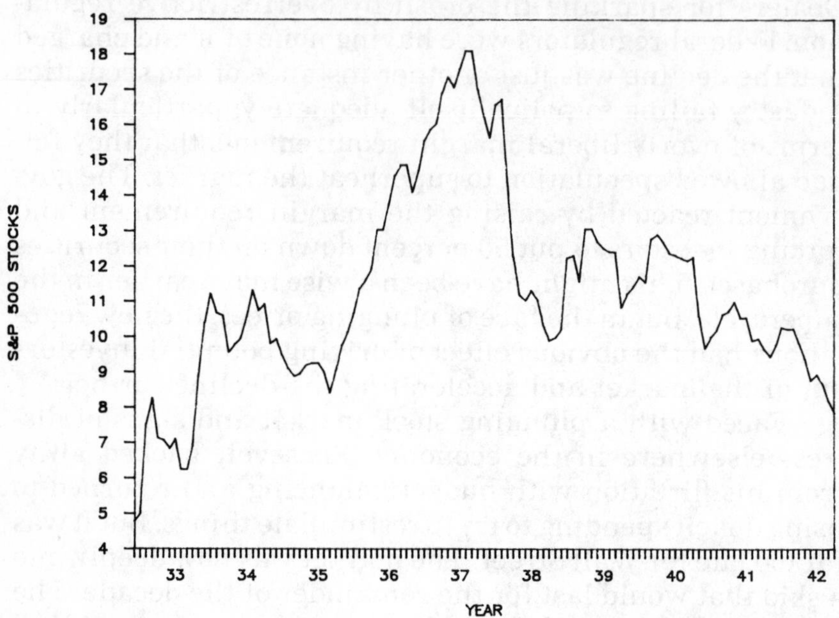

Chart 2.3B. Supercycle Three Adjusted for Inflation

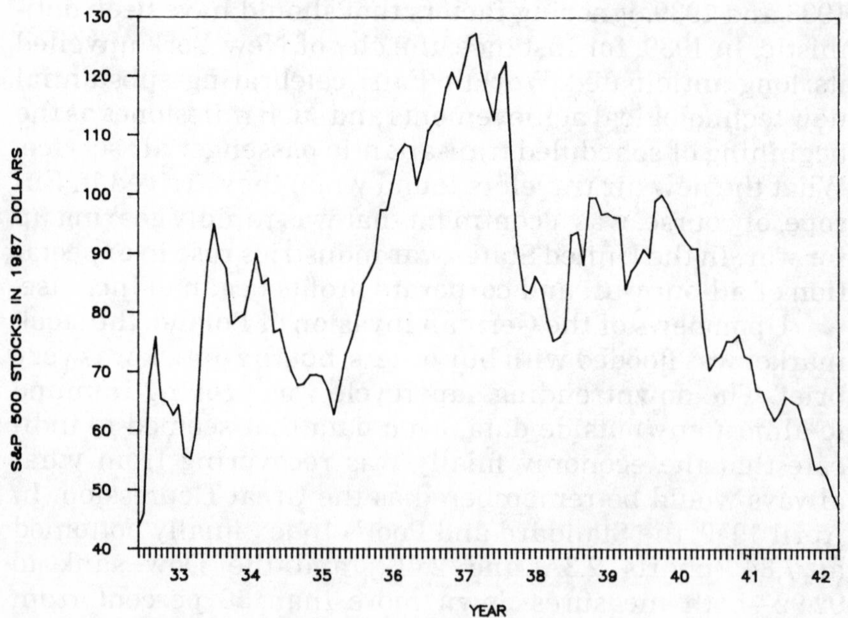

Supercycle Four

War worries kept the stock market on ice in the long months that led up to the nation's first real victory in World War II but with the Pacific victories at Midway and Guadacanal in 1942, confidence began to grow once again. By D-day, June 6, 1944, stock prices had risen sharply, as had trading volumes, and the S&P 500 Index was up more than 60 percent from its 1942 low. And if the anticipation of peace had a salubrious effect on stock prices, its arrival was even better. In January 1946, the Dow crossed the 195 barrier (the 1937 peak), and it crossed the 200 mark by midyear.

Despite this growing confidence, the economy was sailing through some very treacherous waters. In the latter years of the 1940s, the United States was trying to adjust quickly to the rapid demobilization of its massive war machine, even as the country took its place as the preeminent economic power of the postwar world. The almost inevitable result of these sweeping changes, and the superheated economy they sparked, was a phenomenon that most Depression-reared Americans never had seen before: inflation. Consumer prices rocketed more than 30 percent in 1946 and 1947. Indeed the prices that were being recorded at the beginning of 1948 were twice the level they had been at the beginning of the decade. And then the nation had a whiff of deflation going into 1949.

Reacting cautiously to these unprecedented economic developments, investors took a wait-and-see attitude, and supercycle four took its first breather. Through the middle of 1949, the Dow oscillated between 160 and 190. Then in the middle of 1949, after it was becoming apparent that the economy had survived its brush with deflation, investors began to conclude that there would be no new Depression, and the supercycle resumed its climb.

In 1952, General Dwight D. Eisenhower was elected president of the United States. He was to be at the helm during the greatest period of prosperity the nation had ever seen. As if anticipating this rosy future, the Dow reached nearly 300 by the end of 1952, while the S&P 500 advanced to more than 26.

The end of the Korean conflict signaled another demobilization period in the economy, but even more important it signaled the end of all wartime economic controls. When, for good measure, the Eisenhower administration also threw in a tax cut, the economy reached a rolling boil. The nation's corporations spent millions expanding their facilities to meet the growing demand, and the Federal Reserve accommodated this industrial expansion by increasing the money supply.

The strong bull market carried prices up sharply through 1956, pushing the Dow through the 500 level, while the stock exchanges struggled mightily to keep up with the increasing demand. By now, stock market trading had become so commonplace on main street that even the radio columnist Walter Winchell had taken to giving stock tips on his evening broadcasts.

Two of Winchell's more notable stock picks were Eastern Airlines and Bell Aircraft. This was not the last time that investors were well advised to buy aircraft and high-technology stocks. In October 1957, the United States awoke to find Sputnik, a new artificial moon launched by the Soviets, beeping its way through orbit. As soon as the shock wore off, investors began picking up strong signals from Washington that the space race was on. This led to a strong boom in technology stocks, which in turn led to a further acceleration of the bull market. By 1959, with the Dow approaching the 700 mark, the joke on Wall Street was that not only had the future been anticipated by the surging prices but the hereafter as well. Boom mania was afire throughout the land, but the supercycle was far from over.

The early sixties saw the growing domination of the nation's stock exchanges by large institutional investors—banks, mutual funds, corporate and union pension funds, and investment trusts. The coffers of these large institutions were swollen by more than a decade of prosperity, and they began to accumulate enormous portfolios of stocks. The presence of these huge institutions gave investors a sense of safety. Surely with the vast capital pools contributed by these institutions acting as its foundation, the stock market must be invincible!

Mutual fund sales soared ahead, reaching a record of $813.1 million in the fourth quarter of 1962—twice the level of the same quarter only five years before. The market suffered through several down-shocks sparked by unexpected news in the early sixties and always bounced back. Even the most dramatic shock, the assassination of President

Kennedy, set back the market only momentarily. As the news of the Dallas shooting broke, the market plunged 24 points, but by the end of the next trading day the Dow was up 32 points.

Fueled in part by the expanding war effort in Southeast Asia, the business cycle within the economy continued to expand well into 1966, and another bull market continued with it. Before the end of the year the Dow was flirting with the magic 1000 level, but 1967 was filled with bad news. As the Vietnam War intensified, it also continued to grow more expensive. Finally, to fund it, along with the wide range of Great Society social programs he had instituted, Lyndon Johnson was forced to ask for a surcharge on individual and corporate income taxes. Meanwhile, as the gout of government spending continued, inflation rates and interest rates began to rise.

The stock market declined into 1967 with the Dow eventually hitting a low of 786, but the boom still had life. As stock prices began to rise again, reassured investors piled back into the market by the millions. The beginning of this supercycle was by now so far gone in the mists of time that it had become almost impossible to remember when stocks were not a nearly riskless path to prosperity.

It was the "go-go" era on the nation's stock exchanges, and young stockbrokers began to flock into the nation's brokerage houses to help deal with the astonishing level of demand for stocks. The number of registered representatives working within the brokerage industry doubled between 1965 and 1968, and unfortunately, many of them were too inexperienced to keep up with the amount of paperwork for which they were responsible. Finally the level of chaos reached the point where the exchanges were forced to close on Wednesday to catch up with accumulated paperwork, and brokerage houses were strictly forbidden from advertising for new business or from opening any new offices.

It made little difference. Stock prices rose steadily throughout 1968, despite more bad news than any market could be expected to absorb in one year: The Tet offensive in Vietnam showed the endless futility of the Vietnam War; assassins took the lives of Martin Luther King and Robert Kennedy; Lyndon Johnson was forced out of office by the rising tide of antiwar sentiment in the country; race riots continued in major U.S. cities throughout the summer; the cost of living was increasing. Still the market climbed. By December, the S&P 500 Index had reached a new high of 106.5 while the Dow was again near the 1000 mark.

At the end of 1968, boom fever was raging through the stock market. The supercycle was now almost a quarter century old and the growth of the economy was so large it was almost incomprehensible. The supercycle had increased the value of a share of IBM stock from $.25 to $75; Texas Instruments had gone from under $2 to over $72 a share. Other gains were equally dramatic: Sears and Roebuck from $2 to $77, National Cash Register from $1.50 to $77, Eastman Kodak from $1.50 to $58, Eastern Airlines from $2 to $62. Polaroid had rocketed from $.07 to more than $133 a share; Xerox from $.04 to $109. Even utilities like American Electric Power had climbed from $2 to $48 a share.*

It was a heady time, and if there were people who were looking hard at disturbing signs such as the price/earnings ratio (as measured by the S&P 500) which had climbed over the years from less than seven in 1950 to more than eighteen in 1968, they weren't making much noise. Most investors greeted 1969 with the confident expectation that stocks would crash through the 1000 level and move on to new heights.

They didn't. By January 20, 1969, the Dow had fallen to 920 and by the end of the year to 770. The final blow to the upward trend of the twenty-six-year-old supercycle had come. Faced with resurgent inflation throughout the economy—inflation that was far outdistancing the 2 or 3 percent rates that had been the maximum the country had seen since the early forties—the Federal Reserve took action by raising the discount rate to banks. Soon the prime rate charged by the nation's largest banks had reached the previously unheard of level of nearly 9 percent. In May 1970, the Dow fell to 631—the same place it had been on the day John Kennedy took the oath of office in 1961. Mutual fund sales had fallen to half of their 1960 levels, and many brokerage firms began to fail.

For a while it looked as though a decline in interest

*All stock prices in supercycles four and five have been adjusted for stock splits and stock dividends through 1986.

rates during the recession in 1970 had served to put the market back on its long upward climb. It appeared that the Dow finally might penetrate the long-sought 1000-point barrier late in 1972, and the S&P 500 moved over 118 in early 1973. But a closer look at the dynamics of the market showed that this apparent good health was largely illusory.

Although it was not widely noticed, the entrance of large institutional investors into the stock market in the sixties had made some real changes in the ability of large market measures like the Dow Jones Averages and even the S&P 500 Index to reflect accurately the actual movement of the market as a whole. Since institutional stock portfolios were managed by professional money managers whose primary fiduciary responsibility was to be sure the fund would not suffer catastrophic losses, those managers tended to invest heavily in well-capitalized blue chip stocks—the very blue chips whose prices made up the Dow and a major part of S&P 500 Index. Under this investment pressure, many of these stocks, particularly the so-called "Nifty Fifty," recovered quite nicely for a brief time in the early seventies. The Nifty Fifty included Eastman Kodak, which rose to $101 in 1973—$43 a share higher than its 1968 peak; Sears, which rose to $120; and Xerox, Polaroid, and IBM, which all rose to new highs.

But most stocks never came close to returning to their 1968 peaks. Eastern Airlines, for example, managed to reach only $32 by the end of 1973, far under its 1968 peak of $62. General Motors, after seeing its price rise from $4 to $114 in 1968, could only manage $85 in 1973. Control Data closed the year at $40, down $42 from its 1968 peak, and Litton only managed a $27 close, down from $127 at its 1968 peak. And with the renewed inflation of the early 1970s factored in, even most of the Dow stocks were under their peaks.

That inflation, fought futilely by the Nixon administration through a series of wage and price controls, and lashed still higher by an Arab oil boycott, finally reached double-digit levels and the Federal Reserve had no choice but to fight back. When it did, interest rates shot upward.

The Dow fell steadily in 1973, dropping from a high of 1052 in January to a low of 788 in December. Despite a prime rate that topped 12 percent, inflation continued to roar ahead throughout 1974, advancing more than 15 percent. By December 6, 1974, the Dow had sunk to 578—the level at which it closed back in 1959. The S&P 500 fell to 67 which, in real terms, wiped out all of the gains scored since 1954 (charts 2.4A and 2.4B). By the end of that dismal year, Polaroid had plunged from its peak of $150 to $14, Control Data from $82 to $5, Litton from $127 to $3, and American Power from $48 to $14. Eastman Kodak fell to $38 in 1974, Texas Instruments to $40, Xerox to $49, and IBM to $38, all down more than 50 percent from their peaks.

At the end of 1974, there was no sign of the trading frenzy that had once gripped Wall Street, and the supercycle ended with many stockbrokers driving taxicabs or standing in unemployment lines.

Supercycle Five

Supercycles, as we have seen, always start out in an atmosphere that is distinctly gloomy, but the Wall Street landscape at the beginning of supercycle five approached total ruin. The exchanges continued to function, and stock market quotations continued to flash onto TV screens during the evening news, but the nation had a new glamor market: real estate. With inflation still out of control, and with stock prices lying quiescently in the pits, real estate markets from coast to coast began to soak up huge amounts of capital. And even beyond real estate's reputation as a dependable inflation hedge, there was the fact that the special tax breaks offered by real estate investment grew more and more valuable as inflation pushed investors' incomes into higher tax brackets.

As housing prices took off, so did a number of stockbrokers, leaving their firms to get real estate or insurance brokerage licenses. The large stock brokerage houses they left behind tried to survive by diversifying their offerings to the public. They also moved to tap into the real estate juggernaut by offering real estate partnerships and real estate investment trusts. But as stockbrokers' faces and lunch breaks grew longer, supercycle five was picking up steam, almost imperceptibly at first, but steadily.

The fact was that stocks were dirt cheap—and not just

Chart 2.4A. Supercycle Four

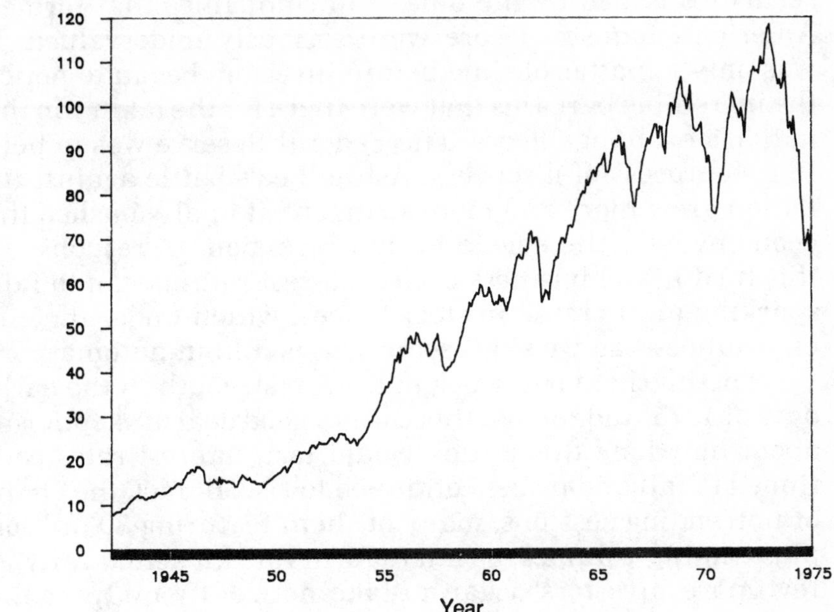

Chart 2.4B. Supercycle Four Adjusted for Inflation

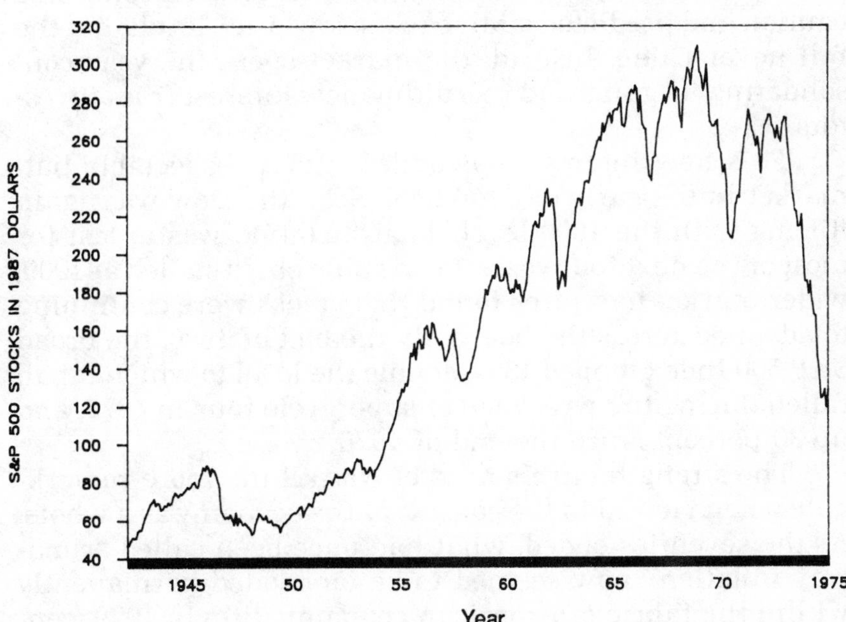

the cats and dogs of the over-the-counter markets. The securities issued by the blue chip companies that formed America's industrial core were seriously undervalued. It was only a matter of time before investors began to notice the incredible bargains that were there for the taking on the nation's exchange floors. The Federal Reserve was to help in this process of discovery. As the Fed's battle against inflation grew more and more stringent, it finally pushed the economy over the edge and into recession. In response to this turn in the business cycle, interest rates began to fall, sparking an increase in stock prices, which under the circumstances—as we shall soon see—is all but automatic.

The market visibly began to gain strength in the early days of 1975, and though there was a good deal of skepticism about how long this uptick would last, interest rates continued to fall and prices continued to rise. In fact, the chain of uptrending sessions, many of them featuring 30 million plus trading volumes, began to form into an actual rally. A few more investors began to take notice. By midyear the prime rate had fallen from its high of 12 percent to 8 percent and the Dow soared more than 300 points to the mid-850s. For the remainder of the year, market bears counseled caution and predicted a fall back to low price levels, but the fall never came. Instead, the market spent the year consolidating its gains and recruiting new interest from investors.

This new interest snowballed into a respectable bull market in the early days of 1976. Soon the Dow was again flirting with the 1000 level. That flirtation was to last for most of the next four years, but as blue chips stalled at 1000, wider market measures found that stocks were continuing to advance across the board. By the end of 1980, the broad S&P 500 Index topped 135—double the level to which it had fallen during the wreckage of supercycle four in 1974, and up 30 percent since the end of 1976.

The strength of this market was all the more remarkable when viewed in the context of the economy as a whole. As the seventies ended, what had once been called "runaway inflation" now seemed to be embedded permanently within the fabric of American economic life. In 1979, consumer prices advanced nearly 12 percent, and in 1980 they increased more than 14 percent. In response, Paul Volker, the conservative new chairman of the Federal Reserve, declared a "no holds barred" war on the inflation rate. When a moderate increase in the discount rate failed to cool the jets of inflation, he acted to push up interest rates still further. By the fall of 1981, the prime lending rate had shot out of sight, advancing over the 21 percent level. Three-month Treasury bills were yielding more than 15 percent, and so were long-term government bonds. Since stocks were yielding much less, their prices should have fallen, and they did, but the decline was far less than anyone could have anticipated. By the end of 1982, the S&P Index had slipped back from its 135 peak but only by 26 points, closing the year at 109.

What had happened? An interest rate spiral like this one should have sent the market to new lows, but it had done little more than superficial damage. Why? There were a few concrete reasons. The booming real estate market of the late seventies had cooled off dramatically, and high interest rates had clobbered both the precious metals market and the bond market. But the most basic reason why stock prices remained relatively stable had to do with the peculiar—and by now familiar—behavior of supercycles. Supercycles are stronger than even the strongest of business cycles, and even though the business cycle downturn of the early eighties was one of the strongest our economy had seen for some time, supercycle four had driven stock prices so low that years later after several sharp rallies stocks were still dirt cheap. Corporate earnings had advanced sharply in the years since 1974—in fact, the price to earnings ratio of Standard and Poor's 500 Index was exactly the same as it had been during the gloomiest days of 1974. Moreover, when the raging inflation of the intervening years was taken into account, stock prices actually were lower than they had been in 1974 (charts 2.5A and 2.5B).

A stock market measure that was gaining attention at the time showed similar results. The so-called "Q-ratio" attempted to measure a company's assets with its replacement costs. In 1982, the Q-ratio of the average American corporation was 55 percent,[8] which meant that the market value of the company, as measured by the price of its stock, was much cheaper than its underlying assets. Although the Q-ratio of the average company in 1982 was somewhat higher than the low of 47 percent it had marked at the end of supercycle four, it indicated that stocks were still a bar-

Chart 2.5A. Supercycle Five

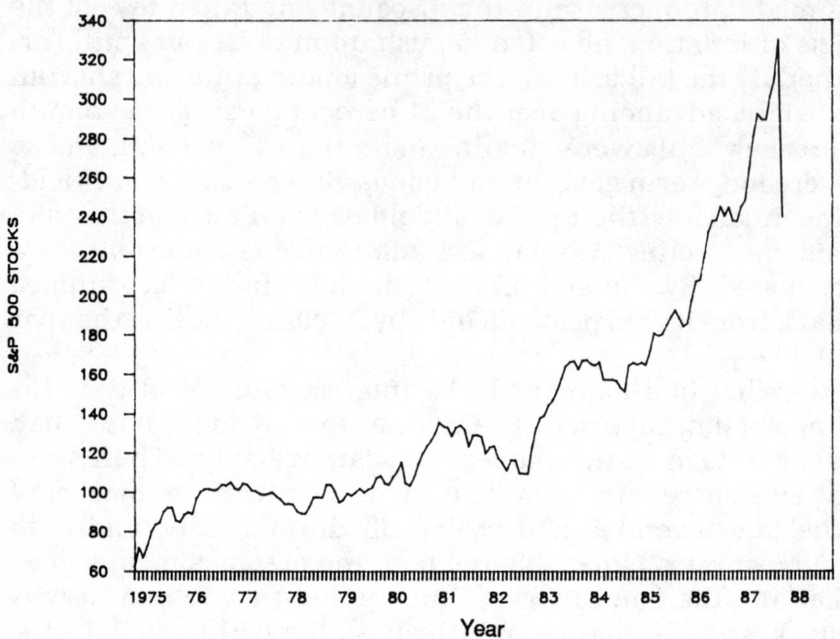

Chart 2.5B. Supercycle Five Adjusted for Inflation

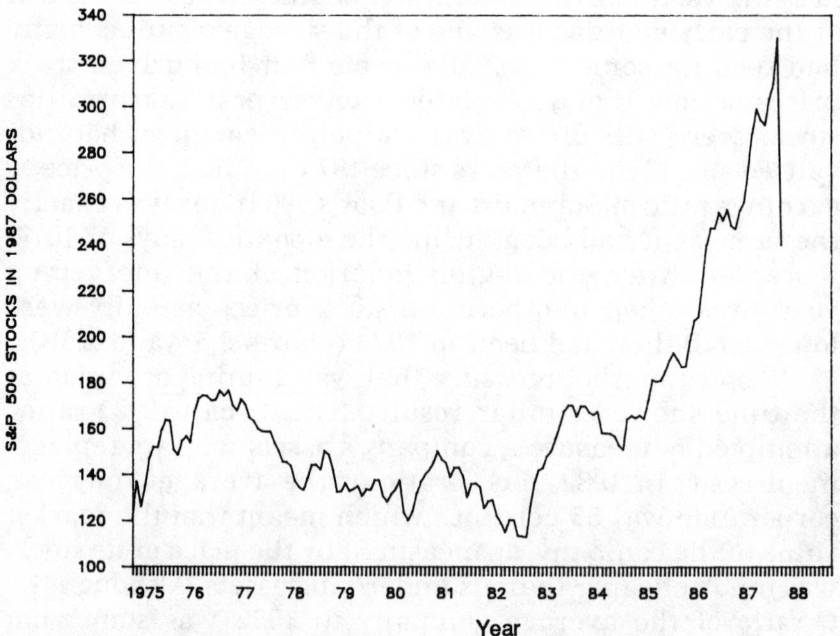

gain. (At the height of supercycle four in 1968, the average Q-ratio was 110 percent, indicating that securities were overvalued.)

Of course, the fact that the market value of most U.S. corporations was substantially less than the value of its assets was of interest to more than just stock market investors and money managers. It also attracted the attention of corporate raiders who were interested in acquiring companies at deflated prices and then liquidating them to capture the underlying assets. In order to avoid such corporate homicide, many corporations had to buy back their own stocks, which pushed prices significantly higher. So it was obviously to the advantage of investors to own stock in companies that might be takeover targets. Soon even the flimsiest rumors of potential corporate takeovers were enough to cause rapid increases in the price of a stock.

However, not all corporate takeover attempts were aimed at selling off the assets of a captured company. Corporate mergers and acquisitions reached a historical high in the 1980s. Across the country corporate managers didn't have to look beyond the merger news in their daily newspapers to realize that they were going to have to trim the corporate fat. They were realizing that unless they made better use of their corporate assets, they would find themselves becoming takeover bait. The annual rate of return on the physical assets of America's corporations had fallen to a low of 4.7 percent in 1982, but prodded by increasingly widespread takeover fears, corporations began to shape up their operations and productivity began to increase—and increased productivity meant increased profitability.

Having already impressed investors with its behavior in the face of interest rate adversity in the early eighties, the stock market was poised to surge ahead. Beginning in 1982, a recession was underway, bringing interest rates down. By the end of 1982, the prime rate had fallen below 11 percent. Moreover, Volker's war against inflation appeared to have been successful; the consumer price index advanced only 3.6 percent in 1982. This was enough good news for the market, and in the early fall of 1982, the Dow finally smashed through the 1000 barrier for good.

It never looked back. A short-lived rise in interest rates in 1984 led the market to consolidate for most of that year, but from then on the trend was always up—sharply up. A market that had tried for years to crack the 1000 mark permanently sailed through 2000 in the early days of 1987. By June it had crossed the 2400 mark while the S&P 500 climbed over 300. Many individual companies scored even more dramatic gains: IBM climbed to $167 a share, up 340 percent from its 1974 low; Texas Instruments was up 400 percent to $203; Xerox had doubled to $80; General Motors tripled to $92. Since 1974, Polaroid had climbed from $14 to $85, Control Data from $5 to $35, and Litton Industries from $3 to $98.

In the face of all this good news, financial analysts and Main Street investors alike began to wonder how long it could last. But as they looked back on the data from 1986, the experts found ample grounds for continued optimism. By the end of that year, the annual rate of return on corporate physical assets had reached an average of 7.7 percent, just a bit under the 8 percent level that had been recorded at the height of the booming sixties.

As American corporations succeeded in trimming the fat in their operations, earnings could be expected to increase sharply with only a modest improvement in the economy. By the end of 1986, economists were predicting healthy increases in corporate profits through 1988. Even the relatively conservative Alan Greenspan, destined to replace Volker as chairman of the Federal Reserve, was forecasting a 10 percent yearly growth in earnings on S&P 500 stock through 1988. Other forecasts ranged as high as 18 percent. Meanwhile, inflation had all but disappeared, and at the end of the year the prime rate was at nearly 7 percent, three month Treasury bills were paying only 5 percent, and bond yields were equally low.

On August 25, 1987, the New York Stock Exchange closed for the day with the Dow notched in at 2722.42. It was a new high, but it drew little attention. This was the era for new highs on Wall Street.

The great bull market of the 1980s was almost exactly five years old on that late summer day. In those sixty months, it had dumped 3.3 trillion dollars into the portfolios of large and small investors. And in the process it had entirely changed the face of Wall Street. The advance of profits was so magnificent and relentless that it had all begun to seem routine, especially to a whole new generation of young traders who came to maturity during the upward movement of a supercycle now twelve years old.

So champagne corks weren't flying on August 25. The Dow's new high did not make it onto the front pages of most newspapers where headlines were detailing ominous developments in the Persian Gulf. But the date was to be remembered later. It was the day the bull market—and the supercycle of which it had been the centerpiece—turned.

The downturn started, as it always does, with the action of a few worried traders. And as the market scaled its final, unbelievably lofty peak, there were several distinctly worrisome signs despite a wealth of positive news. These signs could all be found within one economic folder marked "Debt."

Supercycle five was a fabulously powerful economic engine, but a stock market supercycle was still not large enough to overcome the foolishness that was afflicting economic decision making in America on large and small levels. Government spending was continuing to hemorrhage, consumer debt was skyrocketing, and measures of the balance of trade were continuing to set new—awesomely negative—records. Throughout the year, the bond market continued to respond to the Reagan administration's only apparent strategy for dealing with the negative trade balance: allowing the dollar to weaken further. As the dollar fell, fears of potential inflation grew, and bond yields advanced.

Finally on an early autumn morning in 1987, the financial ticker noted that the yield of a thirty-year Treasury bond reached a lofty 10.4 percent. Most investors paid little attention to this significant statistic, however. Their minds were on other things. The date was October 19, 1987—Black Monday.

3

Understanding Supercycles

In the days following the 500-point collapse of the Dow on October 19, 1987, the market seesawed back and forth rapidly—and so did the prognostications of the experts. No one seemed to believe that the market was likely to reach the 2700 level again anytime soon, but there was speculation that the bear market obviously underway with a vengeance would be relatively brief. Though the media was noting haunting similarities between the path the Dow was traveling immediately after the crash and the path it had traced in 1929, few market professionals were allowing for the possibility that an equally severe downturn could occur in the 1980s. They were wrong. In fact, the events of the late summer and early fall of 1987 marked more than just the advent of a particularly severe bear market. They also marked the peak of supercycle five.

Just what are these supercycles that travel so ponderously through the fortunes of stock market investors? And why do they always seem to escape the notice of almost everyone until it's too late?

Our quick journey through the history of the stock market in this century has shown clearly that at virtually any moment the vast majority of the nation's stock securities were moving in the same direction. They were either moving upward in long spirals of good fortune, or they were falling—often precipitously. The inescapable conclusion that must be reached by any study of the American stock market is that it is incapable of keeping prices from going to extremes. In bull market after bull market, investors have been told that prices were bound to go even higher, no matter how high they were already, and that the market simply was reacting to the nation's ever increasing fortunes. And the beginnings of each of the catastrophic downturns that the market has experienced over nearly a century were greeted with assurances that this was but a "correction," a brief period of "profit taking." Though their information reached them on the screens of computer monitors rather than in the pages of newspapers read by gaslight, the investors who were ruined by the collapse of the current stock market supercycle should be able to feel a distinct kinship with their predecessors.

There are many reasons why most investors have not recognized or prepared for stock market supercycles over the years. First, we all want to believe that prosperity is permanent. When our investments are rewarded handsomely, we want to believe that we can depend on those rewards to continue.

Second, we are lulled by the passage of time. Supercycles differ from other powerful economic phenomena because they tend to operate over relatively long periods of time. Even the most furiously cyclonic of the supercycles we saw in chapter 2 took ten years to play out; most of them took longer to run their inevitable course. It's hard to remain vigilant during a period of long-term prosperity, but that's exactly what's required in order to extract maximum profits from the stock market.

Third, the stock market employs a vast army of workers, and that army swells dramatically during long bull markets. Although these brokers, technicians, and market experts might remember the lessons of previous stock market collapses and speculate about when bull markets will turn bearish, they have entrusted their livelihoods to the stock market, and thus are dedicated to the proposition that the market is a fundamentally rational instrument. They will admit, and even predict, that the market will turn downward occasionally. They will counsel their clients about how to hedge against these downturns. But it is difficult for them to face the fact that stock prices not only can go to destructive, fundamentally irrational extremes but they do. And when they do, investors suffer not downturns but disaster.

What most stock market experts never admitted before the recent collapse was that the American stock market, with all of its computerized information sorting capacities, is as vulnerable as ever to the destructive frenzy of boom/bust cycles. Just as the physics of the ripple made by a pebble in a still pond is the same as the physics of a tidal wave, the anatomy of a supercycle is the same as that of any cycle of boom and bust. They are built on the same set of basic human emotions that fuels any boom and bust, the same combination of hope, greed, fear, and most important, anticipation. The difference is one of scale, and as anyone who has experienced a raging tsunami can tell you, sometimes the scale makes all the difference. Stock market supercycles are megaboom/bust cycles operating within a vast and complicated market.

In the beginning days of a supercycle, there usually isn't much optimism. Supercycles start on the most dismal of days and are launched by investors who see that prices already have been far more battered by conditions than can be justified. As more and more investors follow the lead of these early trailblazers, the market begins to rise. Soon the rise of the market itself begins to attract attention and more investors. Eventually the market develops a life of its own and becomes very noisy. Stocks surge up above the fold of the nation's business pages, and one begins to hear endless discussions of interest rates and exchange rates and the balance of trade. But beneath the hubbub is one stark and totally ignored fact: The actual reason why prices are going up is that they are going up. "You can't argue with the tape," shrugs yet another set of investors as they throw even the most rudimentary of cautious impulses to the winds. Soon the increases become cyclonic. With accelerating prices comes even more attention from the public and the media, and caution from market experts that there soon will be corrections and technical downturns in the market.

When the first signs of the turn at the top of the supercycle appear, they are understood to be healthy corrections. But soon it becomes clear that the corrections are lasting longer and longer. The market is not adjusting; it is falling. Gradually, the emotion that is given financial dimension on the trading floors of the nation's security markets changes from hope to fear. Early profit taking changes to panic selling as investors jump ship. By now, the experts are acknowledging the presence of a bear market, but already are speculating hopefully about the next upturn. But the upturn doesn't come. It doesn't come, in fact, even when prices have collapsed to levels far below anything justified by even the most bearish economic news. Finally, when almost no one is listening any longer, the faint voices of the few remaining experts are correct. Yet another upturn is about to come.

We would like to think of the stock market as a well-oiled machine, its prices adjusting smoothly to changes in the economic, political, and international environment. We would like to believe that dealing with the market is little more than the watching of cause and effect playing out in the glowing phosphors of a video display terminal. But this is not the market that we have or ever could have. The stock market is a mysterious and often perverse mechanism because it is controlled not by cause and effect but by anticipation. It responds not to what is occurring at the moment but to what millions of individual prognosticators believe will happen in the future.

Stock market supercycles in this century have been sparked by investors who predicted accurately a number of momentous economic events: the industrialization of America at the turn of the century, the new era of prosperity that was established in the 1920s, the end of the Great Depression in the mid-1930s, the emergence of America's economic dominance in the postwar world, and the reevaluation of America's corporate assets by stock market investors that began in the mid-1970s, along with the abatement of inflation in the 1980s. In each of these cases investors bought into the market because they anticipated that future events would make their investments more valuable.

The trouble is that because future events are anticipated in stock prices, the actual arrival of these expected occurrences is almost irrelevant. In fact, when long-anticipated positive economic events do take place, they often begin to strike caution in the hearts of investors who begin to doubt that the future will be any brighter than the present. As these cautious investors begin to hedge their bets, other investors begin to notice that the market is not reacting as strongly to positive economic news as they had anticipated, and the caution spreads. Some investors stop buying. Others begin to sell. Gradually, prices begin to level, sparking even greater skepticism. And inevitably, the tide of the supercycle begins to ebb.

The anatomy of a supercycle is exactly the same, except in degree, as the anatomy of the boom and bust cycles of any of its constituent stocks. We can examine the forces that create a supercycle, therefore, by looking closely at the forces working on one of the securities that flashes across the ticker on any day.

To illustrate, let's take a blue chip security issued by a solid, reliable company we'll call General Technologies. We are investing in a climate that is offering investors 8 percent returns for safe investments, so as we examine General Technologies' stock, we will be trying to ascertain if we can expect a safe 8 percent return from it as well. In stocks, returns come in two ways: in cash dividends, and in increases in the price of the stock itself. In the case of General Technologies, the prospects look good. The company has experienced a steady, reliable growth, and its dividends have been growing at a rate of 3 percent a year for a number of years. However, recently there had been a spate of rumors that trouble was brewing in the company; while those rumors were completely baseless, the resulting nervousness had depressed the price of General Technologies stock to \$12.50 a share. Looking at that price, and discovering that the company is paying \$1.00 a share in dividends, we discover that we can get our 8 percent return from dividends alone (\$1.00/\$12.50 = 8 percent), so we decide to buy the stock.

After another year of solid growth, more and more investors come to believe that the bearish rumors about the future of General Technologies were groundless, and become convinced that General Technologies' history of 3 percent annual dividend growth will continue in the future. Given that assumption, it is logical to assume that the price of the stock itself will expand by at least the same 3 percent.

In fact, that very assumption will cause the price of the stock to grow even more. Here's why.

When we bought our General Technologies stock we made no assumption about growth in the price of the stock itself. We simply satisfied ourselves that the dividend would not fall below $1.00 a share, and that the price of the stock would not drop below the $12.50 a share that we paid for it. But if the investors who might buy our stock have come to believe that the stock price itself will advance by 3 percent, they will be willing to factor that growth into the 8 percent return they will be expecting to receive for their money. Since the dividend, which now has grown to $1.03 a share, need only represent 5 percent of the sales price rather than 8 percent, these investors should be willing to pay $20.62 (20⅝) a share for our General Technologies stock ($1.03 equals 5 percent of $20.62).

So we see the dramatic effect growth assumptions have on prices. When we bought General Technologies, we had no growth assumption and were willing to pay $12.50 a share. But investors who believe that the price of General Technologies will increase by 3 percent in a year would be willing to pay $20.62 for the same stock. Thus a 3 percent growth assumption has resulted in a price increase of 65 percent!

If we expand our experience with General Technologies out into the market as a whole, we can see why supercycles occur in the stock market. The bottom of a bear market always is surrounded by considerable gloom. Interest rates and unemployment rates are usually quite high; the economy seems stagnant at best. But a few investors already are beginning to vote their confidence in the resilience of the economy by tentatively buying back into the market. At first they buy high-yield stocks with little or no expectation of price growth, but the arrival of fresh capital into the market does produce some modest growth in prices. Soon investors begin to assume that these increases in prices probably will continue. Even these very modest growth assumptions immediately deposit premiums in the price of stocks, and soon the premiums themselves become the reason for expanded growth assumptions.

Unfortunately, those premiums represent the unstable core of a supercycle's reactor. In our example we saw how a 3 percent growth assumption about the price of a share of General Technologies' stock increased the price of that stock by 65 percent. That 65 percent increase in the price of General Technologies' stock will, of course, justify a much more optimistic growth assumption than 3 percent. If that growth assumption was to increase only another 2 percent—certainly reasonable after a year that saw a 65 percent price increase—the cash dividend contribution to an 8 percent return would need only to be 3 percent. The 5 percent expected increase in price will contribute the rest of the 8 percent return. But what a difference this change in assumptions makes on the price of our stock. An investor now can pay $34 a share and still get the 3 percent yield from the $1.03 in annual dividends that the share will pay. And, naturally enough, such a new surge in the price of the stock will only fuel new and higher growth assumptions, and a self-fueling spiral of increasing prices, growth assumptions, and premiums. Prices rise faster than earnings and dividends, price/earnings ratios expand, dividend yields drop, and the boom gains a life of its own.

We saw in chapter 2, for example, that the ratio of prices to earnings of the blue chip stocks that make up the Dow averaged less than eight in 1974 at the very bottom of a bear market. At the end of 1986, however, that ratio of price to earnings had more than doubled, and was standing at more than eighteen.

At the heart of an accelerating supercycle, optimism is converted to cash. And as this cash flows through the books of investors, it gives a sense of permanence to a phenomena that is nothing more than a mood—a hunch about the future by a collective of millions of conjurers from Wall Street to Main Street. And moods can switch, as we have just seen, often with devastating swiftness.

When growth assumptions flatten, the effect is just as dramatic as when they expand. An investor who paid $34 a share for General Technologies will be in big trouble if he cannot find another investor willing to assume a 5 percent continued growth in the price of the stock. If investors cautiously lower their growth expectations to 3 percent, they would demand a 5 percent yield from the $1.03 in dividends. This would force the price back down to $20.62. As might be expected, a price drop of that magnitude will eliminate any assumption of growth, and the price will fall to $12.87 (12⅞) in order to give investors an 8 percent yield on the $1.03 in dividends ($1.03 equals 8 percent of $12.87).

Note that all of this activity had almost nothing to do with the actual fundamental conditions affecting the stock, which did in fact register a 3 percent increase in yield over the period of a year. In our example, and in the very real world of booming supercycles, prices go up because they are going up. Positive fundamental conditions are quoted frequently to explain rapid price growth but, as every downturn proves, the positive fundamentals have been anticipated long ago by rising prices, and now they are serving only to blind investors to the fact that the market has become speculative.

We have discovered and traced five massive supercycles that have rolled through the stock market since the turn of the century. And we have seen that, with the notable exception of the boom and crash of the late 1920s and early 1930s, virtually none of these supercycles had made their way into the memories of stock market investors whose fortunes were decimated by the Crash of 1987. How can that be? How is it possible that this most statistically accessible of markets also would be the site of such profound historical ignorance?

In part, the answer is caught up in the human psyche's capacity for self-delusion. In our excursion through stock market supercycles we saw time and again how investors in the most dangerously superheated and speculative markets managed to convince themselves that they were investing with no speculative intent, even as they sought the inflated returns that only the most speculative of markets can generate. The history of financial markets is not taught in our schools, there are very few books on the subject, and even few well-read adults have had any genuine exposure to the history of money and trade—exposure which would equip them to anticipate the dynamics of a market.

But beyond ignorance and the natural desire of investors to assume that their investments are being made soberly and judiciously, the stock market itself presents a significant amount of obfuscating evidence. It is true, as all investors know, that stock market prices, like those of other markets, tend to move in broad trends. There are, as we know, bull markets and bear markets. The problem is that an investor, who is scanning the market data looking for indications of trend changes, may not notice that the cycles of bull markets and bear markets are themselves moving within a broader and much more fundamental trend—a supercycle. Unfortunately, an investor who is aware of the cycles of bull and bear markets, but who hasn't noticed the larger supercycle within which those cycles operate, is like an astronomer who after discovering that the earth is round and rotates upon its axis, doesn't notice that it also revolves around the sun.

As we saw in our historical journey through supercycles of the past, the upside of a supercycle is not without occasional downticks, each of which probably worried significant numbers of investors at the time, but the energy of an uptrending supercycle is too strong to be denied. The bull market periods are much stronger than the bear market periods and the supercycle continues to move upward. We also saw that when a market peaks, it is virtually impossible for most observers to tell that the new bear market will be any stronger than the downtrending periods that had gone before. But it is. Suddenly the downward-trending trading sessions are much more energetic than the occasional uptrending sessions until the supercycle eventually ends in a general collapse of prices.

Obviously, therefore, the prudent investor needs to know much more than whether a bull market is about to turn bearish, for if the supercycle is still moving up, that bear market will be relatively brief. Also it is essential to know whether a new bear market is "just a correction" as investors always are being assured, or whether the supercycle has peaked and the crash is beginning.

The peak has come. It came, as it always does, because markets—even the glamorous high-tech, computerized stock market of the eighties—are human instruments. As long as markets are allowed to function freely as the diaries of our collective hopes and fears, supercycles in those markets will always exist. Which is to say that hopeful, confident consumers will always drive stock prices too high, and fearful, anxious investors will, en masse, always allow prices to fall too low. The panic-stricken traders, whose travail the nation watched live and in color during the crash, were actors in a ritual play as formal as a Japanese Noh drama. Though this act is ending, the play will go on.

4

The Stock Market Risk Indicator

We have seen that price breaks on the stock market are perverse; they almost always seem to come in the face of great optimism. That's why so many stockbrokers and investment advisers are "contrarians" who tell their clients that they should beware of optimism and be alert at times when the public is pessimistic. In our study of the operation of supercycles we have seen that this advice is frequently right, and the caution it represents is well founded, but it is also dangerously simplistic.

The problem with a pure contrarian philosophy is that it falls into the same trap as blind optimism: It treats the market it is examining as if it existed in splendid isolation. Supercycles turn for one simple reason: Prices are too high. But how high is too high? Too high is when prices no longer reflect the underlying fundamentals that launched them on their upward path. Prices are too high when price rises themselves have become the reason for investor optimism. There is nothing wrong with investing in markets during a time of widespread optimism, if that optimism is based on solid underlying economic, social, and political fundamentals. But the key to safe investing is to determine as closely as possible the exact moment when prices have pulled their anchors from the bedrock of fundamental conditions and have set sail onto the stormy and dangerous seas that will, sooner or later, result in their demise.

There are few forces that are more important to a market's destiny than the amount of capital that is available to it. The larger forces of supply and demand may produce a setting for strong price increases, but if sufficient investment capital is not available, those prices will not materialize. Thus, all markets are in competition with each other. In a normal situation, capital will flow easily between markets as their underlying conditions change, but if a market becomes dangerously superheated it will absorb a larger proportion of available investment capital than it otherwise would. This change will be reflected not only in its prices but also in the prices of competing markets, which will be lower than their underlying fundamentals would indicate they should be.

Logically, therefore, we should be able to come up with tools for predicting when prices in a given market are too high and are in imminent danger of collapse, tools based on the relative prices of competing markets. For instance, let's look at the stock market and its foremost competitor for investment dollars, the housing market. In order to get the real picture over an extended period of time, and to account for the fact that more dollars are chasing investments these days than decades ago, we need to adjust both of these markets for inflation. Chart 4.1 shows monthly stock and housing prices since 1895 in October 1987 dollars (housing prices have been divided by 1,000 so that they can be displayed on the same scale).

What does this tell us about the relationship between stock and house prices over the years? To find out, let's set up an equation in which we divide the Standard and Poor's 500 Stock Index average by the median price of a new house for each month over these years. What this equation reveals is an elegant financial minuet as each market has taken turns outperforming the other. The results are plotted on chart 4.2. (See appendix A for the exact formula.)

There are many reasons why one market may be outperforming another at any given time, and the fact that stocks may be doing better than houses at any given time

Chart 4.1. Houses versus Stocks (Adjusted for Inflation)

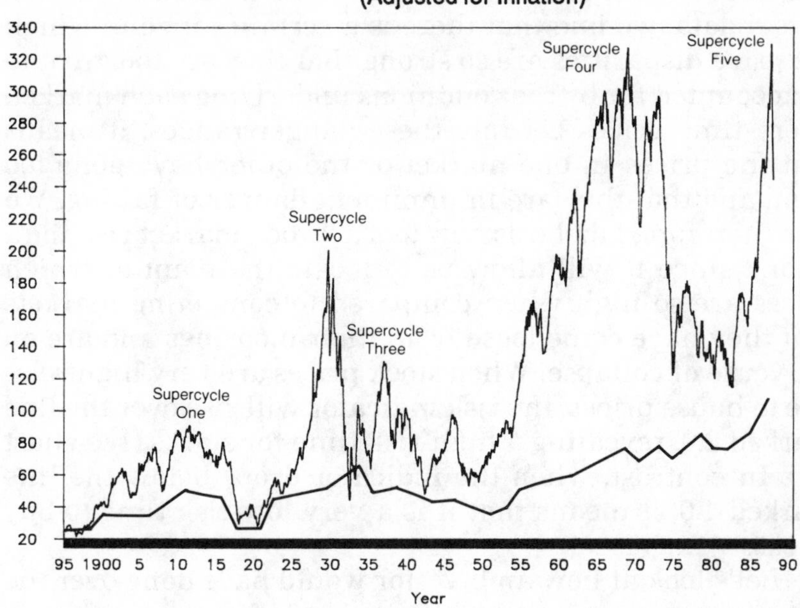

Chart 4.2. Stock Market Risk Indicator (1895–1987)

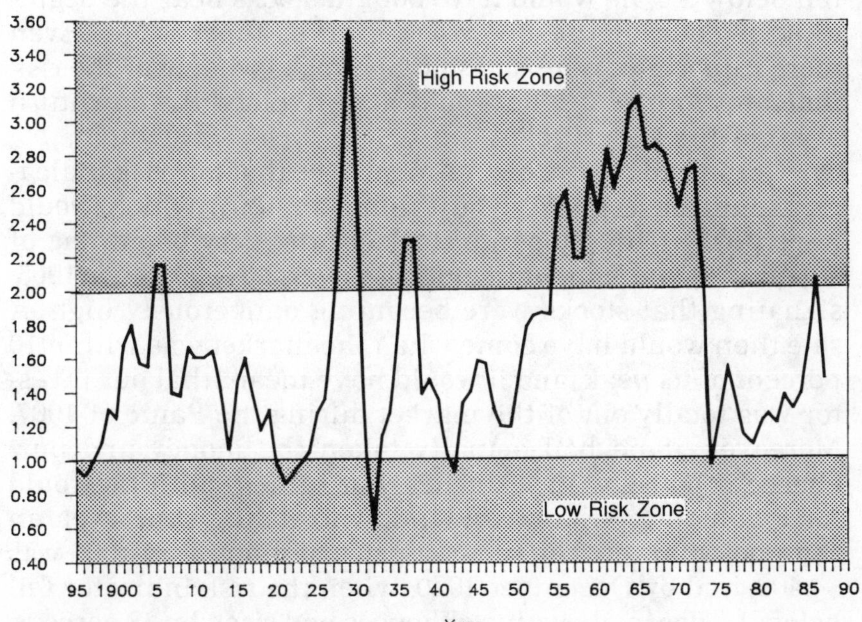

Note: See appendix A for exact formula.

does not necessarily indicate that the stock market is in a dangerous boom condition. However, as we look at the historical data, we find that there is a certain range in which the price disparities are so strong that they are too great to be accounted for by the conditions underlying each market. Every time prices get into these danger ranges, it means that the prices in one market or the other have gone too high, and that they are in imminent danger of falling. We can, therefore, label this new tool a "stock market risk indicator," since it will allow us to locate the point at which prices are so high when compared to competing markets that they have come loose from their moorings and are on the verge of collapse. When stock prices are very high relative to house prices, the risk indicator will rise over the line marked 2.0, revealing a high-risk time for stocks (see chart 4.2). In contrast, when the indicator drops below the line marked 1.0, it means that it is a very low-risk time to buy stocks.

Let's look at how an investor would have done over the last ninety years if he had used this indicator as his sole guide in determining when to buy stocks and when to sell them. He would have done very well indeed. If our investor were to have purchased stocks every time the risk indicator fell below 1.0, he would have bought stocks near the beginning of each of the five stock market supercycles. Even more important, if he had sold his stocks whenever the risk indicator topped 2.0, he would have avoided the downturn of all of the supercycles.

Going back to the beginning we see that our risk indicator would have given a buy signal in 1895, which would have put our investor into stocks at the very beginning of supercycle one. The indicator rose over 2.0 in October 1905, signaling that stocks were becoming dangerously high. A sale then would have come when the market was within 10 percent of its peak, and it would have meant that our investor was totally out of the market during the Panic of 1907. Moreover, if he had actually taken the money and purchased a house with it during that same month he would have done more than avoid a downtrending supercycle in the stock market. The median price of a house in 1906 was $4,400, and by December 1920, when the risk indicator fell below 1.0 again, the value of houses had risen by 38 percent. Investing the proceeds of his fortuitous real estate holdings back into the stock market when the S&P 500 was 6.81, our investor would be back in the market just as supercycle one was finally hitting bottom and supercycle two was beginning—just in time for a ride on the spirited stock market of the Roaring Twenties. By the time the next sell signal was recorded, in April 1928, our investor's capital would have nearly tripled. And this figure could be multiplied by the leverage so freely used during that era, typically 90 percent.

The Great Crash of 1929 was part of an economic catastrophe of such magnitude that the housing market also was affected. But if our investor had decided once again to put all of his stock earnings into houses he could have comforted himself well, because by the time the next buy signal was recorded, his investment in houses had declined only by 15 percent compared with the 85 percent loss he would have suffered by remaining in stocks.

That next buy signal came in May 1932 as the risk indicator slipped below 1.0 again, only three months from the low of 5.01 recorded on the S&P 500 and the low of 41 on the Dow Jones Industrials. It signaled the beginning of supercycle three in stocks, an upturn that would multiply the value of our investor's portfolio by 2.5 times by August 1936, the next time the indicator entered the sell zone. Again, the relatively small amount of money in the Depression-ravaged economy kept the housing market from booming during the stock market's misfortune, but our investor would have made a slight profit by investing in houses as he read about the stock market's crash in the newspapers.

The largest supercycle the stock market had seen yet dawned in 1942, and our investor was right there, having been alerted by a buy signal in March, one month from the bottom. This fourth buy signal was not contradicted until April 1955, and those who were lucky enough to be part of supercycle four from the beginning, like our investor, saw their portfolios increase 4.6 fold.

The sixties were years of dramatic economic expansion for the U.S. economy and the stock market continued to climb, but following the advice of the risk indicator, our investor was not in the stock market. He was in the sizzling housing market in which his money would nearly triple again by the time the next buy signal came, in October 1974. Here our investor, as trusting of the risk indicator as he would no doubt be by this time, and as wealthy as it would have made him, still would be forgiven a little doubt as he pulled his money out of the real estate market and put it into stocks just as supercycle five was beginning. And those doubts must have increased sharply as our investor listened to his friends talk about the killings they were making in real estate. But when real estate prices began to flatten in the early eighties, supercycle five was surging through America's stock exchanges and was still going strong. At the beginning of 1987, as stocks rocketed through the untested 2000 barrier, people were wondering how long it all would last.

Our investor was not nervous. By now he had learned to simply sit back and watch his faithful risk indicator. As 1987 dawned, there was little indication of trouble. In January, the risk indicator stood at 1.24, far from the danger level. But as the year progressed, the stock market began to rocket into the trading stratosphere, and the readings from the risk indicator began to shift rapidly. By mid-August, the Dow had topped 2700, the S&P 500 had topped 330, and the risk indicator rose to the danger level. The message was clear: Stocks had finally become so overvalued in comparison to competing markets that a crash was inevitable. Our investor, undoubtedly to the amazement of all his friends, sold out of the roaring bull market. His portfolio had increased fivefold during the boom of supercycle five. He was to lose no sleep when, less than two months later, the market went into free-fall.

And what's the bottom line? Chart 4.3 shows those signals plotted next to the path of stock prices. The figures show that over the entire ninety-year period, stock prices have outperformed housing prices slightly. Just based on the price growth of each investment market and assuming no leverage was used, a $10,000 investment would have grown to $225,000 in houses and to $565,000 in stocks. Although an investor who started with $10,000 in 1895 could have made money by putting his money in either stocks or housing and simply leaving it there over such a long period of time, if he had followed the signals of the risk indicator he would have made twenty-four times more money—the difference between the $565,000 the stock market would have yielded by itself and the $13,350,000 the risk indicator would have provided. Imagine the results if we factor in the

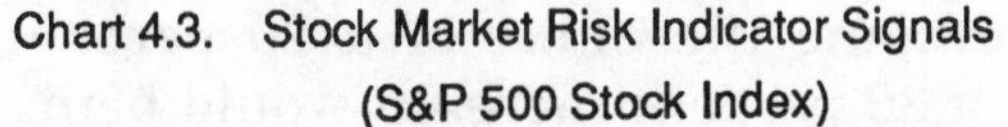
Chart 4.3. Stock Market Risk Indicator Signals (S&P 500 Stock Index)

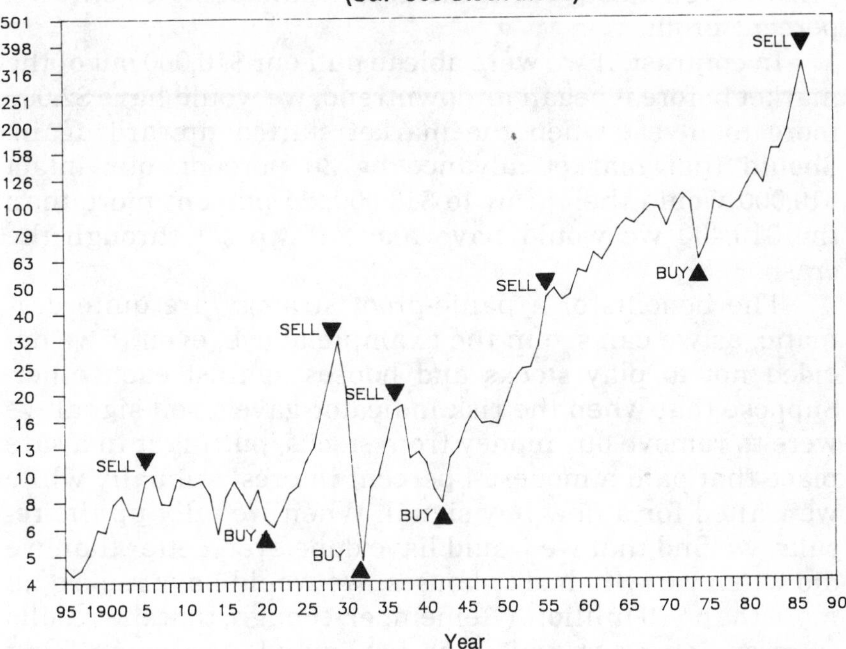

leverage that could have been used with both stocks and houses!

These figures illustrate once again the reason why it is so important to remain aware of the supercycles that are at work within markets: The downward plunge is always much faster than the upward trend. As important as it is to get aboard a supercycle when it is beginning its upward climb, latecomers can still join in the profits, but tardiness in leaving a market can be disastrous. How disastrous? Well let's look at the effect of a 20 percent decline in prices, 3 percent less than the market suffered on Black Monday alone. While common sense would tell us that all we would need to do is wait for another 20 percent upturn, in fact, it would take even more. If we had started with $10,000, the 20 percent downturn would have left us with only $8,000 to invest in the next uptrending market. If that market were to increase in value by 20 percent, we would have $9,600—and we would still be 4 percent below where we had started. In fact, we would need a 25 percent increase in prices to overcome the effect of a 20 percent decline in prices. Even a 30 percent increase would bring us only a 4 percent profit.

In contrast, if we were able to pull our $10,000 out of the market before it began its downtrend, we would have $2,000 more to invest when the market started upward again. Should that market advance by 30 percent, our intact $10,000 would then grow to $13,000, 25 percent more than the $10,400 we would have made if we sat through the crash.

The benefits of a panic-proof strategy are quite dramatic, as we can see in the example above, even if we decided not to play stocks and houses against each other. Suppose that when the risk indicator gave a sell signal we were to remove our money from stocks, putting it in a safe place that paid a modest 4 percent interest annually while we waited for a new buy signal. When we tally up the results, we find that we would have done even better than we did when we switched to houses. We would have racked up more than $20 million. (Remember, though, that the results from switching to houses do not include the magnifying effect of the leverage that can be used with houses.)

Now I am aware that most investors are used to the daily deluge of news and statistics, the mass of price quotations, projections, and speculations about the market that fill the pages of the *Wall Street Journal* and other financial pages. They pay close attention to the inflation rate, the balance of trade, the federal deficit, the interest rates. But when a supercycle is about to turn, none of these factors are as important as the simple fact that prices have soared too high.

5

The Crash of 1987

In the tumultuous days following Black Monday, it seemed as if there were as many explanations for the crash as there were financial prognosticators. On and on the postmortems droned with fingers being pointed at everything from inattention in the White House to computerized program trading. Some commentators noted in stentorian tones that the market had broken because prices simply had gone too high. This, of course, was true but it did nothing to explain the timing and the fury of the price collapse.

Lost amid all the sound and fury was the single most important set of figures for understanding the crash: the steadily rising interest rates as measured by the yield on long-term bonds that had been in evidence for most of 1987. Yields on long-term Treasury bonds stood at 7.5 percent in January 1987. On October 19, they had risen above 10 percent.

The market had been reacting subtly to this inexorable rise for several months before the crash. Although the Dow Jones Industrial Average was setting new all-time highs routinely, the utility average was not following suit. Soon the transportation average also was failing to confirm the new highs. In fact, each rally was slightly less enthusiastic than the one before, and each was bringing fewer and fewer stocks with it.

The crash of 1987 was no accident, and its cause is apparent. The market went down because interest rates were too high. To see why rising interest rates always set the stage for falling stock prices (and vice versa), let's look back at the example we explored in chapter 3.

You'll recall that when we investigated the potential purchase of shares of General Technologies Company, we were seeking an overall return of 8 percent on our investment. We saw that if this return was to come entirely from a cash dividend we would be willing to pay $12.50 a share for a dividend of $1. We also saw, however, that if we were willing to trust that the stock would grow in value by 3 percent, we could pay $20 a share. Though the $1 dividend would now represent only a 5 percent cash return, the 3 percent growth assumption would bring our total return to the necessary 8 percent return. The point of this exercise was to show that a growth assumption of only 3 percent would result in a 65 percent increase in prices.

But growth assumptions are not the only volatile factor in the pricing equation. What if, in this example, the amount of return we were expecting were to be revised downward from 8 percent to 5 percent. This also would justify an increase in the price of the stock to $20, even without a growth assumption. If a growth assumption were to be added, the price increase would increase still further. And, of course, these price increases would justify even higher growth assumptions.

This is what happens to the stock market when interest rates drop. Since the stock market is in competition with other markets for investment dollars, it must match the returns offered by other investments. When interest rates fall, the decline is reflected in other investments, ranging from Treasury bills to bank certificates. These yield declines change the environment within which stocks are judged, and investors are satisfied with a smaller return.

Of course, as the events of 1987 proved, this same process works in reverse. As interest rates rise, alternative investments begin to offer higher returns. These returns must be matched by stocks which, in turn, serve to drive prices down. In the case of General Technologies, as our required return grows from 5 to 8 percent, the price of the stock will decline from $20 to $12.50. And, of course, as prices decrease, growth assumptions evaporate, leading to further price declines. Therefore, to predict the short-term movement of the market, it is necessary only to know which way interest rates are heading.

By the middle of 1987, the direction that interest rates were moving was becoming quite clear. That direction was up: the economy was inexorably coming to grip with the awesome mega-debt of the 1980s.

As early as the end of 1986, the balance sheets of large and small American corporations were recording a debt that had reached a staggering $1.2 trillion. This represented a growth of more than 35 percent in only six years. Much of this increase was a direct result of the financing of huge corporate takeovers, or the attempt to fight against acquisition. In either case, the debt load was eating up an increasing chunk of corporate earnings.

And if debt growth in the private sector was a growing concern, it was peanuts compared to the country's national debt. In the six-year period beginning in 1980, corporate debt increased by 35 percent, but the national debt doubled. In 1986, the federal government's spending binge was rocking along at the rate of $1.9 million per minute, $419,900 a minute more than it took in. The result was a record $221 billion deficit, which, when added to the string of deficits that had gone before, raised the total national debt to $2.2 trillion. Perhaps the only way this nearly incomprehensible figure can be rendered intelligible is to point out that to pay it off each adult U.S. citizen would have to pay $13,000, up from $12 in 1910, $325 in 1940, and $1,800 in 1970. Every day in 1986, the government was forced to spend $512 million for interest to finance this debt. By year's end, the government had spent more on interest than on health, teacher training, and employment development combined. Indeed, it spent more on interest alone than the total of the entire federal budget in 1969. Even in 1987, despite the usual noises from Capitol Hill, no end to the spending was apparent as the nation's politicians looked ahead to the election year of 1988.

Chart 5.1 shows the dramatic growth in the size of federal budget deficits from the beginning of 1961 through

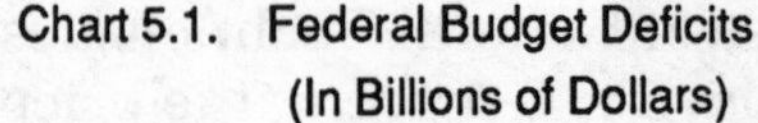
Chart 5.1. Federal Budget Deficits
(In Billions of Dollars)

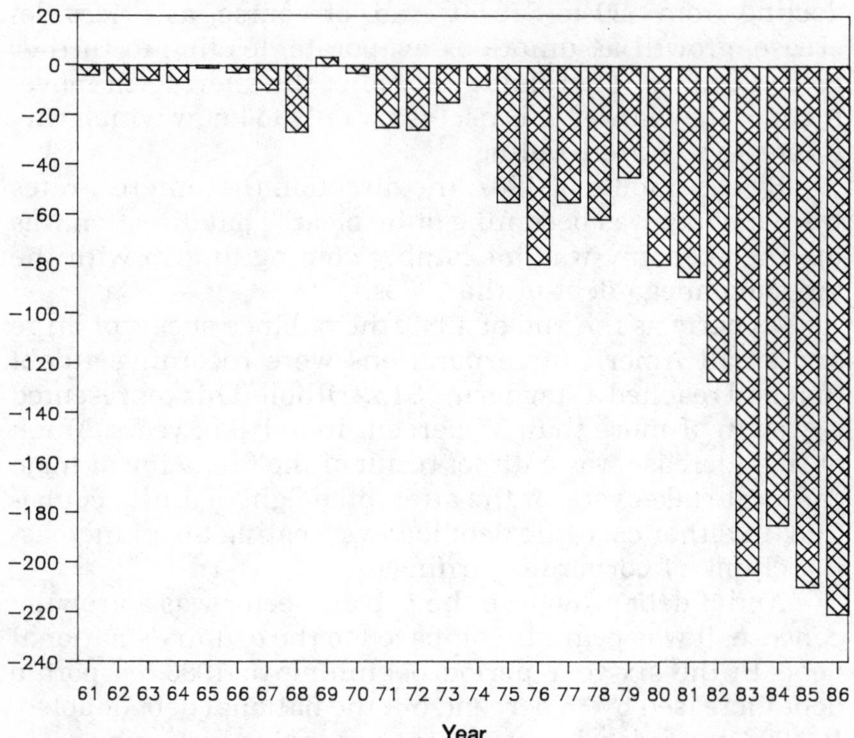

Source: Office of Management and Budget

1986. Notice how dramatically they have increased in the 1980s. When Ronald Reagan embarked on a huge program of military spending upon taking office in 1981, he presumed that he could finance it by cutting back sharply on domestic programs and stimulating the economy's "supply side" through sweeping tax cuts. The scheme didn't work. Lawmakers balked at sharp cuts in domestic spending, and despite the fondest hopes of supply-side theorists, the revenue side never came close to catching up.

The huge amount of money that the federal government has needed to finance the national debt has had some unprecedented effects on the economy. One was an increase in the level of real interest rates (the level of interest rates after subtracting inflation). Chart 5.2 shows the level of real interest rates, as established by the average yield on three month Treasury bills adjusted for inflation, for each year

Chart 5.2. Real Interest Rates: Three Month T-Bills

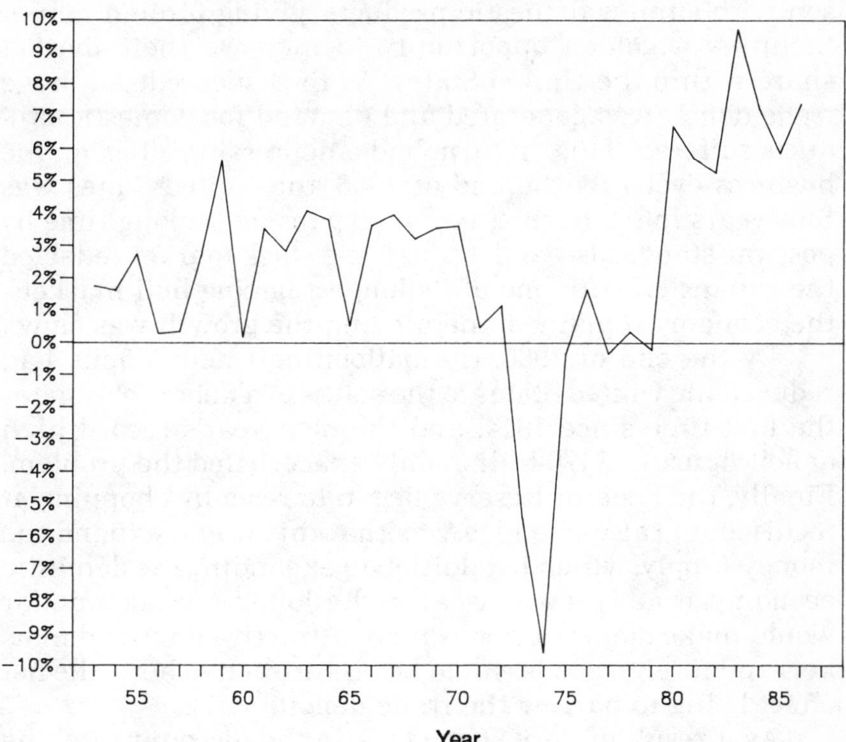

since 1952. You'll note that through the first two decades of this chart, real interest rates bounced around from near zero to a high of no more than 6 percent. In the seventies, when inflation was at record highs, real interest rates hovered around zero, occasionally falling into negative figures. Beginning in 1979, however, and continuing throughout the 1980s, real interest rates have soared to record highs.

These new high levels of real interest rates had two immediate effects. On the plus side, they lured foreign investors to finance the national debt. In 1986, even though interest rates had declined from their sky-high level of the early 1980s, they were still high enough in real terms to interest foreign investors in financing more than $60 billion of U.S. Treasury debt. This meant that they were financing more than a fourth of the federal deficit, as opposed to just 4 percent in 1983. On the negative side, as foreign investors sought to turn their currency into dollars so they could buy U.S. Treasury securities, the dollar tended to strengthen. A strong dollar makes foreign products cheaper in comparison with similar domestic products, giving foreign manufacturers a golden opportunity to increase their market share within the United States. As they succeeded, a huge trade deficit was generated and demand for domestic products suffered. This, in turn, had a depressing effect on the business cycle. By the end of 1986, the United States was four years into a business cycle expansion—a long time by postwar standards—and, though the stock market reflected the expansion with one of its longest lasting bull markets, the economy remained anemic and the growth was slow.

By the end of 1985, the ballooning trade deficits had reduced the United States to the status of a debtor nation for the first time since 1914, and the next year's record high deficit figure of $170 billion only exacerbated the problem. Finally, the Federal Reserve began to react by chopping at its discount rate. The idea was that this would expand the money supply, which in addition to expanding the domestic economy, would serve to weaken the dollar. A weaker dollar would make domestic goods more attractive on world markets and foreign goods would be less attractive here, the net effect being to narrow the trade deficit.

As a result of very sharp cuts in the discount rate, the nation's money supply grew 9 percent in 1985 and then grew at a rate almost double that in 1986. This 17 percent growth in the money supply was a far greater rate than anything the United States had seen before in modern times, even in the inflationary seventies. There always had been a threat attached to any move by the Fed to lower the discount rate: A big increase in the money supply always had preceded an increase in inflation. Chart 5.3 illustrates this connection. The growth rate of the money supply is shown by the solid line on the chart. The inflation rate is shown by the shaded area. You can see quickly that each increase in the money supply has been matched by an increase in the inflation rate within a few years. But despite this historical evidence, the inflation rate remained dormant through 1986 and showed only small increases in 1987.

The Federal Reserve's strategy seemed to be working, at least at first; the strong dollar collapsed in 1986 and 1987 and the economy began to show a more spirited growth while inflation was held at bay. However, a serious problem

Chart 5.3. Inflation versus Money Supply Growth

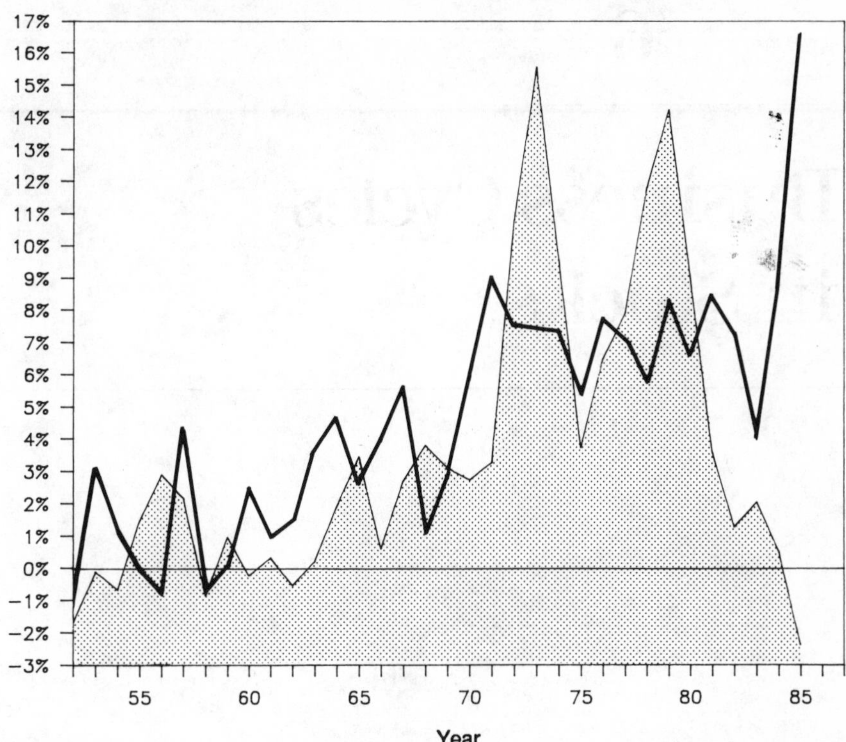

began to develop in 1987. A crashing dollar meant that foreigners began losing money by investing in U.S. Treasury securities. As a result they began cutting back their purchases. Meanwhile, the Treasury, still in need of huge amounts of capital to finance the federal budget deficit, continued offering Treasury securities in record volumes at weekly Treasury auctions. The obvious result was a dramatic increase in bond yields. To make matters worse, the trade deficits remained stubbornly high. As investors began to see the dilemma that the nation was in, the stock market crashed, marking the peak of supercycle five.

6

Business Cycles in Stocks

If supercycles are the solemn, inexorable seasons that roll through the environment of a market, business cycles are the highly visible, sometimes serene, frequently blustery fronts and storms that we actually perceive as weather. Since an investor is like a sailor preparing to set out to sea, it should go without saying that it is essential he know the season before he sets out. But also it is obvious that a knowledge of the season is, by itself, no guarantee of smooth sailing. The balmy seas of summer can be whipped into a cyclonic frenzy, and a placid weather front can smooth a midwinter's chop.

The stock market risk indicator has given us a panic-proof tool to determine the investment season in the stock market. This information is all-important; there will be no heat waves in January, no blizzards in July. But in our search for fair winds, we need to know more than the season. We must be able to predict the weather. We need to chart the barometric pressures within a market, to figure the intensity of its shifting winds, to determine its temperature. For this we will need to learn how to use some new and even more sensitive tools.

In chapter 4, we saw how the massive volume of statistics that flood forth from Wall Street and Washington can serve to blind investors to the all-important movement of supercycles. But with our reliable risk indicator firmly in place to give us ample early warning of supercycle shifts, we can turn our attention back to these statistics and determine how they can help us to predict the microclimate through which our investments will travel.

Interest rates are the pulse of the market, a pulse that can be read accurately by paying close attention to the business cycle. Interest rates are nothing more than an indicator of the demand and supply balance for money. The economy, as it swings through its business cycle between expansion and recession and back, determines the demand for money, and the Federal Reserve System controls the supply. When the economy enters a recession, consumption is sluggish, businesses are cutting their inventories, and factories reduce their output. In a situation where the volatile economic players are sitting out of the action, demand for money and credit declines. In the face of this reduced demand, interest rates also fall.

Meanwhile the Federal Reserve Bank pursues its goal of keeping the economy out of a full-scale depression by lowering the interest rate it charges to banks (the discount rate). This has the effect of allowing banks to lower interest rates still further. All of these actions combine to increase the money supply, and eventually money becomes so plentiful and cheap that important economic actors are lured back into the game. When this happens, a recession is well on its way to being over.

From recession to recovery to expansion—economic activity begets more economic activity; higher employment leads to increased demand until that demand begins to outdistance the economy's ability to produce goods and services. Soon too much money chasing the available goods and services results in inflation. In order to check the inflation, the Federal Reserve is forced to reduce the money supply by increasing its discount rate. As the supply of money contracts, it becomes more expensive. Interest rates rise until they eventually choke off the economy's expansion and the economy slips into recession, bringing inflation rates down with it. With the cooling of inflation, the cycle is poised to start all over again.

Given the effect of interest rate movement on the market, one can see why stock market movement has always seemed so perverse. Just when the economic news seems to be turning unremittingly gloomy as the economy is heading into the recessionary phase of its business cycle, interest rates come down and stimulate the stock market. Conversely, just when the economy is looking rosy, interest rates start heading up again and start to depress the market. No wonder casual investors so frequently have found themselves buying optimistically into a market just as it peaked, or staying out of a market as it launched itself into a new bullish phase.

And so we see that interest rates are more than the visible tracks left by a business cycle; they are also the means by which the business cycle affects stock prices. It follows, then, that in order to determine the direction of stock prices in the months ahead, it is necessary to determine the direction of interest rates. And to determine the direction of interest rates, it is necessary to decipher the direction of the business cycle.

Fortunately, the government regularly gives us the data with which to make the judgment. I have found that when eight of the government's leading economic indicators are compiled together in a "diffusion index" they function with amazing accuracy as predictors of the birth of a new business cycle, and thus, of the beginning of a new bull market in stocks. These eight leading economic indicators include the number of labor hours devoted to manufacturing each week, the number of new orders received by manufacturers, the number of newly organized businesses, the value of Standard and Poor's 500 Stock Index, housing starts, vendor performance, changes in industrial inventory, and changes in business and consumer credit.

To construct our diffusion index we will observe changes in each of these indicators over a six-month period. We will give a value of one point (1.0) to any indicator that moves up over the period. For every indicator that is unchanged we will attach a value of one-half point (0.5). If an indicator falls, no value will be attached. The sum of all of these figures will be expressed as a percentage of eight. If, for example, six indicators are up at the end of a six-month period, one is unchanged, and one is down, the diffusion index will be 6.5÷8 or 81 percent.

The Commerce Department has been compiling these indicators since the early 1950s. Chart 6.1 shows the performance of our diffusion index of leading indicators over those years. You'll note that there are times when the diffusion index drops to zero. This indicates times when all eight of the leading indicators were lower than they had been six months before. In yet another example of the perverse nature of stock market forces, each of these depressing times actually turned out to be an excellent time to get into the stock market (shown by the circles on the graph). By the time a battered economy had painted all eight economic indicators into the negative, the bear market had bottomed out and was ready to rise. One of the most significant times was when a buy signal was recorded in November 1974, which was exactly one month before the Standard and Poor's 500 average hit its low. The next buy signal was recorded in March 1980, again only one month before that year's bear cycle bottomed out.

Chart 6.1. Diffusion Index of Leading Indicators

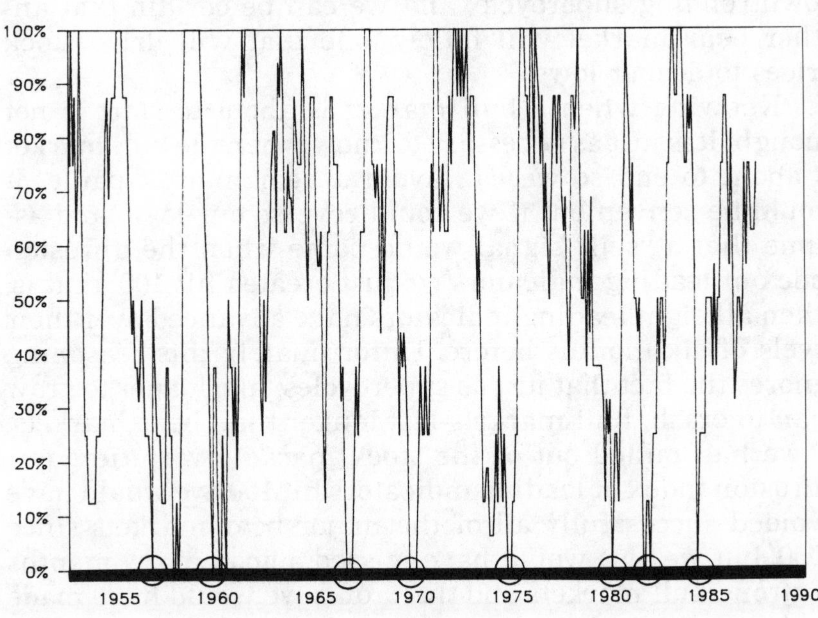

We have, therefore, determined that our diffusion index of leading indicators is a good indicator of the bottom of a business cycle. In order for all eight leading economic indicators to fall below levels they experienced six months before, it is pretty certain that the economy as a whole must be in a fairly severe recession, which will have had a strong effect on the one economic factor not measured by the composite index: interest rates. As we have seen, the decline of interest rates is the primary fuel for the launching of a new bull market.

As a practical matter, it takes the Commerce Department about one month to publish the leading indicators, which is the soonest we can act. Fortunately, the historical results improve somewhat if action is taken one month later than the signal. The results are not quite as good if the delay is two months, although they are still not bad. Thus, one month after the diffusion index of these eight leading indicators hits zero will be the best time to buy stocks. If this happens after the stock market risk indicator has fallen below 1.0, it will announce a new bull market that will also mark the commencement of a new supercycle. However, if the diffusion index of leading indicators hits zero before the stock market risk indicator has fallen below 1.0, then it will be signaling a bull market that is merely interrupting a downtrending supercycle, and we can be certain that another bear market will follow, one that will drive stock prices to deeper lows.

Knowing when a bull market is about to start is not enough. It is just as necessary to know when the bull market is about to end so we can avoid a bear market panic. It would be convenient if we could reverse our logic and assume that a "sell" signal would come when the diffusion index of leading indicators we just created hit 100, that is, when all eight leading indicators have advanced over their levels of six months before. Unfortunately this reasoning ignores the fact that just as supercycles take longer to grow than to crash, bull markets last longer than bear markets. If we had pulled out of the stock market every time our diffusion index of leading indicators hit 100, we would have avoided successfully all of the major bear markets since 1950, but we also would have missed a good many months of strong bull markets and the profits we would have made during those months.

Given the fact that it usually takes several months for a bull market to mature and peak even after the diffusion index of leading indicators has hit 100 percent, it makes intuitive sense that the problem is that *leading* indicators won't work for our sell signals. If a diffusion index of leading economic indicators is so accurate in describing the bottom of a business cycle, doesn't it stand to reason that a set of *lagging* indicators would reveal when the market has peaked?

Fortunately, the Commerce Department does publish a regular, if much less well known, set of lagging economic indicators. These include the number of weeks that idle workers have been on unemployment, the ratio of manufacturers' inventories to their sales, the labor cost of each manufactured unit, the prime interest rate, the number of outstanding commercial and industrial loans, and a ratio comparing the amount of consumer debt to growth in personal income.

Chart 6.2 shows a diffusion index constructed from these six lagging indicators. Prior to the late eighties when budget deficits started choking the economy, a reading of

Chart 6.2. Diffusion Index of Lagging Indicators

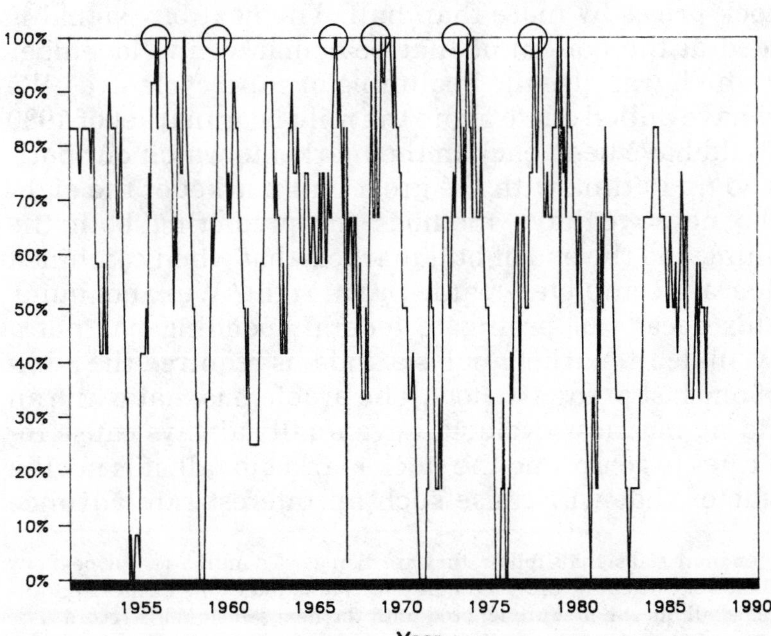

100 percent functioned as a reliable sell signal. Happily, this set of sell signals turned out to be timed very well for the last three decades (shown by the circles). By basing our decisions to buy on when the diffusion index of leading indicators hit zero, and our selling decisions on when the diffusion index of lagging indicators hit 100 percent, and waiting one month to act in each case, we have a finely tuned, panic-proof, market-predicting instrument.

If we had followed the signals from our diffusion indexes over the last three decades, we would have done very well indeed! To begin with, we would have been in the stock market during the long majestic upswing that marked the beginning of supercycle four throughout the early and mid-sixties. The sell signal recorded in September 1968 not only signaled the peak of that business cycle but also the peak of supercycle four.* If we had followed it, we would have taken our profits when the S&P 500 was just six months away from turning, and just before a price break that was to hammer stock prices down a full 25 percent. A buy signal would have put us back into the market in time for the bull market that began in 1970, with a sell signal getting us out in June 1973. At that point, we would not only be out of the market with huge profits but we would have avoided the panic that marked the end of supercycle four, a drop that cut stock prices by more than half. The next buy signal is recorded at the bottom of that bear market in November 1974 (which was also the beginning of supercycle five). We would have pulled out to avoid the mild bear market of 1980 but would have been back in the market to watch our portfolios go up in time with the great bull market of the eighties. So now we have methods for predicting both the beginning and the end of bull markets that when combined together are completely panic proof, right? Well, not quite.

This decade of profligate federal spending has put a new wrinkle in market analysis and has required the addition of one last predictive tool. The problem is that while an expanding business cycle will eventually always cause interest rates to go up, and the stock market to fall, it is not the only factor that will cause such an interest rate advance

*When more sell signals follow, they are disregarded until after the next buy signal. Likewise, when the diffusion index of leading indicators flashes multiple buy signals, all but the first are ignored until the next sell signal is recorded by the diffusion index of lagging indicators.

these days. As long as the U.S. economy continues to suffer under huge deficits, the megadebt itself will exert a strong upward pull on interest rates from time to time.

There have been two times so far in the eighties when the Treasury's borrowing has pushed up interest rates before natural business cycles were allowed to do so. The first instance was in 1984, when Treasury bond yields soared over 13 percent and the market subsequently slid 5 percent. The other occasion was in August 1987 at the peak of supercycle five and just before the Crash of 1987. In both these instances, the diffusion index of lagging indicators did not flash a sell signal because the economy was still below its business cycle peak. Another indicator did, however. This indicator, when used alongside the diffusion index of lagging indicators, will enable you to avoid bear market panics like the one that ripped through the market in 1987. I call this indicator the Treasury bond–discount rate spread index.

This indicator measures the difference between the discount rate set by the Federal Reserve and the yield on long-term Treasury bonds. Whenever this difference becomes greater than 3.75 percentage points—that is, whenever the yield on long-term Treasury bonds becomes more than 3.75 percentage points greater than the discount rate—it is time to sell, even if the diffusion index of lagging indicators is still below its sell signal of 100.

During the week ending March 16, 1984, long-term Treasury bond yields rose to 12.28 when the discount rate was 8.5, a difference of 3.78 percentage points. In the weeks that followed, the difference became even greater and the market fell through July. At the end of the market's decline, the diffusion index of leading indicators flashed a buy signal by dropping to zero. The bull market resumed. Bond yields and the discount rate came down, and the difference narrowed through the spring of 1986, but it soon began to widen again. During the week ending September 4, 1987, the spread climbed over 3.75 again to 3.93. That was within two weeks of the peak of the great bull market of the 1980s, and investors who heeded this warning escaped the plunge that followed.

Throughout all of 1987, the diffusion index of lagging indicators never rose above 50 percent, but bond yields rose sharply due to the Treasury's exorbitant demand for financing. Thus, as long as the Treasury is forced to sell large quantities of Treasury securities to finance a large federal budget deficit, we will need to keep track of the times when this activity becomes so great as to have the same impact on interest rates that a maturing business cycle does. The Treasury bond–discount rate spread index will give us that warning. (We will also need to keep an eye on the diffusion index of lagging indicators for sell signals, just in case the business cycle is allowed to function undaunted by government borrowing in the future.)

As we pointed out in our discussion of the stock market risk indicator, remember that the importance of these financial tools lies in their ability to allow us to avoid bear market panics. To see how an investor armed with our tools would have fared, take a look at the signals shown in table 6.1 and plotted on chart 6.3. (See appendix B for updating procedures for both diffusion indexes as well as the Treasury bond–discount rate spread index.) A look at the bottom line using these indicators highlights the superior investment results of panic-proof investing.

If an investor had put $10,000 into S&P 500 stocks in 1950 and had done nothing else, he would have a portfolio that would be worth $148,104 in November 1987. Had he

TABLE 6.1
BUSINESS CYCLE SIGNALS

Buy Signal (Leading Indicators)	*S&P 500*	*Sell Signal*	*S&P 500*	*Gain (%)*
Start 1950	16.88	March 1956[2]	48.05	184.66%
October 1956[1]	45.76	August 1959[2]	57.05	24.67%
November 1959[1]	57.23	May 1966[2]	86.06	50.38%
September 1966[1]	77.81	September 1968[2]	103.80	33.40%
November 1969[1]	91.11	June 1973[2]	105.80	16.12%
November 1974[1]	67.07	September 1977[2]	93.74	39.76%
March 1980[1]	102.97	April 1984[3]	157.30	52.76%
July 1984[1]	151.09	September 1987[3]	329.40	118.02%

[1] Diffusion index of leading indicators
[2] Diffusion index of lagging indicators
[3] Treasury bond–discount rate spread index

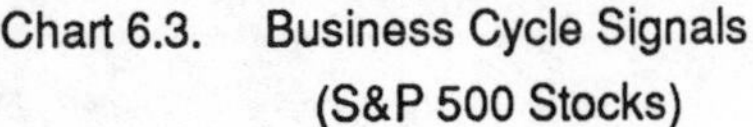
Chart 6.3. Business Cycle Signals (S&P 500 Stocks)

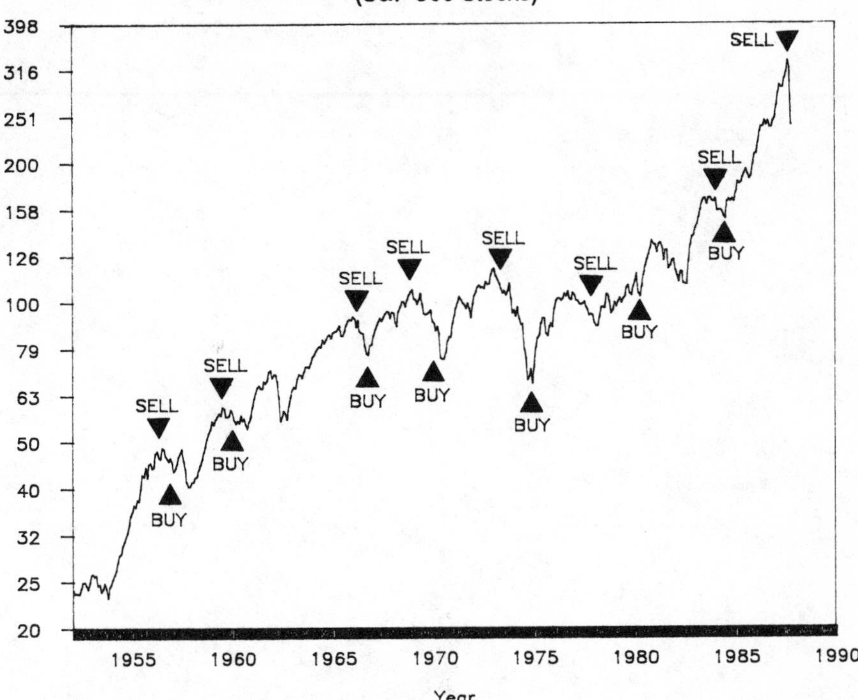

taken advantage of the signals described above, however, and put his cash in the bank or in Treasury bills at a mere 5 percent between the times when sell and buy signals were recorded, his investment would have grown to $529,205, more than 3.5 times more.

It is important to realize that most of this difference is due to the avoidance of the bear market panics in the seventies, after the peak of supercycle four. During the fifties and sixties—the boom phase of supercycle four—avoiding the bear markets certainly added to profits. But those bear markets were small niches in a steep uptrend. When supercycles peak and begin downtrending, however, bear markets become deep gorges. The bear market panics that lie ahead during the rest of supercycle five are not likely to be an exception.

HOW TO PROFIT

I

Winning with Stocks and Options

7

Inflation or Deflation?

For all its noise and energy, the stock market crash of October 1987 was just a part of the collapse of the market's fifth supercycle, and the duration of that collapse will be measured in months, not days. Of the previous four supercycles in this century, two have seen their declines accompanied by surging inflation (supercycles one and four) whereas deflation accompanied the demise of the other two. It is of extreme importance to investors to find out which of these two scenarios will accompany the collapse of supercycle five.

While deflation is a possibility that can't be ruled out entirely, it is highly unlikely in today's political climate. Given the choice, most Americans would vote for inflation over deflation, and politicians know it. Therefore, they would be very unlikely to adopt the austerity measures that were adopted by the government after the peak of supercycles two and three. And, in fact, in the wake of the Crash of 1987, the Federal Reserve has relaxed its monetary policy dramatically. The answer, then, is that the current collapse of supercycle five will result in sharply increased inflation.

This will be the case whether or not our leaders manage to shrink the federal deficit.

There has been a good deal of talk in the days since the crash of the absolute necessity to reduce the federal budget deficit, and this is all to the good. The deficit is causing huge problems for the U.S. economy. Since the crash, interest rates here have dropped sharply while the dollar has plunged to all-time lows against the currencies of Japan and West Germany. The dollar's decline has been exacerbated by the fact that Japan and Germany have been resisting stimulating their domestic economies. They do not want to risk reigniting inflation simply to help the United States accommodate its uncontrolled government spending. Should the United States manage to show that it is making substantial progress in trimming its deficit, the Germans and the Japanese would be more willing to cooperate in stabilizing the dollar by stimulating their economies. This would, in turn, result in a more favorable balance of trade for the United States and a stronger dollar.

But would even this most hopeful of scenarios manage to allow the U.S. economy to escape the ravages of rekindled inflation? Many economists and politicians think so, having been lulled by the fact that stimulative monetary practices by the Federal Reserve didn't rekindle inflation in either 1986 or 1987, but their thinking would be dangerously in error. To understand why, it is necessary to look at one of the most frequently ignored economic fundamentals.

There are a growing number of analysts these days who point to the negligible inflation rate during the last few years of loose monetary policy and argue that this shows that inflation is not a threat to our economy. What they forget, or ignore, is that the level of consumer prices is influenced not only by the supply of money in the economy but also by how fast that money is spent. The rate at which money is circulated is known as "velocity," and it is every bit as important as the size of the money supply. This relationship is expressed by the equation: $M \times V = P \times T$, where M is the supply of money, V is the velocity of the money supply, T is the volume of transactions in the economy, and P is price. If you multiply the number of transactions times the level of prices, you arrive at the total dollar value of the economy, known as the gross national product (GNP).

First, let's look at the left side of the equation. Clearly if the money supply expands dramatically it will have a profound effect on the product of $M \times V$ and thus on the right side of the equation or the GNP (and, depending on the level of transactions, on the inflation rate). It will, that is, unless there is a sharp drop in the velocity at which that money supply is circulating through the economy as has been happening during the debt-choked eighties.

Chart 7.1 shows the velocity of money since 1952. Until 1980, the American money supply circulated at a rate that grew by an average of 3 percent a year. This rate of increase was so consistent that economists soon began to assume that it was a constant, and it began to disappear as a variable in the inflation equation. But then came the 1980s and the necessity to finance a gargantuan federal debt. As Treasury bill and bond prices were depressed by the Treasury's huge sales needed to finance the federal debt, real interest rates

Chart 7.1. Money Velocity
(GNP Divided by Money Supply)

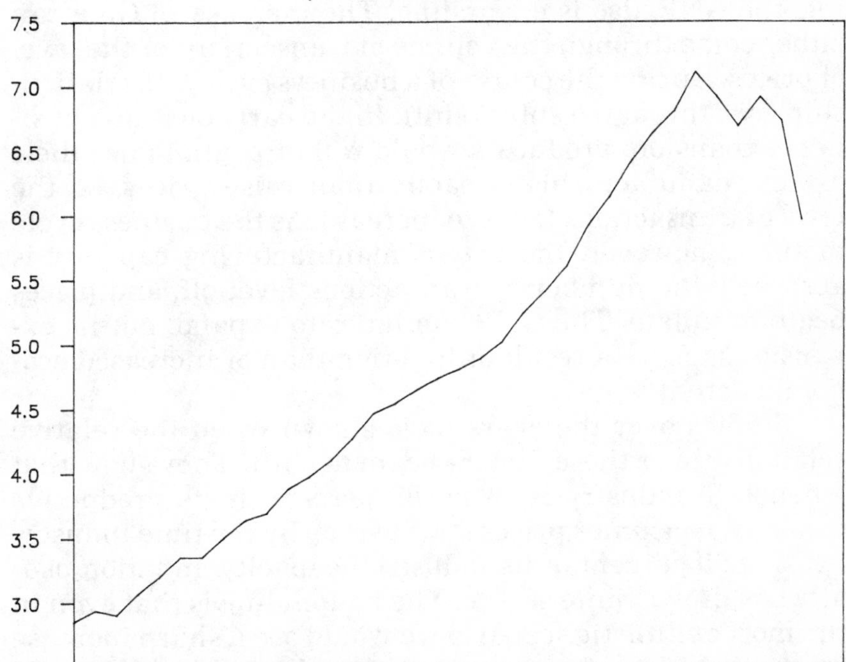

rose and the velocity of money began declining dramatically.

Put simply, money velocity is the measure of whether Americans are spending money or holding it. If people are saving or investing money rather than spending it, their actions will lower the velocity of the money supply. In a situation of high inflation rates and low interest rates there is a strong incentive to buy consumer items rather than to save and invest. In a time of low inflation rates and relatively high interest rates, the situation is reversed. Buying decisions often are deferred in favor of the relatively high return offered by savings instruments and other investment vehicles. This is what has been happening in the eighties, and money velocity has slipped a full 17 percent.

Should American policy makers make substantial inroads into the size of the federal deficit, the upward pressure on interest rates that has been constant during most of the 1980s will be relieved. But this would have the inevitable effect of stimulating consumer spending, which would increase the velocity of money.

As we saw above, when the product of $M \times V$ is expanding, the GNP also is expanding. The increase in GNP can either come through the volume of transactions or the level of prices. During the course of a business cycle this relationship goes through a subtle shift. In the early days of a business expansion, producers would rather begin to use their excess manufacturing capacity than raise prices, so the level of transactions tends to increase. As the business cycle matures, however, the excess manufacturing capacity is absorbed, the number of transactions level off, and prices begin to inflate. The GNP continues to expand, but its expansion is more a result of inflation than of increased economic activity.

Studies over the years have shown when the relative relationship of these factors begin to shift. They show that when U.S. industry is using 85 percent of its productive capacity, consumer prices start to rise. By the time industry is using 90 percent of its industrial capacity, inflation usually has grown quite severe. The bottom line is that even in the most optimistic scenario we would see a sharp increase in the velocity of money that would combine with the greatly increased supply of money so far, as well as the inevitable increase in the future, to spark a resurgence of inflation.

At this writing, there appears to be almost no chance that dramatic action will be taken to reduce the budget deficit beyond the relatively modest Gramm-Rudman goals and the prospects of a balanced federal budget seem bleak indeed. Therefore, it is necessary to examine the other possible scenario—that of red ink. The result is bound to be the same: increased inflation.

A despairing look at the prospects for budget balancing need go no further than the Social Security system. Although it was originally designed to be a government-administered pure insurance scheme, guaranteeing that what an individual paid in during his working years would be returned to him upon retirement (along with accumulated earnings), politicians have long since severed any actuarial linkage between income and expenditure and have turned the Social Security system into a safety net for all Americans. Thus, Social Security has graduated into a giant Ponzi scheme, promising benefits to millions of retirees while mortgaging the incomes of workers who are not yet born. By the end of 1986, the cost of Social Security soared to $210 billion, which by itself equaled the entire budget deficit in 1986. Even though it has become a budgetary monster, complete with built-in automatic benefit increases each year, there are only a handful of legislators who are willing to entertain the thought of trimming Social Security even slightly. Even in the days following the Crash of 1987, when public concern impelled Congress and the administration to try to work together to cut government spending, Social Security was still a sacred cow. And only a few more politicians argue seriously for meaningful reductions in defense spending.

Beyond all of this, however, and towering over every discussion of economic or political priorities, is the actual cost of financing the national debt. In 1986, a year of relatively low interest rates (given the context of the high-interest-rate eighties), the government spent $187 billion on interest alone. This expenditure is increasing along with the increasing federal debt, and it will increase further as interest rates rise.

Social Security, defense, and interest on the national

debt amount to 70 percent of all government spending. And there are other sacred cows, including military and other federal pensions that have automatic cost-of-living adjustments with nowhere to go but up. When these items are figured in, the amount of the federal budget that is politically immune to change is 85 percent. Even if Congress were to decide to eliminate totally the other 15 percent, axing programs like highway maintenance, farm price supports, student loans, and expenditures on the federal criminal justice system, there would still be a deficit.

As Congress struggled to find a way to meet Gramm-Rudman targets, they quickly found themselves hard up against these implacable budget realities. For a while some thought went into selling off government assets, but the effort was halfhearted. While there might be some short-term relief, there would be a loss of future income from the vanished assets. It simply was not an answer for the imponderables that lay behind the budget deficits. As House Budget Committee Chairman William Gray put it, "It's like selling your garage to make this month's mortgage payment. What do you do next month?" Largely unremarked upon was the fact that asset sales simply serve to drain capital out of the private sector, which has the same impact as a direct funding of the deficit.

Even in the extremely unlikely event that somehow federal politicians cut spending sufficiently to meet Gramm-Rudman goals, the deficits are not very likely to disappear. A more than cursory look at the economic assumptions behind the Gramm-Rudman forecasts reveal that they are widely optimistic. These forecasts, for instance, assumed that interest rates on federal securities would remain at 5.6 percent until 1990. But given the nature of the business cycle and/or the upward pull exerted on interest rates from financing the budget deficit, this assumption is absurd. At the peak of the last business cycle, interest rates on three-month Treasury bills were 15 percent. If interest rates go to anywhere near that level again, the yearly deficit could be as much as $400 billion more than the forecasts. That potential error is itself greater than any deficit we have seen so far.

Given the extent of this gloomy news, it's no wonder that so many budget analysts are agreeing with former budget director David Stockman's bleak forecast of $200 billion plus deficits for "as far as the eye can see." The only solution Stockman sees is a massive tax hike. Unfortunately, tax hikes have proven to be politically unpalatable. And a tax hike of the size necessary to make any sort of dent on the problem would have a profoundly negative impact on the economy.

Without meaningful progress on cutting the deficit, our foreign trading partners are not going to be sympathetic. They will be less willing to risk an inflation explosion at home so we can continue to be irresponsible. Without this cooperation, we will have no choice but to monetize our own deficit, to increase the money supply sufficiently so that there are enough dollars in this country to buy our own Treasury securities. The Federal Reserve will have to keep its discount rate low to ensure that there is an adequate money supply to finance both the national debt and the basic needs of the economy; otherwise interest rates will be pulled upward by the Treasury's financing demands and the economy could slide easily into a deep recession or depression. Already we can see the massive increases in the money supply that have been necessary so far to satisfy the Treasury's needs and to keep an anemic economy alive. The simple fact is that the unbridled growth of the national debt has forced, and probably will continue to force, unprecedented increases in money supply growth, which inescapably must lead to sizzling inflation.

8

Protecting Your Portfolio

Supercycle five is past its peak and has started its inexorable decline. From history we know that the downtrend will not end soon. Stocks have gone down for many years after the peak of past supercycles. The shortest period of decline (supercycle two) was slightly less than three years; the longest (supercycle one) lasted fourteen years; the average supercycle decline lasted seven years. Thus, it is likely that there are at least several years of hard times lying ahead for the stock market, and it is important that we become familiar with the ways in which we can protect our stocks against, and even profit from, the declining markets that lie ahead. In this chapter we will concentrate on the strategies that will protect your portfolio from deteriorating stock prices. It will be necessary to understand these basic concepts in order to implement the strategies covered in chapter 9, which will enable us to profit directly from the downtrending phase of supercycle five.

The best means available to investors who are trying to profit from a market that is trending downward is a trading device which, though it has existed for decades, has been formally organized only since the early seventies: stock options. Stock options have been traded in an organized manner since the spring of 1973 when the newly created Chicago Board of Options Exchange first listed call options for sixteen stocks. Soon three other exchanges were formed, in Philadelphia, San Francisco, and New York, and by the mid-eighties the number of stocks on which options trade had grown to more than five hundred. As options markets have grown, so have the number of trading strategies that are available to owners of common stock, and as the stock market heads into hurricane latitudes, it is important for us to have all of these strategies firmly in mind.

A call option on a stock is exactly the same as an option on a piece of real estate. When you buy a stock call option, you buy the right to purchase 100 shares of a particular stock at a designated price, during a designated time period. The reason you would want to buy such an option is because you think that the stock's price will go up during the designated time period and thus you will have purchased the right to acquire it at a below-market price. This simple gamble represents the most obvious and accessible level of the options market.

Suppose for a second that you and your neighbor are discussing investments over your backyard fence. He owns 100 shares of General Technologies stock with a market value of $51 per share, but he's unhappy. He thinks that his General Technologies stock is going nowhere. However, you have strong reason to believe that the price of General Technologies is about to go up dramatically. Given your hunch, you could buy the 100 shares of General Technologies from your neighbor for $5,100. Or, perhaps you could persuade your neighbor to sell you an option to buy his stock anytime in the next three months for $50 a share. For this right, you will pay him $600 immediately. By selling you such an option, your neighbor will pocket $600 while you will capture all of the upscale potential you see in General Technologies, at a risk of only $600. If General Technologies were to rise to say, $60 during the three-month life of your option, you could exercise the option, sell the stock, and realize $1,000 on an investment of only $600—a profit of 66 percent. Note that if you had purchased the stock outright at $51, the $900 profit would represent only 17.6 percent on an investment of $5,100. This is the leverage and limited amount of risk that makes call options so attractive to investors. Of course, in order for you to make any profit at all, the stock will have to move at least from $51 to $56—a fairly substantial move.

As for your neighbor, he will be protected to the extent of your $600 investment against any downward movement in the stock. But it is clear that he also will profit if the price of General Technologies is essentially unchanged at the end of the three-month period. If, for instance, the stock is $51 in three months, you could exercise your option to buy at $50, and thus recoup $100 of your $600 investment. He will have gained $500 (you gave him $600 for the option and $5,000 for the stock itself for a total of $5,600; the market value of the stock alone was $5,100, hence a $500 profit). That $500 represents a 9.8 percent return for just three months.

So we can see that while call options can give an investor who is very certain that a stock is about to rise sharply a relatively low-risk, high-leverage way to play his hunch, it is the seller who is most likely to profit from options. For the buyer to profit, the stock's price must rise sharply—in the case of our example, a full 9.8 percent in three months, but for the seller to profit it can stay the same, advance, or even decline somewhat. Given the fact that stocks have advanced, on average, less than 5 percent per year during this century, investors who are gambling continually on advances in stock prices in the range of 9.8 percent over three months (39 percent annually) will not win very often.

Clearly, your neighbor is employing the superior strategy for the long-term. And in actual practice, he is not necessarily forced to give up his stock even if it is above $50 a share at the end of the call period. The reason is the existence of the options market itself, which makes it possible for call options to acquire a market value of their own. This value is determined by the price of the underlying stock, the length of time left during which the option can be exercised, and the dynamics of the marketplace. (For simplicity's sake, we will ignore commission costs in the discussion that follows, though they can become a significant factor in some strategies.) Your neighbor can go to the market and buy an option that is identical to the one he sold. The original sale and the purchase offset each other, and there would be no outstanding call against your neighbor's stock. His profit or loss, in that case, would be determined by the difference in price between the call option he sold and the one he bought.

It is important to realize that as long as a premium exists in the price of the option, your neighbor can be assured that no one will exercise their right to buy his stock. When he sold the option at $600 while the stock was at $51, the intrinsic value of the option was $100, because it gave you the right to buy 100 shares of the stock at $50. The rest of the option's price was a premium of $500. The premium is at its greatest at the beginning of the option period, declines gradually until finally, in the last hours before the option expires, the premium vanishes. If the stock is $51 at that time, the option will sell for $100 with no premium. Your neighbor can be assured that no one will exercise the option until the time on the option nearly has run out, because as long as there is a premium attached to the price of an option—and there always will be so long as there is time remaining on the option—anyone desiring to actually possess the stock would first sell the option on the option exchange in order to capture the premium, and would then buy the stock on the open market.

Say, for instance, that you decided you wanted to buy your neighbor's stock. You could exercise the option and buy his stock for $5,000. But if you did that you would be throwing away the $500 premium on the option itself. Therefore, if you wanted to actually buy 100 shares of General Technologies, you would sell your option for $600 and then use that money to help buy 100 shares in the stock market at $51 a share. That $600 would allow you to buy the 100 for $4,500.

Although your neighbor can be assured that no one will exercise the option he has sold as long as there is any premium attached to its price, as the option approaches the end of its life and its premium disappears, he will have to decide whether he wants to give up his stock. If the price of the stock is still above $50, and if your neighbor decides he doesn't want to lose his position in General Technologies, he will have to buy another call option to offset the one he sold. Yet by then he already will have made his profit. There are three ways the price of General Technologies could go during the three-month options period. Let's see what each will do to your neighbor's fortunes.

First, let's assume that the price of General Technologies has risen to $60. At that point a call option will be selling for $1,000. (There is no premium—we are too close to the exercise period for that; this is just the difference between $50 and $60 on 100 shares of stock.) If he buys this call option, your neighbor will realize a loss of $400—the difference between the $600 option he sold and the $1,000 option he bought. But this will allow him to keep his stock, which has appreciated $900 in value since he originally sold the call option. Therefore, he still is $500 ahead—an annualized return of 39 percent.

But what if the stock price is still $51 at the end of the option period? In that case the call option will cost $100 to purchase and your neighbor still will realize an overall gain of $500. Of course, if the price of the stock drops below $50, the call option will be worthless and simply will expire. In that event your neighbor will pocket the $600, which will help offset his loss on the price of the stock.

You can see that because the options market allows options themselves to be traded, your neighbor has been able to continue holding, and collecting dividends from his stocks while generating cash by writing options. This strategy is known as "covered option writing."

Covered option writing is a very conservative approach to owning stocks. In fact, because this strategy functions as a downside hedge, it is actually safer than just owning stocks, and in a sluggish market the profit potential is pleasingly high. All of this safety and stagnant market profit potential is purchased at a price: Investors following this strategy give up the ability to make a killing on very dramatic increases in stock prices. In a roaring bull market, therefore, this strategy may limit profits, although, as we have just seen, they are still substantial. But now that supercycle five has peaked, we should be worrying less about limiting further bull market killings, and worrying more about hedging ourselves against a downtrending market.

There is another similar strategy that is somewhat more aggressive, but that will give us even more protection and more profit potential. Let's return to your neighbor's situation. He is trying to protect the value of his 100 shares of General Technologies that is currently selling at $51. If your neighbor is nearly certain that the price of General Technologies is about to fall, he might be well advised to sell two call options on his stock. From the sale of the two options he now has protected himself against a $1,200 drop in the price of his stock.

But what if he's wrong? What if the stock doesn't drop? Actually he is still in very good shape. If at the end of the three-month period the price of the stock hasn't changed and is still selling at about $51, he will have to buy two call options to cover the ones he has sold. These options will be worth $100 each so he will show a profit of $1,000 ($1,200 on the original sale less the $200 it has cost him to buy). This represents a 19.6 percent return (a 78 percent annualized return) on his $5,100 worth of General Technologies stock. (You'll note that the second call option he wrote was not covered, that is, he did not have a second 100 shares of General Technologies to back up the option. This means that he will need to satisfy basic margin maintenance requirements in order to pursue this strategy. Those requirements are detailed in appendix C.)

And if the stock goes up? Well, let's see what would happen if the stock was to go up to $57 at the end of the three-month period. At this point, two new options would have to be purchased for $700 each. This would represent a $200 loss, but in the meantime the stock will have appreciated $600, so there will be a net profit of $400. This represents an annualized return of more than 31 percent. In fact, even with this strategy, which is designed to protect against the downside, the stock would have to increase to $61 at the end of the three-month period before your neighbor would be thrown into a situation where he would receive a loss.

The strategy we have just explored is known as "ratio writing," and it is best used in a diversified portfolio. As we have just seen, stocks can move in a wide range with this strategy while still bringing in profits.

To see the potential benefits of ratio writing, let's look at a stock portfolio that could have been established in the first half of 1987. The portfolio shown in table 8.1 has 100 share blocks of four stocks: Northwest Airlines (NWA) at $63 a share, Burlington Northern (BNI) at $67, United Technologies (UTX) at $48, and Boeing Aircraft (BA) at $53. The total value of this portfolio is $23,100. In pursuit of our strategy we will sell two call options on each of the stocks at an exercise price (called a "strike price") just a few dollars above the current price levels and with a life of three to four months each. This would result, as table 8.1 shows, in an income of $3,550.

Table 8.1 goes on to show how our strategy would fare under a variety of market conditions. If the prices of all of our stocks were to remain below the strike prices of our call options at the end of their respective lives, we would pocket the $3,550, applying it to any losses that we may have been handed by the stock prices themselves. If the net prices of the underlying stocks remained unchanged, this return would annualize out to 53 percent. If the underlying stocks were to lose 5 percent, our return still would amount to an annualized rate of return in excess of 35 percent. If our

TABLE 8.1
RATIO WRITING

	NWA	*BNI*	*UTX*	*BA*	*Total*
Number of shares	100	100	100	100	
Stock price ($)	63	67	48	53	
Investment ($)	6,300	6,700	4,800	5,300	23,100
CALL OPTION					
Life (months)	3	3	4	4	
Strike price ($)	65	70	50	55	
Option price ($)	4.25	5	4	4.5	
Number of options sold	2	2	2	2	
Cash received ($)	850	1,000	800	900	3,550

Change in Stock Price (%)	*Profit or Loss ($)*				*Total ($)*	*Annualized Return (%)*
	NWA	*BNI*	*UTX*	*BA*		
20	(10)	260	240	240	730	11
15	305	595	480	505	1,885	28
10	620	930	720	770	3,040	45
5	935	1,265	960	1,035	4,195	62
Unchanged	850	1,000	800	900	3,550	53
−5	535	665	560	635	2,395	36
−10	220	330	320	370	1,240	18
−15	(95)	(5)	80	105	85	1
−20	(410)	(340)	(160)	(160)	(1,070)	−16

stocks dropped 10 percent—our return would be 18 percent. Even if our stocks were to drop a full 15 percent—equivalent to a drop in the Dow of more than 300 points from a level of 2000—we still would be in the black. And even in a situation where the market drops more than this, our strategy has the potential for keeping losses low. In a time when stock prices are falling rapidly, we can write more options against our stocks, or simply close out all positions and wait out the storm.

And if prices go up? Well, as we have seen, if these price increases are moderate we will pull in substantial rates of return: a 62 percent annualized rate of return in the event of a 5 percent increase in stock prices; 45 percent with a 10 percent increase; 28 percent with a 15 percent increase. But the amazing thing about this strategy is how far stocks can rocket before we start seeing our profits disappear. Even a 20 percent increase will return an 11 percent annualized yield. And if the market begins to mount an advance of this magnitude or greater, we always can close out our option positions before the expiration period is up.

Interestingly enough, a sharp rally in the market reduces the premiums from options. This is because a great number of the traders who buy options do so because they represent leverage. But as stock prices outdistance the strike prices of the call options—putting those options "in the money"—they become more expensive. And as they become more expensive, their value to speculators declines, and so do their premiums. Thus, even when stocks advance sharply when we are ratio writing, our losses will be reduced, and could be offset totally, by the decay of those premiums.

Had an investor implemented the transactions shown in table 8.1, he would have watched three of the four stocks increase sharply as the Dow Jones rocketed to 2700. Yet, in the case of all four stocks, he would have shown a profit had he just waited until the day the options expired and bought back the uncovered calls while letting the covered calls expire or be exercised. In total, he would have realized a profit of $1,602, which would represent an annualized rate of return of 23.8 percent.

The bottom line: In a situation where the market reasonably can be expected to either stay stagnant or decline moderately, ratio writing offers substantial potential for profit, and even if the market starts moving more violently—either upward or downward—it still is possible to close out your option positions and shift to more adequate strategies.

In this chapter we have discussed strategies that will hedge our stocks against declines. Now let's look at ways to profit directly from downtrending markets.

9

Cashing in on the Crash

The decline of supercycle five is likely to be so widespread that only the rarest of stocks will go unscathed. Don't gamble on having such a stroke of luck. But even if you decide to sell everything and forget about stocks and options for the next few years to concentrate on the other promising markets discussed in the chapters ahead, don't quit reading yet. You can ring up handsome profits directly from the crashing market even as you move most of your investment capital to greener investment fields.

It is always said that the best, and often the only, way to make money during a time when a market is crashing is to short-sell stock. Though always said, in practice it is done rarely. If you have ever short-sold a stock, you are one of a very select group of investors. Although short-selling has been around as a strategy for a long time, it has never been used widely. In part this is simply due to the fact that for many investors the idea of selling a stock and then buying it at a lower price seems to attack some basic law of nature: that you can't sell what you do not own. Moreover, many investors who have tried to short-sell stocks have been burned by the contrary nature of the market. Since the strategy of short-selling only works at a time when a stock's price is declining, many investors have been stung by the market's tendency to anticipate news. By making their judgment of a stock's downside potential on the basis of negative news, rather than on more sophisticated market measures, many have seen their stocks move upward during even the gloomiest of times. For the short-seller, of course, this movement is always a disaster.

About thirteen years ago I watched a colleague experience just this sort of debacle. It was 1974, and the market had definitely turned bearish, so he decided to start shorting stocks.

The first stock he picked to short was International Flavors and Fragrances. Just the name sounded flaky to him. And it was selling at $29 which, based on its current earnings, represented a price/earnings (P/E) ratio of twenty. Although average by today's standards, back then this P/E ratio was outrageously high. The Dow was sinking fast—it was on its way to 550—and even glamorous Dow stocks were selling at P/E ratios of seven. So he shorted 100 shares.

My colleague was a stockbroker and had an electronic quote machine right next to his desk. For the next few days he was punching in I-F-F (the ticker symbol) every five minutes so that he could witness the disastrous fall that he expected this stock to take. Well, despite the rotten market conditions, International Flavors and Fragrances inched upward incessantly—one half of a point one day, three quarters the next, and after a week it was a full three points higher.

The next week was even worse. Instead of fractional points, the stock rose by more than a point most days, and trading volume started to get active. By now the stock had climbed to $38. It was getting ridiculous!

When he shorted the stock originally, my colleague began boasting to his cohorts of his clever idea, but now he was the object of much jocular ridicule in the office. His friends would pass him in the hall and ask how International Flavors and Fragrances was doing, or lean over his desk to watch IFF climbing steadily on his quote machine.

The following week was the last straw. On Monday the stock was up two points and earnings came out after the close. IFF reported fantastic earnings, and I could see that my colleague was sick. It seemed obvious that this news would drive the stock up even further. He wanted his nightmare to end, so he put in an order to buy 100 shares on the next day's market opening. Of course, the wonderful news did cause the stock to leap upward on the opening—to 44¼—which is where he covered his short position, and that, as you've probably guessed, was the high for the year. In the two months that followed, the stock subsequently plummeted to $15 a share as the market crashed in 1974.

My colleague's experience illustrates the problem that many investors have with shorting stocks. In normal circumstances an investor buys a stock anticipating that it will go up. Hopefully, he will be right, but even if he's wrong he has a basic confidence that no stock drops to zero; there is always an underlying value below which no stock can fall. However, an investor that short-sells a stock has no such assurance. Stocks can, and regularly do, skyrocket to levels that are totally unjustified by any underlying fundamentals. They usually will not stay at these inflated levels for long, but any time can be too long for the investor who has gambled wrongly on a decline.

Looking at strategies like the one described above, the nation's options markets decided to introduce an option that would operate virtually identically: the put option. Knowledge of the put option will be essential for investors who want to reap the profits offered by the crash of supercycle five.

As you might expect, the put option is the mirror image of a call option. It gives the buyer the right to sell 100 shares of a given stock at a given price (again called a strike price) for a given amount of time. As the value of a stock declines, the value of a put option increases.

When put options were first introduced in the nation's options exchanges in 1978, their prices corresponded almost exactly with the price of the underlying stock and the cost of a call option on that stock. If, for example, a three-month call option at $30 a share on 100 shares of IFF was $250 when the stock itself was selling for $29 a share, an investor could short-sell that 100 shares while buying a call and this strategy would limit his or her exposure to $350.* Not surprisingly, therefore, put options on IFF would be

*Since the call option guarantees that he can buy the stock at $30 to cover his short-sale, his loss is limited to the $100 difference between $29 and $30 plus the $250 cost of the call option.

priced very close to $350 so long as the underlying stock price remains at $29. If my colleague had been able to buy a put option on IFF in 1974, he would have watched its value decline from $350 as the stock price advanced to $44.25, but since he had limited his exposure to an acceptable $350, he would have hung on and been able to watch happily as IFF finally fell to $15 a share. During the period of the decline, the value of the put would be increasing continually until, when IFF hit its bottom of $15, its intrinsic value would have risen to $1,500—more than four times his initial investment. Moreover, if the decline in IFF had come while a significant amount of the option's time period remained, there would be a premium in the price of the put option that would have increased his profits still further.

In a rapidly declining market, therefore, put options give us a way to make substantial downside profits, while keeping our exposure at a quite acceptable low. Moreover, other recent additions to the options market allow us to limit our risk still further. As my colleague found out to his great chagrin with International Flavors and Fragrances, it always is possible for the price of one stock to defy even the strongest broad market trend, and thus it always is possible that the stock you have decided to short is the one stock that is going up in a bear market. Today, however, in addition to a greatly expanded list of stocks on which options trade, it also is possible to buy put and call options on the broad stock market measures. Index options are being traded currently on the Standard and Poor's 100 and 500 indexes, the New York Stock Exchange composite index, the American Stock Exchange index, and the Value Line composite index.

Options on market indexes work the same way as they do on individual stocks, with one difference: When the option is exercised, money changes hands and not stocks. Suppose, for example, that you were to decide to buy a put option on the S&P 100 Index with a strike price of 290 for, say, $300. If the S&P 100 Index were to fall to 280, on expiration day the option would be worth the difference between 290 and 280 times 100 or, in this case, $1,000. Assuming you did not sell it before then, while it still had a premium, you still would make $700 on a $300 investment.

The use of the S&P 100 Index in this example is not casual; the S&P 100 is currently the preferred options index. Market professionals prefer it because it is based broadly enough that it can be depended on to move in concert with the market (the market has moved with the S&P 500 Stock Index a full 97 percent of the time, and followed the exact moves of the Dow Jones Industrial Average 95 percent of the time). Yet the base is small enough so that market professionals can create a portfolio composed of these stocks, which in turn allows them to use S&P Index options as a hedge against declines in the portfolio itself. For the smaller investor, the presence of these large traders in the S&P 100 Index is a good thing because it makes for a very liquid options market.

One of the problems with buying puts outright is that they have a premium, a premium that will erode naturally with the passage of time. Moreover, as the underlying stock or index drops, the puts become more expensive, which makes them less attractive to buyers wanting leverage, and the premium erodes for this reason as well. We can reduce this problem, and increase our leverage at the same time with what is called a "bear spread," using puts.

A spread in options involves the simultaneous purchase of one option and the sale of another. A bear spread is a kind of options spread that is specifically designed to make us money when the underlying stock or market index declines. Suppose, for example, that the S&P 100 Index is 280. We might find quotations like the following for three-month put options:

S&P 100 INDEX OPTIONS

Strike Price	*Puts—Last (Closing Price)*
280	8½
285	10½

We could create a bear spread by purchasing a put with the higher strike price of 285 for $1,050 and simultaneously selling the put with the lower strike price of 280 for $850. The $200 difference between these two prices (plus the brokerage commissions) is the only money we would need to execute this transaction. This is a conservative bear spread because we don't actually need the S&P 100 Index to decline. As long as it does not go up more than two points, we make money.

As time passes, the premiums will erode on both put

options. Close to expiration date, the price of each put will be close to its intrinsic value. With the S&P 100 Index unchanged at 280, the put with the strike price of 285 (the one we bought) would be selling at $500 because it is "in the money" by five points. The put with the strike price of 280 (the one we sold) would be worthless. Thus, with no movement in the S&P 100 Index our $200 investment would turn into $500—a profit of 150 percent.

If the S&P 100 Index were to drop, say to 275, our profit would be the same. The put with the strike price of 285 would be selling at $1,000 close to the end of the option's life, and the put with the strike price of 280 would be selling for $500—again a difference of $500 and a profit of 150 percent.

But what if the S&P 100 Index rises? In that case we could lose as much as we invested but no more. If the index rose to 285 or higher, both of the puts would expire worthless, and our $200 would be lost. It could rise as high as 283 without suffering a loss, however, because the puts we bought with a strike price of 285 would still be worth $200 near the expiration date.

In this bear-spread configuration, we have taken advantage of the forces that erode the premiums on options. We have done this by selling the option with the larger premium and purchasing the option with the smaller premium. The option with its strike price closest to the market value of the underlying index or stock always will have the fattest premium. Conversely, the option that already is in the money will be more expensive and have a lot of its premium squeezed out of it. The passage of time will erode the price of the option with the largest premium—the option we sold—at a faster rate and this will make us money even if the underlying index or stock doesn't budge.

When you begin to use this bear-spread strategy you will need to find a quick way of organizing information and calculating your potential risk and profit. Table 9.1 shows such a way. (This table is produced in blank form in appendix D). By filling in the information on table 9.1, we can see that the S&P 100 Index has to move up 1.07 percent (three points) before we would begin to lose money. The table shows our profit-to-risk ratio to be 1.5, which means that for each dollar we are risking we expect to make $1.50.

Even in a relatively stable market, this strategy should work many more times than it will fail, and because the

TABLE 9.1
WORKSHEET FOR PUT BEAR SPREADS

(FOR ONE SPREAD ON 100 SHARES)

(A) Price of put option purchased	$ 1,050	(A)
(B) Price of put option sold	$ 850	(B)
(C) Risk: (A) minus (B) equals	$ 200	(C)
(D) Strike price of option purchased	$ 285	(D)
(E) Strike price of option sold	$ 280	(E)
(F) Break-even point: Divide (C) by 100 and subtract the result from (D)	$ 283	(F)
(G) Price of underlying index or stock	$ 280	(G)
(H) Move needed to break even: Subtract (G) from (F), divide by (G), and multiply the result by 100	% 1.07	(H)
(I) Maximum profit: Subtract (E) from (D), multiply the result times 100, and subtract (C)	$ 300	(I)
(J) Profit-to-risk ratio: (I) divided by (C)	1.5	(J)

rewards are greater than the risk, you will make money even if it works only half of the time. We can also employ a more aggressive bear spread by widening the gap between the strike prices of the put options we sell and the ones we buy. Let's expand our newspaper column to get a larger array of choices.

S&P 100 INDEX OPTIONS

Strike Price	*Puts—Last (Closing Price)*
265	3½
270	5¼
275	6¾
280	8½
285	10½

We could purchase one put with the strike price of 285 as we did before, but instead of selling the put with the strike price of 280, we could sell one with the strike price of 265. This would bring us $350. When we put the information on our worksheet (table 9.2), we can see what it looks like.

The first thing we realize is that we are risking $700 instead of $200, and that the stock actually must move down

TABLE 9.2
WORKSHEET FOR PUT BEAR SPREADS

(FOR ONE SPREAD ON 100 SHARES)

(A)	Price of put option purchased	$ 1,050 (A)
(B)	Price of put option sold	$ 350 (B)
(C)	Risk: (A) minus (B) equals	$ 700 (C)
(D)	Strike price of option purchased	$ 285 (D)
(E)	Strike price of option sold	$ 265 (E)
(F)	Break-even point: Divide (C) by 100 and subtract the result from (D)	$ 278 (F)
(G)	Price of underlying index or stock	$ 280 (G)
(H)	Move needed to break even: Subtract (G) from (F), divide by (G), and multiply the result by 100	% −0.7 (H)
(I)	Maximum profit: Subtract (E) from (D), multiply the result times 100, and subtract (C)	$ 1,300 (I)
(J)	Profit-to-risk ratio (I) divided by (C)	1.86 (J)

two points (0.7 percent) by the expiration date for us to break even. Therefore, our risk is slightly higher. But we also can see that the profit potential is higher. If the index drops to 265 or below, we will have a profit of $1,300. This means that for every dollar we are risking we could make $1.86.

In this second, more aggressive bear spread, we are hoping for a sharp drop in the market to make our maximum profit, and we will need a slight drop to break even. The drop from 280 to 265 that is required to maximize profits in this more aggressive bear spread would occur in an environment when the Dow Jones Industrials were dropping in the neighborhood of 120 points. (Generally, a move of 1 point in the S&P 100 Index will be accompanied by an 8-point move in the Dow.)

Aggressive bear spreads do not necessarily need to be limited to index options; in fact, you may find that you will get more action out of individual stocks, particularly those that are priced above $100 a share. Stocks like Texas Instruments, Teledyne, and IBM, can, and frequently do, move ten, fifteen, twenty points in a single week, and often they have greater volatility than broad market indexes. A put bear spread with strike prices far apart on such stocks has enormous profit potential. The same worksheet as we used for index options will help you see which stocks you can trade without exposing yourself to intolerable risk.

So far we have discussed options on stocks and stock market indexes. There is another strategy worth mentioning that is certain to throw off profits. As we have seen, whenever bear markets occur, they are marked by a stiff rise in interest rates. When that happens bond prices automatically go into a tailspin—a tailspin we can turn to our advantage because there are now options trading on Treasury bonds, and put bear spreads will reap huge profits.

In fact, there are options available on both short-term Treasury bills and Treasury notes, as well as on long-term Treasury bonds, but you will find the latter to be much more profitable. This is because the prices of longer-term bonds are much more sensitive to a change in interest rates than shorter-term bonds. Here's why. The yield from a bond is made up of two components: one is the "coupon" payment, that semiannual payment of interest that comes from the government; and the other is the difference in the purchase price of the bond and its face value—the $1,000 that the Treasury will pay to the owner of the bond when it matures. When both components are factored into the return, the result is called a "yield to maturity."

If interest rates are close to the bond's coupon rate, that bond will sell close to its face value; otherwise the bond will sell at either a discount or a premium. With interest rates at 8 percent, for example, a $1,000 Treasury bond paying interest at the rate of $80 per year will sell for $1,000 because $80 is 8 percent of $1,000. But what if interest rates climb to 12 percent? If this is a short-term bond that matures in one year, its price will drop by $36 to $964. Someone buying the bond at that figure will only receive $80 in interest, but when the $36 profit is factored in, the total of $116 is 12 percent of the purchase price of $964. If, however, this is a long-term bond, the price will have to drop much more in order to give investors a sufficient additional profit for each year until the bond matures. The price of a bond maturing in twenty years that paid $80 a year would have to drop to $720 to furnish a 12 percent annual yield to maturity.

Inflationary pressures in the months and years ahead

will cause interest rates to rise in earnest, and long-term bond prices will drop like a rock. If you are positioned in a put bear spread at that time, you will make enormous profits.

Options on long-term Treasury bonds work the same way as other options do, except that the underlying security that is tendered upon the exercise of the option is $100,000 of Treasury bonds. Of course, as we have seen, no one in his right mind exercises options while they still have premiums on them. So in practice, you can be assured that no one will exercise a put option much before expiration day.

Bond prices are quoted as a percentage of their "par," value which is $1,000 in the case of all Treasury bonds. Thus, a quote of 92 means that the bond's price is 92 percent of $1,000, or $920. Any figures to the right of the decimal indicate the number of thirty-seconds. A quote of 92.20 really means 92 and 20⁄32, which is 92.625 percent of par, or $926.25 per bond. The same rules hold for Treasury bond option prices. Therefore, you will have to remember to convert the quotations you get from the newspaper or your broker for both the bonds and the options on the bonds.

There are both put and call options being traded on Treasury bonds with strike prices every two points. A bond trading around 92 usually will have options with strike prices at 88, 90, 92, 94, and 96. A long-term Treasury bond on which options are traded is described in the newspapers as the 7½ November 2016. This means that the bond has a coupon of 7½ percent of par, or $75, of which half is paid on each May 15 and November 15, and the bond matures on November 15, 2016.

In the middle of 1987, this Treasury bond was quoted at 92, representing a yield to maturity of 8.26 percent. A three-month put option on 100 Treasury bonds with a strike price of 94 could be purchased for $325. The put with a strike price of 92 was selling for $250. Table 9.3 uses our familiar worksheet to determine how a bear spread using these puts looked. By purchasing the put with the strike price of 94 for $325 and simultaneously selling the put with the strike price of 92 for $250, we would risk only $75. The bond even could climb to 93.25 before we would begin to lose money, and if the bond's price remained unchanged or declined, we would show a $125 profit for each $75 we had at risk, for a profit-to-risk ratio of 1.67.

TABLE 9.3
WORKSHEET FOR PUT BEAR SPREADS

(FOR ONE SPREAD ON 100 SHARES)

(A) Price of put option purchased	$ 325	(A)
(B) Price of put option sold	$ 250	(B)
(C) Risk: (A) minus (B) equals	$ 75	(C)
(D) Strike price of option purchased	$ 94	(D)
(E) Strike price of option sold	$ 92	(E)
(F) Break-even point: Divide (C) by 100 and subtract the result from (D)	$ 93.25	(F)
(G) Price of underlying bond	$ 92	(G)
(H) Move needed to break even: Subtract (G) from (F), divide by (G), and multiply the result by 100	% 1.36	(H)
(I) Maximum profit: Subtract (E) from (D), multiply the result times 100, and subtract (C)	$ 125	(I)
(J) Profit-to-risk-ratio: (I) divided by (C)	1.6	(J)

Note that this Treasury bond put bear spread makes money with the mere passage of time, just as our first bear spread example on the S&P 100 Index did. Of course, it is highly unlikely that, once the business cycle begins to turn, the price of this bond will go up or merely stay the same. If, for example, the yield on this bond only rose to 9 percent, the price of the bond would drop to 88. At a price of 77 the bond only yields 10 percent. When interest rates reached their height in the last business cycle during the early 1980s, long-term Treasury bonds were yielding 15 percent! That kind of yield would shove the price of this bond down to 51.

Again, you may decide to adopt a more aggressive strategy, selling puts at a lower strike price to allow more room for profit. Or you simply can buy a put with no offsetting sale (in which case I would recommend purchasing the longest term option available at the time).

During bear markets all of the tactics discussed in this chapter will provide profits. Almost any strategy using puts and put bear spreads will provide you with handsome profits. In order to choose, you first need to decide how much risk you want to take. Use the worksheet in appendix D to map out many different spreads so that you can see the spectrum of profit-to-risk ratios and choose the best opportunities.

Some final notes on trading in options: When it comes to actually executing a spread transaction, I have found that I get the best prices by using market orders that are entered before the market opens. This tactic eliminates the bid/ask prices that exist during the trading day. With trading options you'll note that after the market opens on a particular option there will be two prices quoted from the floor of the exchange: the "bid" price and the "ask" price. The bid price is the price for which an option can be sold, and the ask price is the price for which an option can be purchased. The asking price always is higher than the bid price, which is how market makers on the floor of the exchange make their money. A typical quote might be "5½ at ¾," which means you could sell the option at 5½ but you would have to purchase it at 5¾. This ¼ point cost—which doubles when a spread involves two options—is not present at the opening of each option market.

There is, however, one risk in this strategy that should be avoided. Before giving your broker market orders, you should check the size of your order against a normal day's trading activity. If it will not be a measurable part of the market opening, then your market order will be safe. You never should have a problem with market orders for options on the S&P 100 Index, or largely capitalized, high-priced stocks like Teledyne, Texas Instruments, or IBM. But if there is not a lot of trading on the options you are interested in, relative to the size of your order, then you can use a "spread order," which your broker can transmit directly to the appropriate options exchange floor. A spread order specifies both options and the credit or debit that you are willing to accept. For example, the first S&P 100 Index (O-E-X is the ticker symbol) bear spread example we discussed in this chapter (table 9.1) could be executed as a spread order that reads: "Buy one OEX 285 put and sell one OEX 280 put at a debit of two points." In a spread, you really don't care what the price of each option is, but the difference between the two option prices is critical because that is the amount of risk you are taking in the transaction. This spread order defines that difference as a two-point debit, which means that you will pay no more than $200 for one of these spreads.

As you can imagine, there are a great number of spread combinations that I have not discussed. You can, for example, set up a bear spread using calls by selling a call at a lower strike price than the one you are buying. The trouble with this configuration is that the fattest premium always will exist on the call that you purchase. This means that, unlike a put bear spread, the passage of time will not be on your side. I have been buying and selling options actively since 1973 on a great array of underlying securities using all kinds of configurations and strategies, and it didn't take me long to discover that having time on my side was the single most important ingredient of success.

10

The Financial Minuet

If you are like many investors you may prefer not to play the downside of a market. Many investors have a difficult time coping with the relatively complicated mechanisms that must be used to profit from a crashing stock market. Fortunately, however, they can profit from the stock market crash quite handsomely without buying a single put. That's because the stock market does not exist in the universe of investment capital by itself.

Throughout the history of our economy, capital has been on the move in a complicated waltz from one investment arena to another. When it leaves one market, it moves to another, and this time will be no exception.

Near the peak of supercycle five, more than 47 million Americans owned stocks, either directly or through mutual funds. (This compares with 1.5 million stockholders in 1929.) As the stock market crash continues, most of these folks will be pulling their money out of stocks, and handsome profits can be made by any investor who can anticipate where they will be putting that money next.

This task actually is much simpler than it seems, for

the fact is that there are not many capital markets from which to choose. This is not to say that there aren't a galaxy of potential investments that compete to attract attention. There are, and they range over a wide gamut from oil wells to fruit orchards. But for most investors there are only four realistic investment options: stocks, bonds, real estate, and commodities (which include precious metals). Since the continuing crash of this supercycle will have the effect of forcing investors out of the bond and stock markets, it is obvious that a great deal of new capital will be flowing into real estate and commodities.

Such a massive shift is not a new phenomenon. We saw in chapter 2 how a real estate boom served to dampen money from an inflated stock market in 1907, and how the stock market boomed when Florida's land prices eventually crashed. When stocks crashed in the thirties, Depression-era real estate was still out of favor with investors, and capital flowed into bonds. Bond prices zoomed upward, forcing bond yields below the 3 percent level. In the fifties money shifted back into stocks and real estate, where it sloshed between one market and the other. In the inflationary years of the early seventies, the markets of choice in the United States were precious metals and real estate, but through most of the eighties money flowed back to stocks and bonds.

Most investors are aware of the way markets compete with each other for capital, but it is usually a sort of intuitive awareness. They recognize that the talk they hear at cocktail parties sometimes shifts: In the seventies everyone was talking about making profits in real estate, but by the eighties, that talk had faded completely in most parts of the country, replaced by discussions of profits made in the stock market.

I remember the day a friend of mine quit his job as a banker in the early seventies to become a real estate developer. It seemed like a bold move at the time, but he explained it easily. As a banker, he said he had been watching others making killings in real estate, and he could see how they were doing it. They would come to his bank, sit at his cluttered desk, and establish a line of credit. Then he would not see them for a while—only the cash withdrawals against the line of credit. Several months later they would come back with an appraisal of the apartment building they had built with the money. Now they were after a mortgage loan. Because the real estate market was so hot, the property would appraise at a much greater price than it cost to build. The proceeds from the mortgage loan, therefore, would not only pay off the line of credit used to build the property but would leave a tidy profit to deposit in their bank account. And they did all of this with the bank's money!

My friend also could see that stocks were fading and that the real estate market was getting hotter. Adding it all up, he made his move. He used his banking relationships to establish a line of credit and started building apartments. In fact, he built hundreds of apartments in the space of a few years and made his fortune.

My friend hasn't built any apartments for a while. As more and more people started doing what he did, the market became saturated. But he doesn't care. He was in the game early enough to make millions. Now the cash flow from his apartments provides him with a grand life-style, and he spends only a few hours of his leisurely days checking in with his property managers.

In early 1987, I was in Vail, Colorado, participating in an investment seminar for a group of physicians. The seminar was scheduled for the early mornings and the late afternoons to allow for skiing during the day. As I rode up the chair lifts with these physicians, I heard no talk about real estate, but there was a lot of conversation about stocks and mutual funds. One doctor told me that he has been investing actively in mutual funds for his pension plan since 1981, and that he had more than quadrupled his money; he now had more than $800,000 in mutual funds.

In each of these cases, both my friend and the physician did their homework and acted, and they are to be congratulated for that. But what made their success so fabulous was that they were just ahead of a supercycle; they beat the crowd and correctly anticipated a massive shift of capital from one capital market to another.

We have seen through decade after decade that the investment bandwagon is constantly on the move. And just as easily as it rolled over to the stock and bond markets, it can, and will, roll back again to the other capital markets. Astute investors will be there, waiting patiently to make their fortune. Let's see how we can join them in beating the crowd.

II

Winning with Precious Metals

11

Supercycles in Gold

We have seen that the history of the stock market is a history of supercycles; as we soon will see, the stock market is not unique in this. All of our major capital markets compete for investors' savings and they are dominated by supercycles. A chart of any of these markets will show the familiar alpine landscape of booms and busts—except one: gold.

Does this mean that gold is somehow immune to the virus of speculation and panic that create supercycles? Not at all. The long flat line that makes up most of a chart of gold prices over the past centuries simply is a measure of government control of prices. Throughout most of the history of the United States, the price of gold has been controlled strictly. For a good deal of that time, the country was using gold to back its currency and thus had a strong vested interest in preserving the precious metal against the vicissitudes of the market.

Any speculation, however, that gold is somehow endowed with an innate ability to resist strong price fluctuations can be demolished easily by a quick look at its performance during those brief periods when gold prices have been free to respond to the riptides of supply and demand in an unfettered market. We are in one of those periods right now. Since the mid-sixties the price of gold has been allowed to float free, and a glance at a chart of gold prices over that period shows the familiar spike of a supercycle. At the peak of that cycle, gold was selling for more than $800 an ounce, but only a few short years later it had fallen to less than $300 an ounce.*

Clearly this was a boom and bust of supercycle proportions, and it is not the only one we can trace. There was one other period in U.S. history when gold was traded as freely as it is today, and during that time—just over a century ago—the market was dominated totally by a supercycle. That price spasm—a boom that tripled the price of gold—was followed by a crash during which it declined by more than 60 percent.

Despite this clear historical evidence that gold is as susceptible to boom and bust cycles as any other investment object, some economists are not convinced. They point to the fact that gold prices have been languishing for the past few years, going nowhere—either up or down—fast. But equipped as we are with a thorough understanding of the anatomy of supercycles, we have another explanation for these price doldrums. We have seen from our studies into stock market supercycles that a period of flat prices usually indicates that a market has reached the uneasy latitudes in which new supercycles are born.

The fact is that we soon will see a magnificent boom market in gold, one that is perfectly timed to absorb and magnify the capital we should be pulling out of stocks. To understand why, let's take a closer look at the two previous supercycles that have rolled through the nation's gold market and compare them to our current situation.

The roots of America's first supercycle in gold took hold in the currency crisis that coincided with the beginnings of the Civil War. The formation of the Confederate States of America was announced in Montgomery, Alabama on February 4, 1861. On March 9 of that year, only five days after President Lincoln's inauguration in Washington D.C., the

*Precious metals trade in troy ounces. Throughout this book any references to ounces of a precious metal actually mean troy ounces. In physical weight, a troy ounce is 91.15 percent of an ounce.

Confederate Congress issued its own currency and treasury notes.

When the shelling of Fort Sumpter on April 12 marked the formal beginning of hostilities, Northerners and Southerners alike decided that stocks were a risky place to entrust precious savings in a chaotic time, and the stock market saw a disastrous loss of capital. Southern investors moved quickly into the gold market, buying the precious metal with their new Confederate currency. Alarmed that gold was flowing south and Confederate currency was flowing north, northern banks declared that they no longer would accept Confederate currency as legal tender. The effect of this decision was to complete the final rupture of the national economy of the prewar United States.

This rupture was not painless. Though its northern and southern regions had been at political loggerheads for years, the nation had had one interrelated national economy, albeit largely dominated by the more highly developed and industrialized North. At the time of the outbreak of hostilities, therefore, the South was indebted heavily to the North. In fact, at the end of 1861, southern merchants and planters owed northern bankers and manufacturers more than $300 million. When the North was forced by the drain of gold to stop honoring Confederate currency it was suddenly clear that these southern debts never would be paid. As that realization spread, so did a wave of northern bankruptcies. By year's end it was to engulf more than 6,000 separate businesses and severely harm the northern banking system. At the end of 1861, 89 of the 110 financial institutions that once had been operating in the state of Illinois were in the hands of receivers.[1]

In February 1862, the Treasury of the United States suspended the exchange of gold for currency, and issued $150 million in a new currency backed only by the government's good name. These "greenbacks" signaled the departure of the U.S. economy from the gold standard for the first time in its history.

As might be expected, trust in the value of the new federal currency waxed and waned in concert with the Union's success on the battlefield. And the measure of that confidence, or the lack of it, was gold. Investors' attention was now riveted on a gold trading den with the prosaic name of Gilpin's News Room. On this underground trading floor, quotations for gold began to swing wildly. With each of the South's early victories, the price of gold soared higher, since it was clear that a defeated Union would not be likely to redeem its greenback dollars. As the war progressed, and the Union began to score some victories of its own, gold prices cooled somewhat. However, within the fluctuations the underlying price of gold was rising inexorably as nervous investors began to worry that even a victorious North might be so exhausted at the end of the war that it would be unable to repay its greenback obligations.

During the first four months of 1862, the price of the gold being traded at Gilpin's climbed 20 percent to $24.80 an ounce. In July, another $150 million in greenback dollars was issued. When the Confederacy closed out the year with a resounding victory at Fredricksburg, the price of gold jumped to $27.70, and by the end of January 1863, it had topped $31 an ounce. This represented a jump in prices of more than 50 percent.

So inextricably were the prices of gold tied to news from the front that gold traders soon were hiring agents to travel with the armies and send back up-to-the-minute battle reports. Northern gold speculators even had spies in the Confederate army camps who were telegraphing battle plans back to New York where traders often learned about new battle developments long before the generals who were waging the war. This intelligence operation was so sophisticated that the gold market became the best barometer for charting the changing fortunes of the war—to the great annoyance of the Union commander-in-chief. "What do you think of those fellows on Wall Street who are gambling in gold at such a time as this?" thundered the normally probusiness Lincoln. "For my part, I wish every one of them had his devilish head shot off."[2]

Another $100 million in greenbacks were issued by the federal government in 1863. This blizzard of paper served to intensify a spiral of inflation that already had sent wholesale commodity prices up more than 50 percent over their 1861 levels. It quickly was becoming apparent to all Americans that the purchase of gold was about the only way they could protect their purchasing power.

When General Grant won the Battle of Vicksburg on July 4, 1863, the price of gold actually declined. But it was a temporary breather. When Grant failed to capture Richmond in 1864, gold shot upward, reaching an all-time high of $58.90 on July 11. Meanwhile, the furious pace of trading was requiring a more organized market than that represented by Gilpin's News Room, and in October 1864, the New York Gold Exchange was formed. A member described it this way:

> The gold room (as it was called) was like a cavern, full of dank and noisome vapors, and the deadly carbonic acid was blended with the fumes of stale smoke and vinous breaths. But the stifling gases engendered in that low-browed cave of evil enchanters, never seemed to depress the energies of the gold-dealers; from "morn to dewey eve" the drooping ceiling and the bistre-colored walls re-echoed with the sounds of all kinds of voices, from the shrill piping treble of the call boys to the deep bass of [other brokers], while an upreared forest of arms was swayed furiously by the storms of a swiftly rising and falling market.[3]

On the far wall, a large clocklike apparatus ticked up and down with each change in the price of gold. All eyes were riveted on that machine as hundreds of thousands of dollars changed hands during days of frenetic trading. Ironically, however, this new market was to preside over the long but steady collapse of the price of gold—a decline that began even in the face of searing inflation that, in 1864 alone, topped 46 percent.

The Union forces began to take convincing control of the war in 1865, and with the news of each victory the price of gold skidded further. When General Sherman completed his triumphal march to the sea, the price of gold fell to $30 an ounce. It was to remain there, fluctuating in a narrow trading range around $29 an ounce for the remainder of the decade as the U.S. economy worked to recover from the war. Only during a few autumn days in 1869 was there any real action on the market, and that was sparked by financier Jay Gould's attempt to corner the gold market. The attempt, which drove gold prices up over $33 an ounce for a few short days, collapsed on a day that came to be known as Black Friday during which prices fell back to $28 an ounce.[4]

That was not the limit of gold's price collapse. Despite the shining and widely touted promise that was represented by the completion of the transcontinental railroad and the burst of further rail construction that followed it, the U.S. economy was having a good deal of trouble adjusting to peacetime. Wholesale prices had been drifting downward since the end of the war, and by the end of 1872 they had declined by a full 42 percent from their levels in 1864. It was becoming quite clear that the country was in the grip of a serious deflation, and the gold market began to skid. By the end of 1872 it had reached $23 an ounce.

And there the fragile U.S. economy stood at the beginning of 1873. If left alone, the nation might have survived into a new decade of postwar recovery, but it was not to be. The United States, for better or worse, was now a part of an international economy much larger than itself. European financial interests had entered the U.S. economy in a big way during the war, and had stayed on to finance much of the new peacetime economy. The great railroad construction boom of the late 1860s and early 1870s had, for instance, been financed largely by European capital. By now the American economy was susceptible to catching a cold any time Europe sneezed, and in the mid-1870s a distinct sound of sniffling was coming from the continent.

There were several different strains on the European economy. The recently concluded Franco-Prussian War had run up a sizeable tab, as had the unification wars that had raged between Italian states; the construction of the Suez Canal was siphoning off even more capital. Finally, in May 1873, the strains began to show. A money panic hit Vienna during that month, and the repercussions not only spread over the rest of Europe, but also into the United States.

September saw the beginning of a serious run on U.S. banks. The Gold Exchange Bank was flooded immediately with orders from investors who wanted to change their paper money into gold. Faced itself with imminent collapse when it couldn't fulfill these orders, the bank sought and won an injunction forbidding it from completing any more conversions. At the same time, in an effort to instill confidence, President Grant made a highly public trip to New York in order to purchase $13 million in government bonds on the open market. Unfortunately, this grand gesture failed, and when the Treasury ran out of funds for further purchases, the selling resumed. It was called the Panic of 1873, and by the time it finally had exhausted itself in November, it had inaugurated a depression that still stands as the most devastating ever suffered by the American economy.

By the end of that depression in the late 1870s, more than 23,000 business failures were recorded. Unemployment levels skyrocketed and did not begin to decline until well into 1878. By the end of 1877, stock prices had declined by 71 percent. Wholesale prices continued to decline through 1879, eventually falling 32 percent from their already depressed 1873 levels.

Meanwhile, even in the face of this tempestuous economic climate, the downtrending supercycle in gold continued. When prices came close to the prewar price of $20 an ounce, the government acted to return to the gold standard. The Resumption Act of 1875 mandated that $82 million of the $382 million in greenbacks still in circulation be withdrawn immediately. More important, the act specified that the remaining greenback dollars would be convertible into gold at the prewar rate of $20.67 an ounce beginning on January 1, 1879. (Interestingly enough, despite widespread fears that there would be a run on the gold supplies as soon as greenbacks became convertible, only $400,000 was actually converted, which represented less than 15 percent of the remaining pool of greenback notes. To the relief of Treasury officials, their promises of convertibility had proved to be sufficient.)

Thus America's brief flirtation with freely traded gold ended on the first day of 1879, and so did the nation's first recorded supercycle in gold prices. One generation of investors had watched the price of gold swing through a broad arc from $20 an ounce to nearly $60 an ounce, but they all would be long gone before the gold standard was again reconsidered.

Actually, that reconsideration didn't begin in the United States at all, but in depression-battered Britain, where in September 1931, the gold standard was abandoned entirely. Although the United States had been ravaged equally by the worldwide depression, the Roosevelt administration was much more cautious. In the spring of 1933, Roosevelt was forced to suspend the payment of gold for U.S. dollars for several months. Although he was to reinstitute the gold standard by early fall, he attempted to protect the country's gold reserves by raising the price of gold from its pre–Civil War level of $20.67 an ounce to $29.62 an ounce, and then, one month later, to $31.36 an ounce.

When none of these measures proved to be sufficient to

stem runs on the gold supply, the administration took the revolutionary step of trying to find a middle ground between full convertibility and the abandonment of the gold standard altogether. In this new strategy, dollars no longer would be convertible into gold, and no more gold coins would be minted, but the dollar nonetheless would be defined and valued in relationship to a certain price of gold—a price set by the president himself. Having proclaimed this new "gold standard," Roosevelt went on to set the new price of gold at $35 an ounce. He hoped that this would work to offset the steady deflationary plunge in wholesale prices. It didn't do that, but it did introduce chaos into the world's currency markets.

During the late thirties, nations throughout the industrialized world began to compete with each other to devalue their currencies, causing the effective market price of gold to soar 82 percent by the end of 1939. The turbulence in Europe's financial community obviously had not helped quell the political tinder that was soon to explode into global war, and when the allies began to try to envision the world they would rule at the war's conclusion, monetary reform was high on their list of priorities. In 1944, they convened the Bretton Woods Conference and established the International Monetary Fund.

With international currencies on the way to stability, western economists began to consider the possibility of allowing the resumption of a free trade in gold. In 1948, the French opened the first free market for gold that the world had seen for nearly a century. The Swiss followed in 1952 by removing its domestic price ceiling on gold. London's market opened in 1954.

Not that anyone was making much of a killing on these new markets: The conclusion of World War II had left a world that was dominated totally by the United States and its allies, and these powerful economies were dedicated to the preservation of a quiescent gold market. To this end, the United States and seven other western nations formed a consortium they called the London Gold Pool through which they kept the price of gold stabilized at $35 an ounce—buying when it dropped below and selling when it rose above that target price.[5]

The consortium was able to maintain its target price well into the mid-1960s, but by then the increasingly complex international economic situation had begun to seriously strain the alliance. The first blow was struck by the Soviet Union which, in 1966, announced it would no longer trade its gold on the world market. This meant that less gold was available for trade, and the consortium partners were forced to drain their own reserves in order to keep the world price at $35 an ounce. Demand for gold was increasing at a time when one of the world's major suppliers pulled out of the picture.

The second blow against the consortium was struck by France which, early in 1967, suddenly removed its ban on the importation of gold into the country by French citizens. Anticipating this change, the price of gold coins in Paris already had risen more than 10 percent in the final eight months of 1966, so when the ban was lifted, private purchases on world markets more than doubled. Then, in June, the French pulled out of the consortium altogether, forcing the remaining countries to cough up more than a billion and a half dollars worth of gold to keep the $35 an ounce lid on prices. Finally, in mid-March 1968, the cost of stabilization had become prohibitive and the London Gold Pool dissolved.

The collapse of the gold consortium did not, however, end the U.S. government's attempts to control the gold market, and a two-tier market emerged. One tier operated with an "official" price of $35 an ounce, the rate at which the United States would sell other nations its gold and at which it would redeem its obligations to the International Monetary Fund. The second tier was the market in which private investors were buying and selling their own gold—at a much higher price.

Finally in 1968, President Johnson severed the few slim threads that still tied the dollar to gold. The price of gold was now even freer to float upward on international markets, and it did. An ounce of gold sold for an average price of $39 an ounce in 1968 and $41 an ounce in 1969. In 1970, a widespread economic recession dropped the price to $36, but it had bounced back to $41 by the end of 1971. By that time the inflation rate in the United States and many other countries was beginning to become a major concern and the price of gold began to soar. By the end of 1972, it had climbed to $64 an ounce, only to double in the first half of 1973. Rising interest rates and recessions in several major western economies pulled the price back down to $96 in November 1973, but then it started to move again.

Investors in the United States were quite frustrated as they watched the price of gold more than triple in less than six years; U.S. citizens still were prohibited from buying gold. Finally, near the end of 1974, with gold fast approaching the $200 an ounce level, the government announced that it would eliminate its prohibition on gold ownership. For the first time since 1933, it would be legal for American citizens to buy gold.

I remember sitting in a sales meeting at the brokerage firm where I worked in the waning days of 1974, listening to our office manager's excited plans for attracting our share of the hoard of investors he was sure would be flocking to buy gold. But despite an alluring lobby display of gold wafers, the crowds of gold investors never came to our office or to any other. The fact was that European investors, anticipating the entrance of American investors into the market, had run the price up to levels that the market, for the moment at least, could not support, and the price of gold had reached a peak just before American investors were able to climb on the bandwagon.

Moreover, with the stock market languishing at the 600 level in the early days of 1975, and with the fires of inflation having been banked by a recessionary economy, investors were seeing a good deal more growth potential in stocks than in gold. In the short-term they were right—the Dow Jones Industrial Average rocketed upward more than 60 percent in the early months of the year and the price of gold continued to decline, falling to $100 by the middle of 1976—but there was a supercycle beginning in gold that ultimately was not to be denied.

Late in 1976, the embers of inflation began to glow once again and gold prices responded with what appeared to be a grand overreaction. By the end of 1976, gold was up more than 30 percent, and at the close of 1977, it had reached $160 an ounce. Prices soared through the previously impermeable $200 an ounce level in 1978, and a new gold rush was launched. The price of gold roared through the $600 barrier in 1979 and the $800 level in 1980. How high it could go was anybody's guess.

Of course, most investors were guessing that the market would go much higher. By the end of the seventies, the nation was suffering from serious jitters about its inflation rate. Nothing the federal government could do seemed to be working, and the evening newscasts were full of bleak statistics: The inflation rate had been at 12.4 percent in 1978 and 14 percent in 1979, and now the prime rate had climbed over 20 percent in the early days of 1980. During one of those months I remember watching a TV news broadcast that recalled the hyperinflation that struck Germany after World War I. The report was accompanied by grainy newsreel footage showing German citizens pushing wheelbarrows full of nearly worthless currency down gray streets to buy loaves of bread. Was it about to happen here?

In the early days of 1980, as this widespread concern over inflation seemed to be reaching its crescendo, the supercycle in gold prices that had been all but invisible to investors peaked. Prices topped out at $850 an ounce and began to decline. By the year's end this skid was assisted further by encouraging evidence that strong new measures

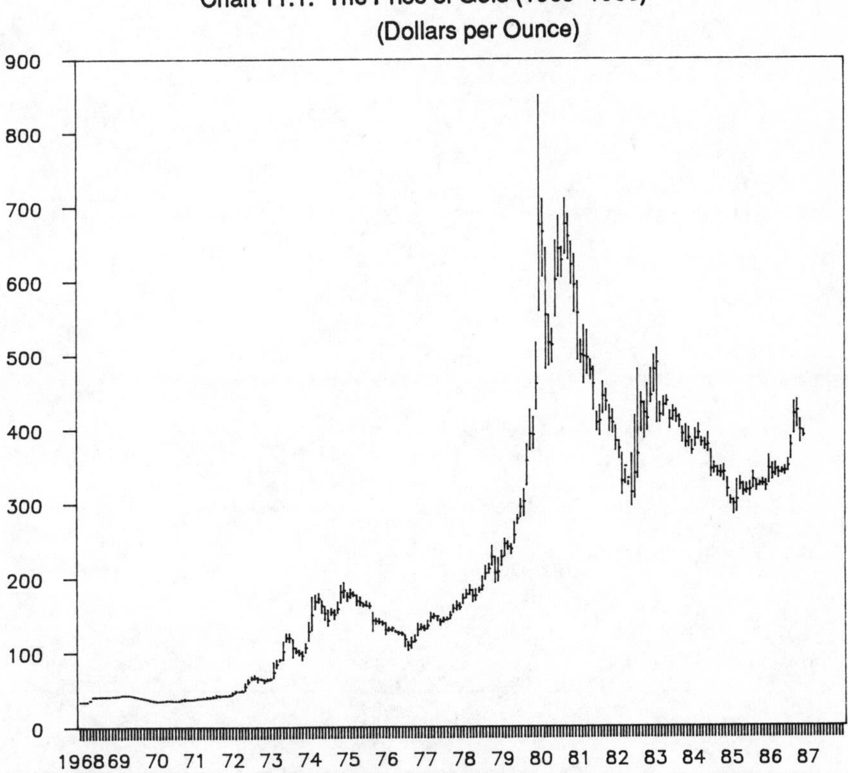

Chart 11.1. The Price of Gold (1968–1986)
(Dollars per Ounce)

Source: U.S. Bureau of Mines

by the Federal Reserve had, in fact, made a dent on inflation. A powerful recession set in, cooling price increases still further. Gold fell back below $600 an ounce in 1980, and closed below $400 in 1981. For the next three years it meandered downward, finally bottoming out at $290 in March 1985.

A glance at chart 11.1 shows the very familiar shape of the supercycle that concluded in the spring of 1985. It also shows that prices have been trending upward again since then. Does this mean that the gold market is in the grip of another profitable supercycle upsurge? Let's look.

12

The Fundamental Value of Gold

It is clear from our study of gold prices in the past that gold is in many ways a unique investment commodity. Whether or not it actually is used to back currency in any given society, gold always has been more than a precious metal with decorative and industrial uses. It has been seen as a way of storing value. While it is true that it has been almost twenty years since gold was last used to settle international accounts, it still has not lost its image as "real money."

Does this mean that it is not susceptible to the supercycle price distortion? The historical answer is a resounding "no." It is clear that as long as the primal human forces of greed, fear, and anticipation are free to act on the price of gold, prices will fly too high, and then sink too low, all the while giving the prescient investor a chance to profit from the swings.

The questions facing every investor who is attuned to supercycle movement are always the same: How high is too high? How low is too low? There are few investors in any market wise enough to know when prices come loose from their underlying fundamentals and become ripe for collapse; there are equally few who are able to part the shrouds of doom that surround a bottomed market and see that prices are just too low.

Still, just as we were able to find reliable signals to tell us when prices are too high or low in the stock market, we also can determine a pivot point around which prices of gold (and several other precious metals) revolve. This is because of gold's close relationship with the world economy.

As we saw in chapter 11, there have been two supercycles in the world's gold markets in the last two hundred years, one occurring during each of the relatively brief periods when there was a free and unregulated market in gold. While the peak of each supercycle was too high and the trough was too low, the average price of gold represented a reasonable value during each of those periods—a price around which prices would swing. If investors during each of those supercycles knew ahead of time what the average price would be for their supercycle, they would have been poised for profit. When the price of gold was above the average, they would have known that they were flirting with danger, and when it was below the average, they would have known that gold represented a bargain. We can have this perspective on upcoming supercycles by using the past supercycles as a reference. Here's how.

During the first supercycle, from 1862 through 1878, the price of gold swung from $20.67 to $58.90 an ounce, averaging $26.35 an ounce over the period. The next supercycle saw a peak of $850, a bottom of $285, and an average price of $317 an ounce. Obviously, one of the reasons why the prices of the second supercycle moved back and forth in a range that was much higher than the first had to do with inflation. During the first supercycle the wholesale price index averaged 49.78 (as compared with 100 in the base year of 1967); during the second supercycle, one hundred years later, it averaged 252.78. If we adjust the average price of gold during the first supercycle for the inflation that occurred over the years between the supercycles, the revised figure would be $134 an ounce: $26.35 × (252.78 ÷ 49.78). This is closer, but it still is quite a bit under the average price of $317 an ounce that was seen during the second supercycle. Clearly more was working on the average price of gold than just inflation.

The unique quality of gold as an investment quantity is its tight relationship with the currencies throughout the world. Even though gold markets are now unregulated, gold still is seen as the world's supercurrency. As such, its price responds not only to its own supply and demand forces, but also to the supply of goods and services in the world's economies as a whole.

To view gold's unique and fundamental relationship with currency and the global availability of goods and services, let's imagine the world reduced to an island whose economy is composed of money, gold, and goods. If the total of all the paper money on the island is $100, the gold supply totals 100 ounces, and there are 100 pounds of goods, the relationship between the three commodities will be easy to trace. Since there is an ounce of gold for every dollar on the island, gold will be worth one dollar an ounce. One pound of goods can, therefore, be purchased with either a dollar bill or an ounce of gold.

Now let's stir things up a bit. Let's increase the amount of money on the island to $800, double the amount of gold, and increase the amount of goods to 400 pounds. Since the amount of money being printed has far outstripped the growth in goods produced, we can expect that our island will be experiencing inflation. Since the amount of money has increased eightfold while the amount of goods has increased only fourfold, the price of the goods can be expected to double. And what about the price of gold? At first glance, the answer might be expected to be that the price of gold would double as well in accordance with inflation. Since the value of money has been halved, we might well imagine that the price of gold simply would double. But this would ignore the fact that the gold itself has purchasing power. And since there are only 200 ounces of gold and 400 pounds of goods, 1 ounce of gold will now buy 2 pounds of goods. Since the established price of 1 pound of goods is now $2, we can see that in reality, 1 ounce of gold will now buy $4 worth of the island's goods. Thus, 1 ounce of gold is now worth $4. (This reasoning is confirmed when we look at the triangle the other way and realize that the relationship between 200 ounces of gold and $800 in currency also would produce a price of $4 for an ounce of gold.)

With this illustration in mind, we now can see why it is necessary to do more than adjust for inflation if we are trying to truly compare the average price for gold during its two supercycles. In order to determine the true value of gold on our island we also needed to determine how much the supply of goods had outgrown the supply of gold.

When we expand the picture back out to the whole world, the "goods" part of our equation becomes the total supply of goods and services that we call "planetary product." In order to compare the value of gold at two different times, therefore, we must first adjust the prices for inflation, and then multiply that number by the amount the growth in planetary product exceeded the growth in the world's supply of gold. Let's try our new equation out on the average price of gold that was recorded during the two supercycles in gold.

The U.S. Bureau of Mines (a branch of the Department of the Interior) estimated that in 1986 the world's supply of gold was 3.203 billion ounces. Using figures from the bureau and other sources, it is possible to determine that during the period of the first supercycle, from 1862 through 1878, the supply of gold averaged close to 331 million ounces. The amount of gold that existed on the planet between 1975 and 1985 averaged 2.935 billion ounces. In other words, the supply of gold was 8.867 times greater in the second supercycle than in the first.

Experts also have estimated that during that nineteenth-century supercycle, the gross planetary product averaged close to $600 billion.* Through the span of the second supercycle (1975 through 1985), it averaged $12.468 trillion*—20.78 times greater.†

*This figure is expressed in 1986 dollars. Since GNP or planetary product measures monetary value, an increase in planetary product can come from either inflation or an increase in the volume of goods and services. Since we are interested in volume only, we must use planetary product figures adjusted for inflation.

†Information is spotty on planetary product before 1900 because many countries did not compile their GNP figures, particularly when at war. Nonetheless, based on reliable figures compiled back to 1869 for the United States, England, Germany, Switzerland, Italy, Sweden, and Denmark, an annual compound growth rate of 2 percent annually is a very good estimate, and there are reliable figures for each year since 1900. Report number 58, published by the Bureau of Public Affairs of the U.S. State Department, covers the period from 1900 through 1978, showing the growth rate in planetary product to be at a 3.155 percent annual compound rate during that period. An index published by the International Monetary Fund in their International Financial Statistics Yearbook covers from 1978 to 1984 and shows the growth rate to be at a 2.313 percent annual compound rate. Growth in 1985 and 1986 is assumed to have continued at this rate.

By combining these two figures, we can see that the total of the world's goods and services increased by 2.34 times more than its gold supply (20.78 ÷ 8.867). So now we have the whole picture. By multiplying the inflation-adjusted average of the price of gold during the first supercycle by the 2.34 times that the gross planetary product outdistanced the gold supply, we get a new adjusted average price for supercycle one of $314 an ounce. According to our theory, the average price of gold through the second supercycle should be nearly identical, and it is: $317 an ounce—only $3 higher.

With our equation confirmed, we can determine what the value of gold should be in any given year, and this value we will call the "fundamental value." I have charted this fundamental value for every year since 1968 on chart 12.1. These fundamental values are represented by the dots on

Chart 12.1. The Fundamental Value of Gold (Dollars per Ounce)

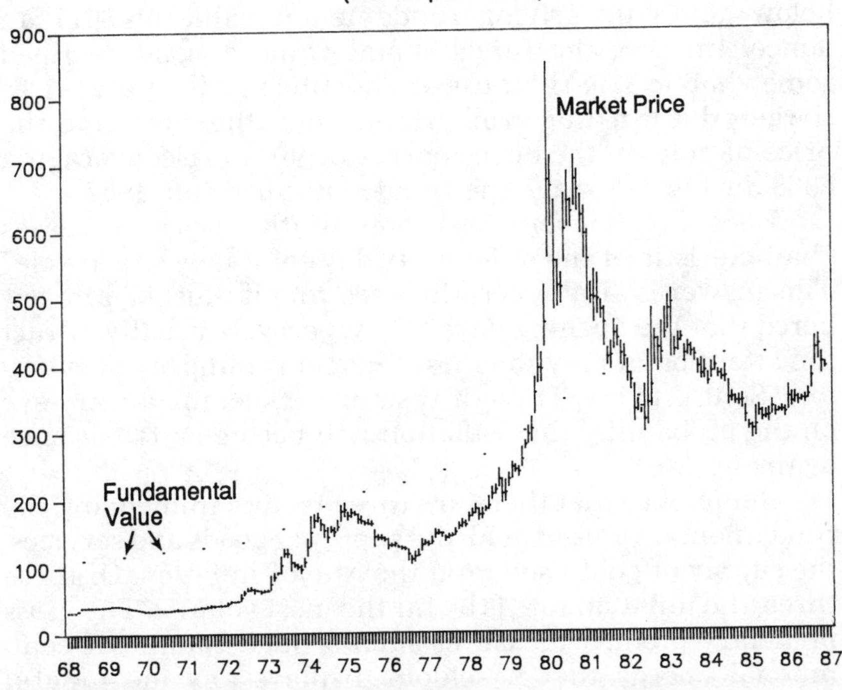

the chart. The chart also shows the monthly range of gold prices and the average of prices for each month over this period.

The chart shows that in the late 1960s the fundamental value of gold was above the market price that the London Gold Pool was trying to preserve; obviously the consortium's collapse simply was a matter of time. Gold's price came into alignment with its fundamental value in 1974—ironically, at exactly the time that Americans had their first crack at buying gold.

It was in 1979 when the price of gold climbed above its fundamental value for the first time and the boom was on. In fact, the boom prices were to fly much higher in the early eighties than they had even during the inflation-wracked years a century before. When adjusted for inflation and changes in the planetary product and gold supply, the peak price of $58.90 that was recorded in 1864 translates to $554 an ounce in 1980. The peak price of gold in 1980 was $850. It didn't stay there long.

By 1985, a five-year-long crash in gold prices was complete. During that year, prices fluctuated between $285 and $341 an ounce for an average of $317 an ounce. This was far below gold's underlying fundamental value of $411 an ounce. In 1986, the fundamental value of gold declined somewhat (to $398) because of a decline in wholesale prices (largely due to a drop in oil prices), but at the same time, the price of gold on the open market began to rise, averaging $368 during the year. The trend continued into 1987.

Does this movement represent the price increases characteristic of the quiet early days of a new supercycle? The answer is almost certainly yes, and it must be remembered that the opening days of a supercycle usually attract the attention of only the most sagacious minority of investors. So it is today. These investors are keeping a wary eye on the probability that inflation will become a factor once again.

Remember that there are three factors influencing the fundamental value of gold: the supply of goods and services, the supply of gold itself, and the rate of inflation. Of these three, the inflation rate is by far the most volatile. The gross planetary product measures such a huge volume of commercial energy that it seldom displays any meaningful short-term fluctuation. And with the perfection of modern mining techniques, the growth of the supply of gold can be predicted fairly accurately. Inflation, therefore, remains the wild card.

As we saw in our discussion of the troubled U.S. economy in the first section of this book, inflation is almost certain to increase over the nearly dormant rates that have been recorded over the past five years. However, to hinge our investment strategies on the premise that inflation will return to the double-digit levels that plagued us in the late seventies could be extreme.

Since it will be impossible to pinpoint accurately what the inflation rate will be over the next few years, it is necessary to project a range of possibilities. Chart 12.2 shows the fundamental value of gold through 1986, and its actual market price performance. It also shows three possible projections of what the fundamental value could be, based on three different assumptions about the inflation rate. One (overly conservative) projection shows an inflation rate that rests at zero through 1995, another projects a 5

Chart 12.2. The Fundamental Value of Gold
(Dollars per Ounce)

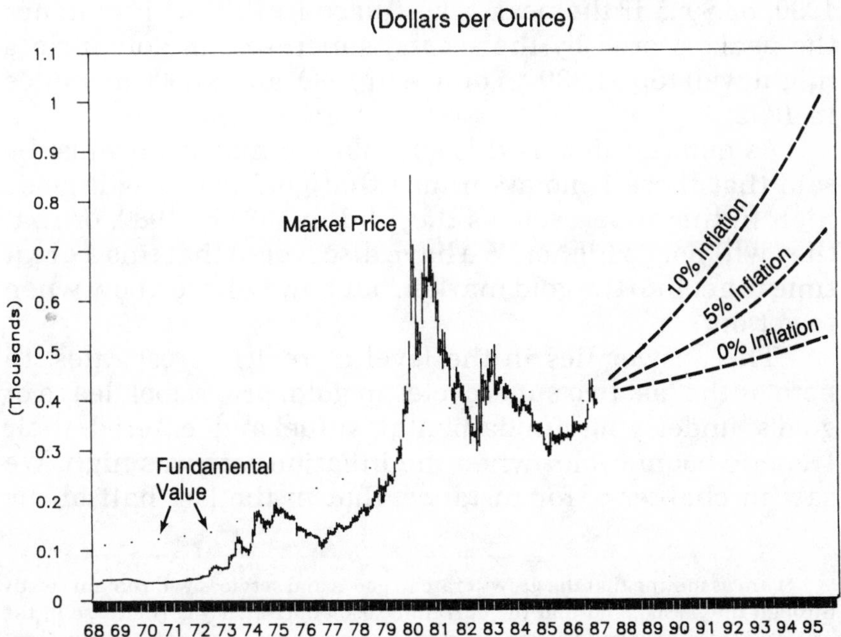

percent annual inflation rate, the third shows a 10 percent rate.*

You can see that the differences between the results are staggering. If inflation somehow manages to disappear entirely through 1995, the fundamental price of gold will be $426 an ounce in that year. But if the inflation rate heats up to 10 percent annually, gold's fundamental value will top $1,000 an ounce.

Before the crash of 1987 the market price of gold was well below its fundamental value. In fact, it was well below its fundamental value even if the zero-inflation scenario were to come to pass. But in the weeks following the stock market crash, the price of gold approached $500 an ounce as the Federal Reserve began to pump money into the economy. As inflation heats up in the years ahead, there will be a great deal of money to be made in gold.

How much money? By adjusting the peak prices of the first two supercycles for inflation at, say, 5 percent annually, and the growth of the planetary product and supply of gold, we can see how high this supercycle might take prices. If the current supercycle were to drive the price of gold as high as the first supercycle did, this supercycle would see prices topping out at close to $800 if the peak takes place in 1990, or $925 if the peak takes place in 1992. If it matches the peaks scored by the second supercycle in gold, prices might well top $1,330 an ounce in 1990, and $1,500 an ounce in 1992.

As entertaining as this speculation may be, it must be said that there is no assurance that gold prices will go as high in this supercycle as they did in 1864 or 1980, or that they will not go higher. We have discovered that this a great time to get into the gold market, but how will we know when to get out?

The answer lies in the level of real interest rates. In both of the last two supercycles in gold, prices took leave of gold's underlying fundamental value and entered their frenetic boom cycles when the inflation rate was high. We saw in chapter 5, for instance, that in the last half of the

*I am assuming that the growth rate in goods and services will remain steady through the period, and that the current 50,000 ounces per year increase in the world's gold supply will remain constant.

seventies, the inflation rate was so high that real interest rates actually declined to less than zero (see chart 5.2). Similarly, the supercycle that ran its course during the Civil War became overheated during the exact years when high inflation rates forced real interest rates into negative figures (chart 12.3). It is no coincidence that the most furious boom times in these supercycles coincided with dramatic declines in real interest rates. The relationship between inflation and the price of gold is even more determinative than we have seen yet.

In this chapter we have looked at how the inflation rate has a dramatic effect on the fundamental value of gold, but just as dramatic is its effect on the psyches of investors who see the precious metal as the ultimate inflation hedge. So confident are these investors in gold's inflation resistance—and so ignorant are they of the perverse nature of supercycles—that their faith adds an artificial premium to the

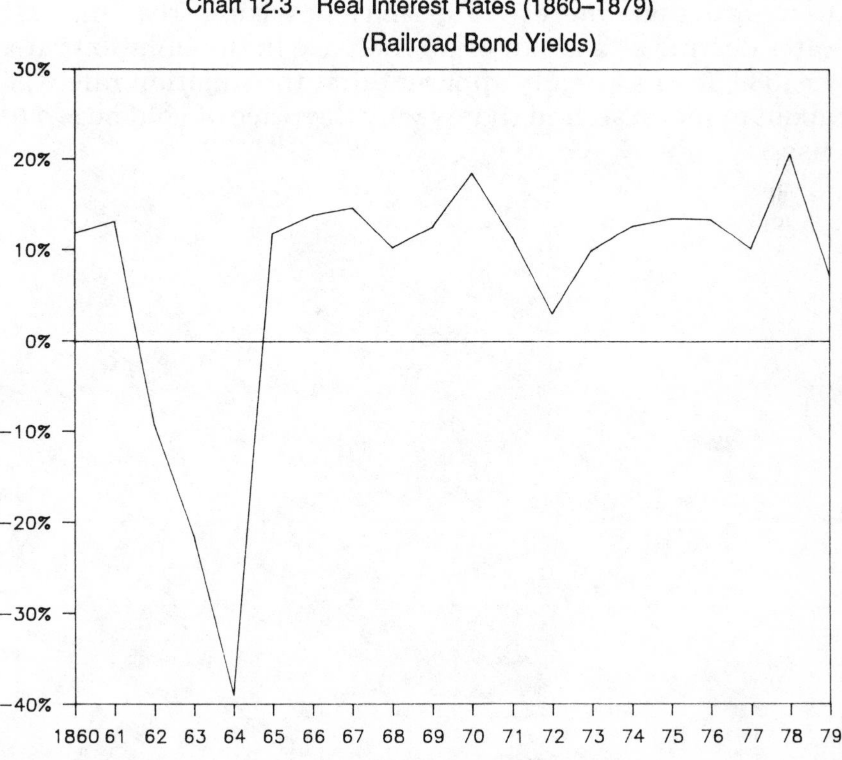

Chart 12.3. Real Interest Rates (1860–1879)
(Railroad Bond Yields)

price of gold. When the supercycle turns, this premium disappears, along with the profits of the faithful.

In both of the previous supercycles in gold, price peaks have coincided with a steep rise in real interest rates in 1864 and 1980 (charts 5.2 and 12.3). And when real interest rates remain high, cooling inflation, gold prices crash.

Therefore, the picture is clear. As in any market, gold prices fluctuate in broad swings around an axis of fundamental value. If gold has fallen below its fundamental value we can invest aggressively when real interest rates begin to decline, but when prices have overshot the fundamental value of gold we must watch carefully for the first increase in real interest rates, for that will signal the beginning of the end. When that happens, we must sell gold to keep our investments panic proof.

Remember that a decline in real interest rates can come from a decline in the level of actual interest rates, an increase in the inflation rate, or a combination of the two. During the expansion phase of a business cycle, even though actual interest rates may be rising, real interest rates decline as a result of an increase in the inflation rate. In 1986, it was already apparent that the inflation rate was about to increase, and that is why the price of gold began to rise.

13

Silver, Platinum, and Palladium

While gold is the premier precious metal, it is not the only one. The category of precious metals also includes silver, and the six metals of the platinum group. In addition to platinum itself, these metals include palladium, rhodium, ruthenium, iridium, and osmium. The last four metals are not familiar to most investors and are not traded widely, but silver, platinum, and palladium are all traded in broad and liquid markets and are definitely worth considering as investment alternatives to the stock market.

Silver, palladium, and platinum all have been subject to the same supercycle pressures as gold—pressures that resulted in parallel supercycles in all these metals between 1975 and 1985. And because they are traded on world markets, accepted widely, and converted into currency, we can use the same analysis that we used for gold. Therefore, by looking at past supercycles, we can determine a fundamental value at any point in time and gauge whether each of these metals is undervalued or overvalued. This will give us a perspective that most investors do not have.

Silver

Like gold, silver's ornamental value was such that it has, since ancient times, been bartered for goods and services. Its value was so widespread that silver was used as a standard for monetary systems as far back as the Roman Empire.

From the beginning, however, there was a much greater supply of silver than of gold. Through the end of the fifteenth century, silver production in Europe was nearly ten times that of gold. Then came the massive silver discoveries that were made in the New World. Silver was first discovered in vast quantities in Mexico, Peru, and Bolivia, and then in 1859, the United States became the world's largest silver producer with the discovery of the Comstock Lode in Nevada. The United States was forced to give up the silver crown in 1900 when new discoveries in Mexico gave it the world production lead.

With all of this silver pouring into the world's economies in the centuries after the discovery of the New World, silver was gradually abandoned as a monetary standard in favor of gold. It did, however, continue to have value as a coinage substance.

Then, early in the nineteenth century, industry began to discover some exciting new applications for silver. A new industry was born when it was discovered that thin layers of silver salts, when exposed to illumination and then subjected to a certain chemical bath, reduced to metallic silver in such a fashion that an image of the illumination was preserved. Throughout the nineteenth and twentieth centuries, more and more uses for this remarkable discovery were made until silver was used widely in products ranging from photographic and X-ray film to photo-offset printing plates.

At the same time, it was discovered that in addition to its strong resistance to corrosion or oxidation, silver had the highest thermal and electrical conductivity of any known substance. This led to its use in switches and other electrical equipment. These applications were in addition to such other industrial applications as mirrors, dental amalgams, bearings, and chemical catalysts. Moreover, it continued to occupy its historical place as a metal coveted for its use in jewelry, silverware, and other decorative objects.

The U.S. Treasury used silver to fashion its currency into the mid-sixties. This gave the government a large vested interest in the fortunes of the silver industry and, in fact, the Treasury was the principal supplier of silver to U.S. industrial producers well into the early sixties. The Treasury's problem was that if silver rose above $1.29 an ounce, the silver content of a silver dollar would be worth more than a dollar. And if the price rose above $1.38 an ounce, the silver content of half dollars, quarters, and dimes would be higher than the face values of those coins. Thus, the Treasury was in a constant chase to keep prices low enough that there would be no massive meltdown of its silver currency. For years, the government kept prices down by stepping up silver production, but by the early sixties it was becoming clear that this strategy was failing. In 1965, the United States began minting half dollars with a much reduced silver content, and quarters and dimes that had no silver content at all. Finally, in 1967, the Treasury announced that it was removing all silver coins from circulation.[1]

From the late seventies through the mid-eighties, silver experienced a supercycle in its prices that roughly paralleled that of gold. After languishing at under $5 an ounce through 1979, the price of silver rocketed up over $50 an ounce in 1980, dropped to $15 in 1983, and settled back below $5 in 1986. During this supercycle the average price was $8.61 an ounce. That was a reasonable price for silver then, although growth in the planetary product and inflation will raise the fundamental price around which the next supercycle will move.

Although industrial demand consumed 168 million more ounces of silver than was mined over the last ten years, industry analysts believe that industrial demand and the amount of silver mined each year will be close to equal in the years ahead. With industrial demand absorbing all of the silver produced each year, the world's supply of silver will remain fairly constant. That means the fundamental value of silver will increase with inflation and the growth in planetary product.

Chart 13.1 shows the average monthly prices for silver

Chart 13.1. The Fundamental Value of Silver (Dollars per Ounce)

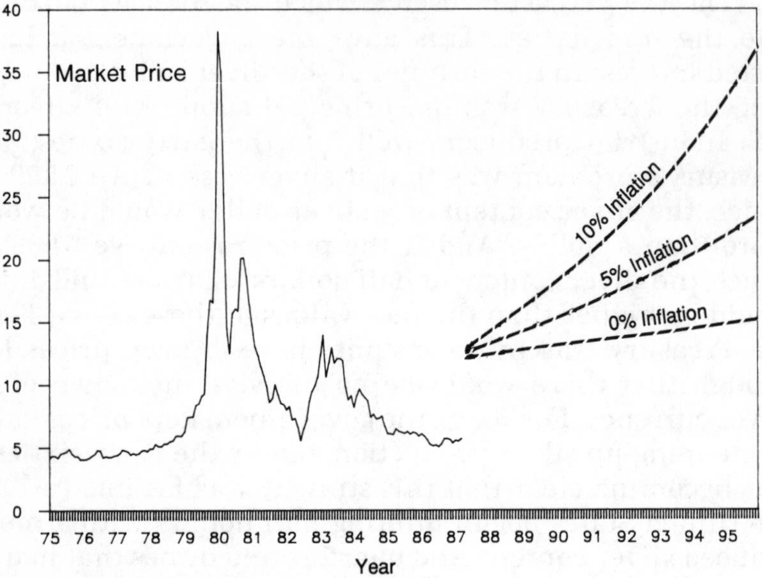

Source: Market prices from U.S. Bureau of Mines

since 1975 along with projections for the fundamental value that we can expect to see in the future. Like the figures presented for gold in chapter 12, these projections are based on three inflation scenarios: 10 percent, 5 percent, and zero.*

Under the most likely assumption that inflation will average five percent annually, the fundamental value of silver will rise from $12.68 per ounce in 1987 to $15.73 in 1990 and $22.50 an ounce in 1995. Even with zero inflation, the fundamental value will reach $12.94 in 1990, and $14.50 in 1995. If inflation heats up to 10 percent per year, silver's fundamental value would rise from $13.29 in 1987 to $18.94 in 1990 and to $34.20 in 1995.

At this writing, silver is $7 an ounce. While it is up from

*In the case of silver, platinum, and palladium, all calculations are based on the underlying assumption that the future growth rate of planetary product will continue in accordance with the recent past, which has been 2.313 percent annually. Thus, in order to determine future fundamental values, the average price of the last supercycle is first adjusted for the inflation that occurred from the midpoint of the last supercycle to the year in question. Then, to account for the growth in planetary product, this result is multiplied by the factor of 1.02313 for each year from the midpoint of the last supercycle to the year in question.

$5 in 1986, it still is considerably below its fundamental value and represents an excellent alternative to stocks. The fact that the price of silver started to advance in 1987 reveals that the next supercycle in silver is already underway.

Platinum

Unlike silver and gold, platinum was entirely unknown to Europeans before the discovery of the New World, though it had been used for decorative jewelry by the native population of Colombia for millenniums. By the sixteenth century, the Spanish conquistadores had not only discovered the beauty and utility of platinum but had recorded major placer deposits in the Choco region of Colombia.

By the beginning of the twentieth century, Canada had become the world's largest producer of platinum, which was produced as a byproduct of its nickel and copper mining. South Africa took over leadership in platinum production in the late twenties when its Merensky Reef mining zone was discovered. In the 1940s, the Soviets began producing platinum from a mining area near the Siberian city of Noril'sk. Soon they had become the number two platinum producer in the world, a position they hold today.

In addition to its decorative uses, platinum has many important industrial applications. The chemical industry uses it extensively. A woven gauze, 90 percent of which is platinum, is used in the oxidation of ammonia to produce nitric acid—the basic component of most nitrogen-based fertilizers, nitrate explosives, and chemical intermediates for processing stainless steel. A similar gauze, also 90 percent platinum, is used to produce hydrogen cyanide, which in turn is used in the production of insecticides and transparent plastics.

Platinum catalysts are vital to the manufacture of common nonprescription pain relievers, and are used by the petroleum industry to make high-octane gasoline and a variety of petrochemicals. And in 1974, automobile manufacturers began to use platinum (and palladium) in the catalytic converters that were designed to reduce the emission of carbon monoxide and hydrocarbons from automotive exhaust. In 1981, the demand for platinum went up still further as the so-called "three-way" converters were devised, which also reduced the emission of nitrous oxide from automobiles. Moreover, these new systems used platinum oxygen sensors to control the fuel mixture so that the converter could operate at maximum efficiency.[2]

Since the mid-1970s, these and many other industrial uses have consumed 99 percent of the platinum that was either mined or recycled in the world outside of the Soviet Union plus the platinum that the Soviets have offered for sale. There are no reliable statistics about how much platinum the Soviet Union produces or how much it consumes. It is possible that there is a considerable stockpile of platinum in Soviet hands. Still, it is not likely that the Soviet Union would use that stockpile to drive down platinum prices on the world market since they derive much needed hard currency from their platinum sales.

Chart 13.2 shows the monthly average prices of platinum since 1975. During its last supercycle, platinum soared from $150 an ounce to over $900 an ounce, and then

Chart 13.2. Fundamental Value of Platinum
(Dollars per Ounce)

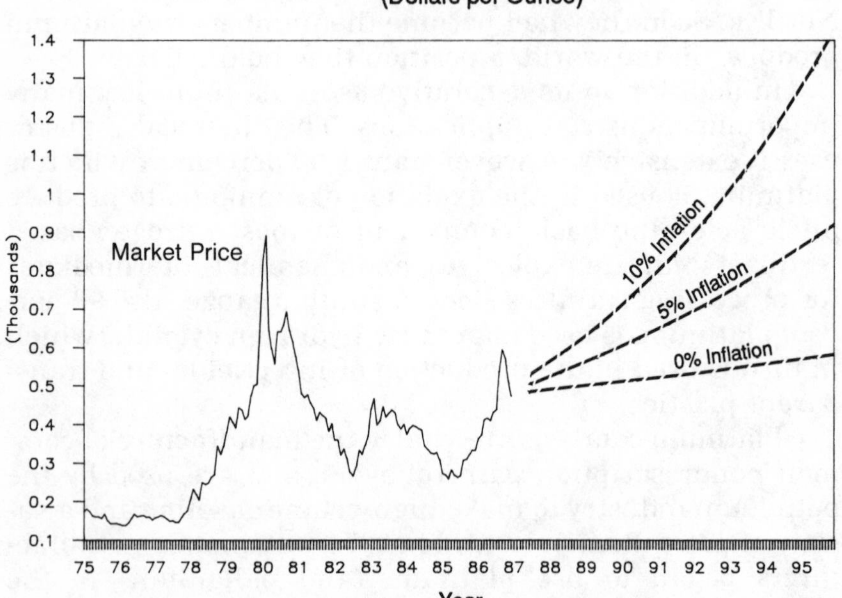

Source: Market prices from U.S. Bureau of Mines

crashed under $300 an ounce. The average price was $336. Since 1985, the price has climbed to $625 an ounce. This chart also shows the fundamental value of platinum under the assumption that the supply of platinum on the world market will not change materially, and again, this means that the fundamental value of platinum will be a function of inflation and the growth rate of planetary product. The three scenarios of inflation are depicted on the chart. If inflation averages 5 percent in the years ahead, the fundamental value of platinum will rise from $495 in 1987 to $614 in 1990 and to $879 in 1995. Assuming no inflation, the fundamental value will rise from $471 in 1987 to $505 in 1990 and to $566 in 1995, and with an average of 10 percent inflation the value becomes $519 in 1987, $740 in 1990, and $1,336 in 1995.

At this writing, platinum is $625 an ounce, which is above its current fundamental value. While there is a very good chance that this supercycle will drive its price still higher, it is not as safe an investment as either gold or silver at the present time.

Palladium

Palladium and platinum share some industrial uses. Both metals are critical materials in the furnaces and vessels that are used to make glass, in the terminals of fuel cells for the catalytic production of electricity, and in printed electronic circuitry. Palladium also is used for its tarnish resistance in dentistry and other medical uses and, although to a lesser extent than platinum, palladium is used in catalytic converters. Moreover, palladium has properties that make it useful in its own unique applications. A major use for palladium is in low-voltage electrical contacts. Telephone switching contacts have typically been 60 percent palladium and 40 percent silver, and more recently the content has jumped to 80 percent palladium. Palladium and silver are used together in capacitors.

In the chemical industry, palladium is necessary in the production of hydrogen peroxide, which plays a vital role in industrial pollution abatement. Palladium catalysts are used in paint emulsions and adhesives as well in as silicone-based products used in automotive fluids and construction materials. Also the metal figures prominently in the synthetic production of vitamins A and B-2, and in a process called hydrocracking, which increases gasoline yields.

As in the case of platinum, over the last ten years these and other industrial uses in the world's market-economy countries combined to consume virtually all (95 percent) of the palladium produced and recycled in those countries plus the quantity that the Soviet Union sold on the world markets. Here again Soviet secrecy is obscuring the total picture, and, in the case of palladium, this is a larger problem because the Soviet Union is by far the world's largest producer. Soviet production was estimated to be 2.5 million ounces in 1985 while South Africa, the world's second largest producer, produced 962 thousand ounces (Canada was third at 158 thousand ounces). Gauging the stability of the world's supply of palladium is speculative because of the enormous role that the Soviet Union plays in the world supply picture.

Still, we can assume that it is not in the Soviets' interest to flood the market from their presumed stockpile, thus forcing down the price of palladium on the world markets. Assuming, therefore, that we can calculate the fundamental value of palladium in the same fashion as silver and platinum, we can check chart 13.3 to find the monthly average prices since 1975 and the results of our inflation projections.

During its last supercycle, the price of palladium rose from under $50 an ounce to $300 and crashed to close at $50 an ounce. Since late 1982, it has meandered upward to around $150 an ounce. The average during this last supercycle was $100 an ounce. Under a 5 percent inflation scenario, the fundamental value of palladium is $147 in 1987, $183 in 1990, and $262 in 1995. With zero inflation the values become $140 in 1987, $150 in 1990, and $169 in 1995. Under the 10 percent inflation assumption the fundamental value becomes $154 in 1987, $220 in 1990, and $398 in 1995. Thus, with palladium close to its fundamental value, it appears to be reasonably priced, and the uptrend in force since 1982 shows the clear beginnings of a supercycle that undoubtedly will carry the price of palladium much higher.

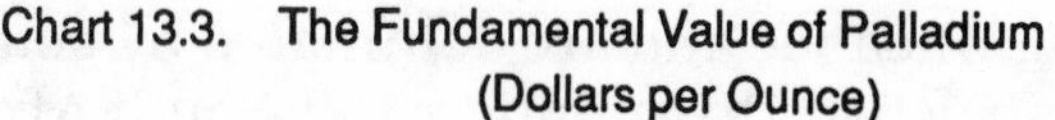
Chart 13.3. The Fundamental Value of Palladium (Dollars per Ounce)

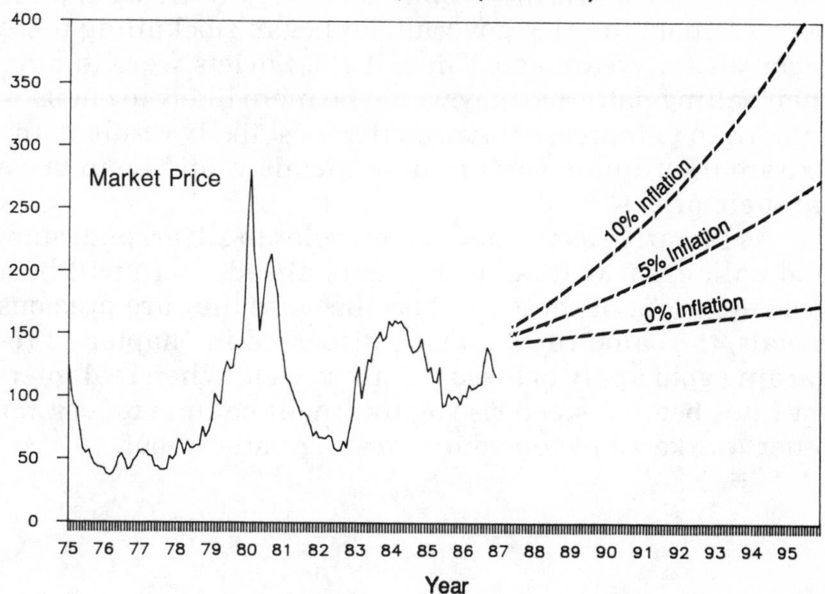

Source: Market prices from U.S. Bureau of Mines

Conclusions

From our analysis of the fundamental values of these precious metals, we can see that silver is undervalued, palladium is reasonably priced, and platinum is overvalued. This can and probably will change as the prices of these metals move up and down with investor expectations. For example, the fact that European auto makers are starting to equip their cars with catalytic converters has bolstered the price of platinum recently. However, as South Africa increases production to meet new European demand, the price of platinum likely will move back in line with its fundamental value.

There will probably be other extraordinary events that will cause near term price swings. It is almost certain that the years ahead will see continued political instability in South Africa, which could translate into extreme volatility in the price of platinum, since this republic is the second major producer of the metal.

Due to the fact that both platinum and palladium have

strategic significance and are dominated by potentially unstable or untrustworthy suppliers like South Africa and the Soviet Union, the U.S. government began stockpiling these metals a few years ago. Thus, if the Soviets were to alter their selling patterns, they would be more likely to cut back sales than to increase them. So the most likely result of any extramarket influences on these metals would be to drive up their prices.

As lucrative as the new supercycles in silver, platinum, and palladium will be in the years ahead, there will be a time to get out of these markets. Because they are precious metals, the same rules that we discussed in chapter 12 regarding gold apply to these metals as well. When real interest rates begin a steep rise again it will be time to look for other markets to keep your investing panic proof.

III

Winning with Real Estate

14

Real Estate Supercycles

Most investors tend to see real estate as a unique investment arena, not at all on a par with stocks and precious metals. They are conscious of prices; they even may frequently congratulate themselves on their foresight when they see how much the equity in their homes or rental properties has increased. But they don't see these profits as being speculative in the least. Surely, the steadily escalating price of real estate can be thought of as the one dependable and unchangeable feature of our troubled economic landscape. Can't it?

Sadly, history's answer is "no." Supercycles of enormous scope and strength are not just a part of the history of real estate in the United States; they *are* that history. Their story is the story of property in America. And if it is a story of the triumphant taming of a continent, the emergence of an economic colossus, it also is a story of repeated catastrophes and smashed fortunes.

Ironically, it is the sheer expanse of land represented by the U.S. continent that has served to blind generation after generation of American investors to the regular ebbs and flows of fortune that have dominated our nation's real estate markets for more than 150 years. Real estate speculation has existed in the United States at least since the days of George Washington. That it didn't *seem* like speculation to the adventurers and homesteaders, who often were the first investors, had to do with the stubborn belief that land prices had nowhere to go but up. That it *was* speculation can be seen from the numerous boom and bust cycles—supercycles in their baldest and most destructive form—that have wreaked havoc in American real estate through a succession of eras including our own.

Take, for instance, the hopeful settlers that stood on the shores of Lake Michigan in 1835. Like the millions of men and women who were to ride similar financial hurricanes throughout the next century and a half, these folks had every reason to believe that the fortune they were staking collectively on the growth of their new community was safe and destined to grow. They were in the right place at the right time, and so was the little lakeside village of Chicago. Although they had no way of knowing it, these folks were about to participate in America's first major land boom, and virtually none of them would emerge with their fortunes intact.

Their story began in 1817, when New York Governor DeWitt Clinton persuaded his legislature to authorize a 7-million-dollar expenditure to build a ditch 363 miles long, 40 feet wide, and 4 feet deep, joining Buffalo's harbor on Lake Erie to the Hudson River at Albany, which in turn flows southward to New York City. Though the idea must have seemed like total madness to more than a few New York residents, the massive engineering project was finished, and on October 25, 1825, a boat called the "Seneca Chief" became the first to wind its way through the eighty-two newly constructed locks of the Erie Canal.

The completion of the canal signaled the opening of the Midwest to settlement. As thousands of settlers flowed into Michigan, Ohio, Indiana, and Illinois, goods to supply them flowed through the canal from the booming manufacturing centers of the East, where factories were finding it increasingly difficult to find workers. In the wake of the western migrations, labor costs began to soar and the young nation had a serious brush with inflation.[1]

The center of the rapidly settling Midwest was the little

village on the shores of Lake Michigan. In 1832, Chicago had only a population close to 100, but a few years later there was hardly a place in the country where the promise of wealth was greater.

Until the mid-1830s, there was no way to get from the Great Lakes to the mighty Mississippi by water. As a result, the much needed freight that was being carried on the river could reach needy settlements only by a tortuous overland journey. But back when the decade dawned, planning had begun for another canal. This one would connect Lake Michigan to the Illinois River, which, in turn, would flow into the Mississippi just north of St. Louis. And on the harbor where this canal would meet the lake was the little village of Chicago. It was not hard to understand how many of its early residents began to be convinced that Chicago was destined for greatness—a city that would become the vital link between the densely populated East and the natural resources of the South and West.

It seemed inevitable: Chicago was about to take its place at the bustling hub of the country. Vast quantities of eastbound grain and livestock soon would be passing through its harbor, as would ore from the cavernous treasuries of Minnesota and Michigan.

With the hopes of Chicago residents came capital in record amounts. Widespread credit was still a relatively new thing in the 1830s, but like many states, Illinois had started chartering its own banks and the new bankers were bullish on the prospects for their region. Real estate loans were available widely, and as this new buying power flooded into the market, land prices skyrocketed. One 80-by-100-foot parcel of land at the corner of South Water and Clark Streets, for instance, sold for $100 in 1832. That same lot sold for $3,000 in 1834, and one year later for $15,000—a 500 percent gain in one year![2]

The boom was on. And what a boom it was. A speculative fever was rampant. A man dressed in scarlet would trot on horseback down the streets, stopping at each corner to announce the next land auction, and his appearance at nearly any time of the day would bring a rowdy crowd of speculators.

On the Fourth of July, 1836, flashing spades inaugurated the ground breaking of the Illinois Canal. On that happy day it would have been hard for any of the celebrants to think about anything but the glorious future that lay ahead for their windy city. But the dark signs were there. Their future metropolis thus far was in existence only in paper; its foundations were little more than a superstructure of mortgage notes and speculation. Before the dream could be realized, the superstructure collapsed.

It was called the Panic of 1837, but the collapse of prices and paper empires continued for more than four years. In the end, land that had been purchased for as much as $10,000 during the halcyon days of 1836 could not be sold for even $100. The state of Illinois defaulted on its bonds and notes, and work on the Illinois-Michigan Canal came to a grinding halt. Chicago eventually would grow to become the city worthy of the visions of those who lived there in 1836, but very few of them would live to see it. It would take another supercycle.

Considering the fortunes looted, the misery caused, it would be easy to surmise that the spasm that struck Chicago and the nation during the mid-1830s would have lived on in the memory of future investors as proof of the dangers of trying to reap the whirlwind of a full-scale boom. Unfortunately, and significantly, it didn't. Within the next fifty years, Americans would fuel two more supercycles. The first was in gold during the Greenback era, and then as the Depression ended in 1879 their attention would switch to stocks. But when the bull market on Wall Street peaked in 1884, capital began moving into real property again, and another supercycle in real estate began.

This time the most frenetic scene was California, where newly constructed transcontinental railroads were dropping off hopeful pilgrims at an unprecedented rate. During the summer of 1886, the population of Los Angeles was mushrooming at the rate of a thousand new residents a month. Some of these new residents were poor fortune seekers from the frosty East and Midwest; others were wealthy opportunists who arrived in private rail cars with huge sums to invest in the raw new state. Soon all were stampeding into auctions to buy real estate that couldn't be plotted out fast enough. They were not interested in the rich agricultural land that was abundant in the paradise of southern California. The land was selling in ten to twenty acre parcels, too small for farming, but perfect for subdividing into city lots that could be sold at a quick profit.

The use of credit became common by the spring of 1887. Twenty-five percent of the purchase price was all that was needed. By summer, a sixty day turnover was bringing $10,000 profit per acre, and buyers were standing in line all night for a chance to bid on a slice of ownership of their city. Places in line alone sold for $1,000! Natives who had sold their land only one year earlier were buying it back at five to fifteen times that original price.[3] Why not? During this booming year land sales in southern California topped $200 million.[4]

Like the Chicagoans who toasted the ground breaking of the Illinois-Michigan Canal fifty years before, the Californians had their eyes closed to the obvious signs of excess. By the middle of 1887, even if the population growth were to continue to rocket, there were enough city plots already to accommodate this growth for the next ten years. Land prices had been bloated by a flood tide of debt, and there wasn't enough money in circulation west of the Mississippi to pay it.[5]

By January 1888, activity in southern California's real estate markets stopped. Then the crash began. By April, prices were dropping weekly, and the sale of anything other than the most productive farmland was impossible. The slide continued into 1889 and brought prices down to one-fourth of their peak. Population growth in southern California continued as before, and prices continued to escalate on California's fruit. Building activity didn't even fall off. But a full generation of land buyers would come and go before land prices would reach 1887 levels again.

Forty years is not a long time within the history of a nation, particularly one as young as the United States, but it is a long time in terms of human memory. Generations pass, wisdom is handed down and ignored, broken dreams are buried, and fresh hopes take root. There may have been a few survivors of the California land bust who still were alive on the day in 1924 when the ten millionth auto rolled off Henry Ford's assembly line. But they were probably not among the swelling hoard of boomsters who were packing their families into flivvers and heading down the newly completed Dixie Highway to Florida.

As we saw in our study of supercycle one, the nation's capital resources began shifting out of stocks and into real property across the country in 1907. By the end of 1924, the real estate market in Florida had moved from a tropical depression into a full-blown hurricane. The population was exploding, bank deposits had tripled in less than five years, and land was selling at such a frantic level that the paperwork of normal escrow was holding up the pace of trading. To keep up with the action, the real estate industry developed a new financial tool called a "binder." A binder was a way for a buyer to hold a piece of property, usually for 10 percent of the purchase price. Theoretically, the binder was to be in effect only until the sale had closed and financing was in place, but in practice most transactions never got beyond the binder stage: In the superheated market, the profits were so immediate and substantial that most Florida property was being resold before the previous sale had even closed.

As the market crested, few owners bothered to hold their land. The binder was enough. This meant that while the boom/bust cycle unfolding in Florida was following exactly the same path as its predecessors in Illinois and California, the market was leveraged to previously unimaginable levels. Through the sale of binders, enormous pools of capital had appeared almost overnight—at least on paper.

The crash came in 1926. By its conclusion, twenty-six Florida cities were in default, hundreds of banks had failed, and the real estate portfolios of virtually every property owner in the state had been devalued to the point of worthlessness. The supercycles were continuing to hit the nation with almost metronomic regularity. And, now that Florida house lots were a bad bet, a supercycle in stocks—supercycle two—began to gather momentum.

By the end of the Great Depression, critical changes had begun to sweep over the American economy. Improvements in transportation and communication had destroyed the almost autonomous regional economies that had been so vulnerable to the ravages of naked booms and busts. Moreover, with the arrival of the New Deal, the government had entered the economy with both feet, as an economic stimulator through its spending policies, and as a regulator with the now fully mature Federal Reserve system. These developments did not mark the end of supercycles within real estate markets. Far from it. But they did eliminate the uncluttered stage which those supercycles had played previously. Now it would be necessary to look far more closely to catch the high stakes act.

As the nation emerged from the dark years of World War II, it seemed clear that the United States was about to enter an era of prosperity so soundly based that no real end could be glimpsed, and riding the crest of this prosperity was American real estate. As the fifties dawned, even the most pessimistic of observers would be forced to admit that the long series of real estate booms and busts now must be safely tucked away in the archives of history. What could stop the market now? There was unlimited space for growth, land was cheap, and environmental worries were an unknown. What could disturb this rosy picture?

The answer was yet another boom, but one with a most unexpected source. As the nation embarked on its unprecedented spurt of home building, with new suburbs sprouting up from coast to coast, the young families who were moving into those new homes were investing in the future in another very immediate way: They were having children, and having them in numbers that never had been seen before or since then. This baby boom was to change the face of the nation in a wide variety of ways, including changing American real estate.

The fifties and sixties were placid years for the real estate industry, but beneath the untroubled surface, this huge new generation represented a powerful rip tide that was moving closer to the surface. By the late sixties, the vanguard of the baby boom had reached the age of independence, leaving home and looking for apartments. As they did so they also launched a series of real estate supercycles, each of them involving more capital (and potential for disaster) than any that had gone before.

When the first wave of baby boomers left home and began their search for apartments, they discovered a cold fact: There were not many apartments there. At the same time, the economy was being buffeted by some powerful new inflationary forces that were having a profound effect on apartment rents. It didn't take investors long to realize that the time hardly could be better to get into the business of buying apartment buildings. Massive numbers of new potential renters were forcing rents up to unprecedented levels, sparking more investor interest than there were opportunities. Pummeled by this rising tide of investor demand, the traditional link between the price of a rental property and the amount of its rental income was strained to the breaking point, and prices of apartment properties began to float free. The rapid appreciation in price attracted still more investor interest, and the boom was on.

In fact, the only factor that seemed capable of cooling the fire was the availability of credit to finance the expansion. Until the mid-1970s, the traditional source for mortgage loans were banks, but with fires of the apartment boom being stoked higher every day, it was soon clear that new avenues for credit were needed. The solution was called a "real estate investment trust" or REIT. These new organizations allowed the relatively limited mortgage market to tap into the comparatively unlimited resources of Wall Street. The REIT, sold as a stock, would borrow money continuously at short-term interest rates and lend out money as mortgages at long-term interest rates. The magic in this idea was the fact that prevailing short-term interest rates were considerably lower than long-term interest rates, and this spread produced handsome profits for Wall Streeters who invested in REITs. This pipeline into Wall Street was a fabulous success! The asset base of REITs roared from $2 billion in 1969 to more than $20 billion in 1973.

Not all the investors that were attracted to the apartment market were individuals. In fact, many of the most active investors in the real estate markets of the late sixties were large institutions run by professional money managers. Looking for ways to protect their capital from an inflation-ridden economy and a slumping stock market, these institutions—including huge union and corporate pension funds—poured their millions into mega-apartment complexes, mortgages, and REITs.

These circumstances actually produced not one but two real estate booms, both triggered by the arrival of baby boomers at the apartment-renting age. The demand for apartments had caused a building and investment boom; the resulting need for credit had created REITs, and now the prices of the REITs were accelerating at a feverish rate. This swirling financial vortex propelled real estate prices to lofty heights, and from the perspective of the nation's board rooms, there seemed to be no end in sight. But there was, and it was going to come sooner than anyone could have guessed.

In 1973, there were many economic shocks, but in that year of the Arab oil embargo and seemingly endless gas lines, there was no development any more destructive to the real estate industry than the inexorable rise in short-term interest rates that led to a severe credit crunch. As short-term interest rates climbed above long-term interest rates, the economic logic of real estate investment trusts evaporated—and so did most of the REITs. Chase Manhattan Mortgage and Realty Trust was one of the few survivors. In 1972, its stock was selling for $70 a share; in 1974, that same share was selling for $4. There have been few crashes in any market that were more precipitous or destructive.

If the REITs had represented a boom within a boom, the large supercycle within the apartment market itself was following suit. In part, the trouble began with the sudden drying up of short-term financing, and the collapse of real estate's treasured pipeline to Wall Street, but beyond that an even more powerful force was at work again.

The first wave of baby boomers, having revolutionized the apartment market, was now moving on into starter houses, and the wind whistled out of the inflated apartment market as they left. Prices plummeted to fifty cents on the dollar in many areas of the country and foreclosures soared. The mood had changed. Now desperate owners were trying to unload properties as quickly as possible. Takers were rare and doom engulfed the apartment complex market. Apartment construction starts thudded to one-fourth of their peak, and in 1976, over 40 percent of the mortgage portfolios of the nation's largest banks were either earning no interest or were earning at greatly reduced rates.

The twin boom/crash cycles represented by REITs and the apartments they helped finance were the broadest based and most destructive in the history of American real estate, but it also is important to note that, unlike other booms we've looked at in this chapter, they largely were ignored by the general public. The news of their existence never made its way beyond the financial pages of the nation's newspapers. Ominously, in the immensely complicated economy of the United States, this supercycle had now gone underground—painfully obvious to the badly burned investors, but largely invisible to everyone else, including the future investors who in all innocence would take their place. So it was that even as the accounting departments of the nation's largest banks and financial institutions burned the midnight oil in an attempt to bury their losses from now-dubious real estate holdings, a shock wave of young Americans were giving up their apartments and moving into the single-family housing market—a market that has yet to recover from their onslaught.

In 1975, the average price of a home in the United States was $39,000. Although this figure represented a sharp gain over the years before, a house of this price would, when financed, require monthly payments that were not much higher than the amount of rent most baby boomers were paying. But while the transition from an apartment to a home was still a smooth one, the situation was worsening steadily.

Americans had discovered that their homes were serving as a dependable inflation hedge, and the tax advantages that Congress bestowed on real estate began to look more and more attractive as inflation pushed up tax brackets. The parents of the postwar generation had thought of their new homes as a consumer item, not as an investment, but a fast-paced market and persistent inflation had changed that.

By the end of 1976, the average price of a home had jumped to $47,200, up 10.9 percent from 1975. One year later it had jumped 13.5 percent from 1975 to $47,900. With housing prices climbing faster than the wages of likely first-time home buyers, lending institutions began to loosen their lending standards. Now, for instance, young adults were allowed to break through the old benchmark that had limited them to a house priced at no more than twice their annual incomes. Soon it was not uncommon to see banks offering mortgages on houses with selling prices for as much as three times the buyer's salary. And, in many cases, the terms of the mortgages had been liberalized.

So it was that a buying frenzy soon was underway even in the face of accelerating prices. The housing market had changed, and, once again, the heady scent of boom was in the air. As stories began to circulate about overwhelmed builders who were no longer accepting new orders, prospective buyers began to panic. In states like California—where more baby boomers lived than anywhere else—newspapers were running photographs that could have been taken a century before. Once again eager buyers were camping out on the unlandscaped grounds of developments-to-be, hoping that they might be able to bid on a chance to own a home, and to grab their piece of the profit pie.

Besides fueling the anxieties of young panic buyers, real estate's rapid price increases had begun to attract swarms of speculators. By the decade's end, banks in many parts of the country were offering mortgages with as little as 5 percent down. It didn't take one of the numerous books on how to make a fortune in the real estate market to realize that by grabbing the equity that was building rapidly in one property, it was possible to buy another, and then another. Soon many people, even those of modest means, had pyramided themselves into ownership of four or five homes. In many cases they were facing a negative cash flow but they didn't care. The rapid appreciation of the properties themselves plus the tax benefits usually more than made up for it.

For three frantic years, speculators and panic buyers continued to stampede into the home market. In 1978, the average price of a home reached $55,500; by the end of 1980 the average price was $72,000. And as the prices went up, a new class of buyers began to enter the market in significant numbers.

For many years, older home owners across the country had been watching the equity windfall that an overheated market had handed them. Soon, many of them were using their newly found wealth to finance their way into bigger and better homes. This trade-up market only added more fuel to the sizzling prices. In fact, in many areas the prices of the most expensive homes in a neighborhood were outperforming those of the starter homes the baby boomers were buying.

By the end of 1980, the American home market was showing every sign of being out of control totally, and many observers began to worry that it would soon reach critical mass. That it didn't was in large part due to Paul Volker's all-out war against inflation. As the Federal Reserve tightened its monetary policy, the loose lending policies of banks and thrift institutions, and the fuel these policies represented to the boom, vanished. Suddenly a 20 percent down payment was the absolute minimum. As interest rates went up, housing prices, while still going up, began to cool. And even a slight cooling was enough to shake the most dangerously leveraged speculators out of the market.

By the time President Reagan was inaugurated for his second term, it seemed that the housing boom had ended—not with a crash but with a whimper. Speculators and overleveraged institutions had been forced into ruin. Although the posted price of new and existing houses had increased fractionally over the four-year period, it was at a much slower rate than inflation and wages. Moreover, sellers had been forced by high interest rates and tight money to help buyers with their financing. Assumable seller financing at discounted interest rates became an essential element of a sale.

The combination of prices that lagged behind the inflation rate and discounted financing meant that the cost of buying housing, in real terms, had declined dramatically—by 25 percent in most areas of the country. By December 1985, the median family income had become more than sufficient to purchase the median house, and houses were affordable once again. Suddenly, just as it had seemed the market might sleep until prices reached their preboom levels, there were distinct signs of stirring. House prices nationally scored a gain of 11 percent in 1986, rising to $100,600. The Northeast led the pack with a searing 18.4 percent rise to $136,000. The West took on new life with an 12.1 percent increase to $126,900. The Midwest turned in a gain of 7.4 percent to $71,500, and the South showed an increase of 4 percent to $92,100.

And so the story ends where it began: in the uneasy latitudes where hurricanes are born. Were the early to mid-eighties just a breather before another cycle of upward-spiraling home prices? What will happen to apartments and office buildings? And what about other forms of real estate such as farmland? We have seen that the real estate market is made up of several subsidiaries that have lives and supercycles of their own. When one is declining, others may be rising. Thus, in our quest for panic-proof investing we need to consider the timing of each of these markets separately. We need to burrow into the elegant structure of their supercycles to see when each will provide us with a good alternative. Let's start with apartments.

15

Apartment Properties

If there is one factor that distinguishes real estate supercycles from those in other markets, it is the outsize importance of two sets of fundamental conditions: population and politics.

We saw in chapter 14 how the arrival of the baby boom generation into adulthood had and is continuing to have a profound effect on the real estate markets. This is not unusual. Population dynamics affect real estate much more dramatically than any other kind of investment, because among the investments we have looked at so far, only real estate has use value. An investor who buys into the stock or bond market does so exclusively to make a profit. And, while decorative jewelry may be a slight factor, few investors in precious metals are looking to make use of their purchases. This is not so with real estate. Though they may be aware of market conditions, and though they may hope that their purchases will appreciate in value, most real estate investors are buying an investment that they are either planning to live in themselves, or are planning to use to make an immediate rental income.

Because of its use value, real estate ownership, particularly in the postwar period, has become extremely widespread, so widespread that real estate always has received much more than its share of attention from politicians. This attention has resulted in a huge volume of protective legislation that has had a very salubrious effect on real estate markets. But behind all of the favorable legislation is an implied threat: What can be given can be taken away.

One evening in late May 1986, Senate Finance Committee Chairman Robert Packwood appeared on the nation's TV screens promising to revise thoroughly and simplify the nation's tax codes. Most of the millions of Americans who were watching the evening news that night paid scant attention including those with substantial investments in income property. They'd heard it all before. In the previous twelve months they had watched two other tax reform bills crawl into the halls of Congress and die. Surely this would be no different. Congress had, after all, been showering a glittering array of tax benefits on real estate investors for years. Was there really a chance that it would creep in like a thief in the night and take them all away?

The answer to the amazement of nearly everyone was "yes." Almost from the first moment that the bill emerged from committee, unusual signs were being read by political pundits, signs that indicated that this bill had developed an unprecedented momentum. Soon only the most stubbornly optimistic of real estate investors were arguing that the bill would fail. Soon, beneath the hoopla and oratory that was accompanying the tax reform bill's progress through the halls of Congress, it was possible to notice the disquieting hush that had fallen over real estate markets across the country.

As we have seen numerous times, supercycles are spawned from a mix of volatile elements that, once bonded together, virtually become invisible. While first-wave investors buy into a market whose fundamentals they have examined closely, later investors frequently buy into strong markets because they *are* strong markets, and a boom climate is established; soon prices are going up because they are going up. Sadly, for many late investors in the apartment market, with the passage of the Tax Reform Bill of 1986, it was clear that the prices of apartment buildings no longer would be going up. As the computers and calculators hummed in paneled offices and cluttered dens across the country, it soon became clear that the damage from the tax reform bill would be heavy. The only question was how far down prices were likely to go.

That question is still being asked today, and not only by those investors who still own apartment properties. We also are asking the question because we are looking hard for new markets where we can buy into the beginning of a new supercycle. The apartment market is a great candidate for our interest: It has been declining since the passage of tax reform and, if it is soon to bottom out, would present some real bargains. Is the apartment market near its bottom? Fortunately, there is a way to answer that question. But first it is necessary to trace this crashing supercycle back to its beginnings.

Not surprisingly, those roots lay in the devastated landscape that had been left behind after the previous supercycle: the apartment boom and crash of the early seventies. The years following the apartment crash saw investors holding apartment properties that were ravaged by debt, vacancies, and negative cash flows. As the news of their distress spread, potential builders and developers got the word, and construction projects were shelved or canceled in every region of the country; as the builders put away their tools and left the apartment market, a new supercycle was born.

In 1976, 258,200 apartments were finished in the United States, down nearly 70 percent from the 774,800 that had been finished at the height of the boom in 1973. As the construction rate dropped, so did the vacancy rate. Helped by high inflation, rents began to rise: 7 percent in 1975, 4 percent in 1976, 6 percent in 1977, 8 percent in 1978 and again in 1979. By the end of the decade, in a development that would have been impossible only five years before, real estate investors and syndicators began to discover that apartment buildings of all sizes—their rents swollen, their prices still depressed—had become a bargain.

As the new decade dawned and inflation sizzled, rent increases became dramatic: 13 percent in 1979, 12 percent in 1980, and 11 percent in 1981. As the rents went up, it became more and more clear to everyone that there was a new, strong surge in the apartment market. And, conveniently enough, just as this hoard of newly interested investors arrived in the market, interest rates began to decline to affordable levels. Euphoria was widespread. If the apartment market could boom through the 1980 credit squeeze and a recession, what could stop it?

As so many saddened investors have seen so often, prices in boom markets tend to break amid just such a climate of unbridled optimism, and indeed, had Congress not intervened in 1981, the prosperous supercycle in the apartment market would have made its inevitable turn in 1982. By then the market was in a full boom state: Prices had become detached from their underlying fundamentals. Even more ominous, beneath all the frenetic activity, those fundamentals were changing.

In 1982, rents nationwide rose only 1 percent; 1983 followed suit. And, despite this slowdown, builders were back at work with a vengeance. More than 370,000 new apartments were completed in 1983, compared with the depressed level of 293,000 in 1982. In 1984, 506,000 new units were completed, and 534,000 more the following year. The low rents and a new building boom would have been enough to turn the strongest real estate market had it not been for the fortuitous arrival of the Economic Recovery Act of 1981. Suddenly investors could afford to ignore clear evidence that rental income had stagnated, because new tax benefits took the place of cash income from rents as a reason to invest.

Passed in the dark days of a deepening recession, the Economic Recovery Act of 1981 was a package of tax measures that were intended to stimulate the economy. One of these changes was a clause that allowed owners of income property to shorten the depreciation life of their properties from forty to fifteen years. Also the tax law provided an accelerated depreciation method that more than tripled the tax deductions investors could enjoy in the early years of owning an apartment building.

The Tax Reform Act of 1986 took these benefits away. In order to assess the damage, first we need to see how much these new tax provisions helped real estate investors in the days before tax reform. Let's look at a typical fourplex in a good neighborhood. If the annual gross rental income from these apartments was $20,000 and operating expenses were $8,000, the property would produce a net operating income of $12,000. In the days before tax reform, a prudent investor easily could have paid $160,000 for this building, and virtually any lending institution would have lent him 70 percent, or $112,000, through a 10 percent mortgage amortized over thirty years. To buy the property, an investor would only have to come up with the difference of $48,000, and although the mortgage payments would soak up nearly all of the net operating income from the property during the first year, leaving only $205 (table 15.1), he would enjoy fat tax deductions amounting to $13,909. And if the buyer were a typical investor with income in the 40 percent tax bracket,

TABLE 15.1
A TYPICAL FOURPLEX

Purchase price	160,000	Cap rate = 7.5%
Mortgage (70%)	112,000	(100*NOI/Purchase price)
Cash down payment	48,000	

CASH FLOW ANALYSIS

	1986
Rental income	20,000
Operating expenses	(8,000)
Net operating income (NOI)	12,000
Debt service	
Principal	623
10% Interest	11,172
	11,795
Cash flow	205

TAX IMPLICATIONS BEFORE TAX REFORM

Income	20,000
Tax deductions	
Operating expenses	8,000
Depreciation	14,737
Interest	11,172
Taxable income	(13,909)

AFTER-TAX RETURN

Cash flow	205
Tax savings (40%)	5,564
Total	5,769
Percent of investment	12.02%

he would realize tax savings of 40 percent of this amount, or $5,564. These tax savings, when added to the $205 cash flow, would raise the after-tax return to $5,769. This figure, 96 percent of which is tax savings, would represent a 12.02 tax-free return on a $48,000 investment in the first year alone.

Of course, our investor would not buy this building for tax reasons alone. He also would need to be assured of a profit when he eventually decided to sell, so he would need to determine not only the price he would be willing to pay, but also what he could be expected to receive from a future buyer.

There are several methods of estimating the value of a property. Of these, perhaps the most frequently cited is the gross multiple method. Using this tool, a potential buyer will divide a property's selling price by the gross rent it can be expected to produce. In the days prior to tax reform, there was an industry yardstick that was applied to gross multiples: A multiple of six was generally considered to be too low, a multiple of ten, too high, but a gross multiple of eight was considered to be worthy of a closer look.

Although the gross multiple method is undeniably convenient and fast, and although it usually produces a figure that is in the right ball park, a quick look back at table 15.1 reveals that there are several important factors that are ignored by using gross rent as the sole measure. Operating expenses, for instance, can vary widely in properties that appear similar in other respects; so can vacancies. Both can have quite an impact on net operating income. For this reason, the best way to measure the value of a property is to use the net operating income itself as the yardstick.

Here's how: If our investor paid $160,000 for a property that had a net operating income of $12,000, he would receive a cash yield that would amount to 7.5 percent of his total investment. In real estate parlance, this figure is known as the capitalization (or "cap") rate. It means that this investor would recoup his cash investment at the rate of 7.5 percent a year. Of course, few investors pay cash for income property, and debt service easily could eat up this income. But in the heady days before the passage of tax reform, that was no problem. As table 15.1 shows, tax benefits made up the difference.

If a 7.5 percent cap rate was sufficient to provide our investor with a nice return (including the tax benefits), it stood to reason that it also would do so for a future buyer. Assuming that rents and operating expenses continued to rise at a compounded rate of 5 percent a year, table 15.2 shows that by 1990 our investor's net operating income will climb to $14,586. For a buyer at that time to achieve a cap rate of 7.5 percent, he should be willing to pay $194,482. (He also would arrive at this figure by using a gross multiple of eight.) After deducting the mortgage value, a real estate brokerage commission of 5 percent, and the taxes on the disposition at a 40 percent tax rate, our investor would have $62,178 to put in his pocket after the sale. Moreover, if he put the annual returns into a money market fund earning 5 percent, he could amass a total of $90,696. For comparison's sake, it's interesting to note that in order to turn a $48,000 investment into $90,696 anywhere else, it would be necessary to find an investment paying a tax-free return of 14 percent.

Before the passage of tax reform, investments like the one I've just described were considered conservative by millions of prudent investors. Unfortunately, most of them lacked the crystal ball that would have allowed them to see the rules were about to change.

The depreciation deductions used in tables 15.1 and 15.2 were calculated using the accelerated depreciation schedule that had been allowed on residential properties prior to tax reform. Tax reform reduced these tax benefits sharply by lengthening the depreciation life to 27.5 years and by disallowing the accelerated method. In practice, this meant that depreciation tax deductions dropped by more than 60 percent. To make matters worse, the few depreciation deductions that were left, as well as the tax deduction for mortgage interest, could be used only to shelter actual rental income, not salaries, interest income, dividends, or capital gains from investments other than real estate.

Tax reform meant that tax advantages were gone, and as we saw with the fourplex, there was very little else in the way of current benefits. The mortgage payments, even at the relatively modest prevailing rate of 10 percent, gobbled up all but a paltry $205 of the property's net operating income.

For the apartment market, the effect of tax reform was

TABLE 15.2
A PRE-TAX REFORM INVESTMENT PROPERTY

Purchase price	160,000
Mortgage (70%)	112,000
Cash down payment	48,000

CASH FLOW ANALYSIS

	1986	*1987*	*1988*	*1989*	*1990*
Rental income	20,000	21,000	22,050	23,153	24,310
Operating expenses	(8,000)	(8,400)	(8,820)	(9,261)	(9,724)
Net operating income	12,000	12,600	13,230	13,892	14,586
Debt service					
Principal	623	688	760	840	927
10% interest	11,172	11,107	11,035	10,955	10,867
	11,795	11,795	11,795	11,795	11,795
Cash flow	205	805	1,435	2,097	2,791

TAX IMPLICATIONS BEFORE TAX REFORM

	1986	*1987*	*1988*	*1989*	*1990*
Income	20,000	21,000	22,050	23,153	24,310
Tax deductions					
Operating expenses	8,000	8,400	8,820	9,261	9,724
Depreciation	14,737	13,380	12,147	11,028	10,013
Interest	11,172	11,107	11,035	10,955	10,867
Taxable income	(13,909)	(11,886)	(9,952)	(8,092)	(6,294)
After-tax return	5,769	5,560	5,416	5,334	5,309
Percent of investment	12.02%	11.58%	11.28%	11.11%	11.06%

PROPERTY SALE IN 1990

Sale price	194,481
(Cap rate = 7.50%)	
Mortgage payoff	(108,163)
Brokerage commission	(9,724)
Disposition taxes	(14,417)
Net sale proceeds	62,178
Overall equivalent tax-free annual return equals	14%

to eliminate the incentive to use leverage until prices fell to the level at which it would not hurt investors to use financing again. As table 15.3 shows, prices had to fall until cap rates rose to match the prevailing interest rates. The price of the fourplex would have to fall to $120,000 to be at a 10 percent cap rate. If we were to buy the fourplex at that price and elected not to use financing, our cash yield would be 10 percent since the net operating income is $12,000. But note that this property is now at a price level which, if we used financing at a 10 percent interest rate, we would see close to the same yield on our cash down payment. Using a 70 percent mortgage, for example, we would have a mortgage of $84,000 and pay debt service payments of $8,846 per year, leaving a cash flow of $3,154. A small part of the debt service would be reducing the mortgage, and this equity build would amount to $486 in the first year. Thus, the total benefit of cash flow and equity build-up would add up to $3,622, slightly more than a 10 percent return on the cash down payment of $36,000. (Plugging in any amount of mortgage will yield the same result as long as property is purchased at the same cap rate as the mortgage interest rate.)

Table 15.4 shows what can be expected to happen if we were to buy the fourplex at $120,000. Tax deductions will still shelter the cash flow, but now the excess, $742, will have to be stored in our accountant's file cabinet until this

TABLE 15.3
EFFECT OF LEVERAGE

Purchase price equals 120,000 (10% cap rate)

Mortgage	0	84,000
Cash down payment	120,000	36,000
Net operating income	12,000	12,000
Debt service		
Principal	0	468
Interest	0	8,378
	0	8,846
Cash flow	12,000	3,154
Equity build	0	468
Total benefits	12,000	3,622
Percentage of down payment	10.00%	10.06%

TABLE 15.4
A POST-TAX REFORM INVESTMENT PROPERTY

Purchase price	120,000
Mortgage (70%)	84,000
Cash down payment	36,000

CASH FLOW ANALYSIS

	1987	*1988*	*1989*	*1990*	*1991*
Rental income	20,000	21,000	22,050	23,153	24,310
Operating expenses	(8,000)	(8,400)	(8,820)	(9,261)	(9,724)
Net operating income	12,000	12,600	13,230	13,892	14,586
Debt service					
Principal	467	516	570	630	696
10% interest	8,379	8,330	8,276	8,216	8,150
	8,846	8,846	8,846	8,846	8,846
Cash flow	3,154	3,754	4,384	5,045	5,740

TAX IMPLICATIONS AFTER TAX REFORM

	1987	*1988*	*1989*	*1990*	*1991*
Income	20,000	21,000	22,050	23,153	24,310
Tax deductions					
Operating expenses	8,000	8,400	8,820	9,261	9,724
Depreciation	4,364	4,364	4,364	4,364	4,364
Interest	8,379	8,330	8,276	8,216	8,150
Taxable income	(743)	(94)	590	1,311	2,072
After-tax return	3,154	3,754	4,384	4,747	5,160
Percent of investment	8.76%	10.43%	12.18%	13.19%	14.33%

PROPERTY SALE IN 1990

Sale price	145,861
(Cap rate = 10%)	
Mortgage payoff	(81,122)
Brokerage commission	(7,293)
Disposition taxes	(5,231)
Net sale proceeds	52,215
Overall equivalent tax-free annual return equals	16%

property or another property generates unsheltered rental income. If the 5 percent rent increases materialize, we will begin to use this excess in two years.

In terms of our annual after-tax benefits, we are not as well off in the early years of ownership after tax reform —even paying as little as $120,000 for the property—as we would have been before tax reform paying $160,000. However, if we sell the property at the end of 1990 at a capitalization rate of 10 percent, our gain will make up the difference, and our overall return will be comparable.

So finally the bottom line is clear: The swift passage of the Tax Reform Act of 1986 caused the value of this fourplex to drop from $160,000 to $120,000, or 29.4 percent. Had an investor been unlucky enough to buy this property with a $112,000 mortgage shortly before the arrival of tax reform, the drop of $40,000 would have wiped out nearly his entire $48,000 investment.

It is clear that the supercycle that produced steady profits for thousands of investors in the apartment market throughout the early 1980s has turned. It should have peaked in 1982, and without an extraordinary boost from Congress, it would have. But with the passage of tax reform in 1986, Congress took back much more than it bestowed in 1981, and in the process, the remainder of optimism that had been holding up the prices of apartment houses across the country was shot down. All that is left is the wait for local real estate markets to begin to reflect the collapse. Slowly, almost all of them will, and when they do you will have a great buying opportunity.

From the moment of its passage, tax reform has been shaking out bargains as distressed owners find that they can't hold out any longer and must throw in the towel. To find these properties, you simply need to shop for prices based on cap rates that are equal to, if not greater than, the prevailing mortgage interest rates. If you can't find sellers in your area who are ready to take your offers, just wait. Probably it is too early. Soon, though, sellers will be forced to accept reality and the time will be right.

As we have seen and will continue to see in our study of supercycles, downturns are always a lot steeper than upturns. Many years of growth are erased in a matter of months. When these downturns come, they always go too far, and bargains are created. If you buy these bargains, you will profit from this market even if it does nothing more than return to normal. Your profits will motivate others at a time when they are seeing their profits vanish in stocks. Pools of capital will be sloshing through the economy, searching for new channels, and a new boom in apartments will be kicked off. Other forces also will be helping you make money in apartments: One will add to demand, one will restrict supply, and the combination will loft prices. Let's look at the demand side first.

Recall that one of the most dominant forces in the apartment boom and bust of the mid-seventies was the entry and exit of the postwar generation. Will that happen again? The answer is thrown into sharp relief by chart 15.1 which charts the rise and fall of the postwar baby boom. Although its importance usually is underestimated, the age structure of the U.S. population is quite visible. The U.S. Census Bureau surveys the number of births in the country each year and publishes the results. Chart 15.1 is a compilation of those results for 1930 to 1984. Most of the attention that has been given to these figures has focused on the boom

Chart 15.1. U.S. Live Births (Millions)

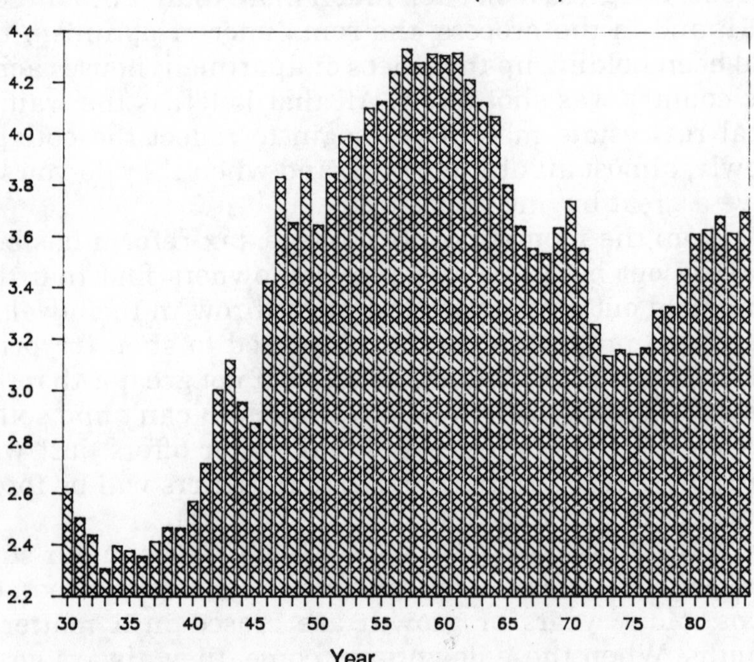

Source: U.S. Census Bureau

in births that took place in the 1940s, 1950s, and early 1960s. Demographers and marketers have followed this leading edge through a series of purchasing booms that began with baby food and moved on through toys, fast food, education, and apartment housing, and each of these markets remained at a rolling boil under the steady flame of their demand until they were replaced by the baby bust.

One thing is sure. The baby boom and the baby bust have distorted the age structure of the United States permanently. As investors we must reckon with this fact in order to be successful, because these demographic forces will continue to have a strong impact on our investments, just as they have in the past. The most important fact to realize is that the future generations will come in waves as well. We can see another wave beginning on chart 15.1 in the early seventies. These are the babies of the baby boom, and when they begin turning eighteen, many of them will start looking for apartments. This means demand for apartments will begin to accelerate in the mid-1990s, and huge profits are ahead.

There is no question that demand for apartments has been on the wane for many years, but chart 15.1 shows that the leading edge of the new wave of young apartment seekers is not far away. In fact, the first of them will be having an impact on the market as early as 1991. Does that mean you should wait until the early nineties before buying apartments? Theoretically yes, but keep in mind that other investors are going to be figuring out these conditions as well. As we have learned, the anticipation of a brighter day ahead is the driving force behind booms. Prices of apartments are likely to begin increasing earlier than changes in actual demand will justify.

There is another reason for not waiting. Beginning in mid-1986, the new construction of apartments began to drop sharply. As this trend continues, the supply of suitable apartment housing will fall short of demand. Any fall-off in building can become a powerful fuel for a new boom. Without excessive building, sooner or later the market will become tight again even without the very positive changes that are building on the demand side. We have seen how tax reform has had a very negative effect on the prices of existing apartment buildings, accelerating a supercycle crash. But it also has had a strong impact on the supply side of the equation by making new construction impractical. Let's take a closer look at the construction industry to see why.

In the first quarter of 1987, the median monthly rent for a typical apartment in the United States was $456, or $5,472 per year. Operating expenses for apartments generally run 40 percent of gross rental income, so the annual net operating income from the typical apartment was $3,283. At a 10 percent cap rate, this apartment would sell for $32,830. If we asked a builder today to build us an apartment house for $32,830 per unit, including the purchase of the land, we would likely find a ticky-tacky hovel on the outskirts of the city dump.

The Commerce Department estimates that the typical apartment in the United States is 742 square feet. The average cost of construction per square foot is approximately $42 for a typical low-rise garden apartment building. The cost of land, improved with sewer, water, and electrical utilities ranged from $15 to $30 per square foot for good locations in most cities. Prime locations cost more. Let's assume that we are going to build a typical apartment house, and can find a good location for a price near the bottom of this range. We can save money on land costs by constructing a two-story building, which is typical of apartment buildings, but we will need to dedicate approximately 20 percent of the land for decorative landscaping, various easements, and recreational areas. This means we will need 0.6 square feet of land for each square foot of apartments we build. For the typical 742 square foot apartment, we will need 445 square feet of land, which will cost $6,675. When this cost is added to the actual construction cost, the typical apartment will cost $37,839 to build. By the time we add landscaping costs, architectural and engineering fees, permits and other miscellaneous costs, we would be lucky to get away with $40,000 per unit. The median net operating income of $3,283 would represent a cap rate of only 8.2 percent. As long as mortgage interest rates are hovering around 10 percent, the typical apartment property cannot be built at a price that would make sense in the wake of tax reform. It is easy to see why construction starts of apartments peaked at 66,200 units the month before Senator Packwood emerged from his congressional chambers with his tax reform bill, why they immediately dropped 28 percent in the next six months, and why starts have continued to plummet ever since.

The figures presented in this chapter so far are national figures. Local forces can and frequently do override national trends, and you will find substantial variation as you travel the country and examine different neighborhoods and locales. A mini-survey of land prices in your area of interest will give you a good sense of land costs. Talk to a few local builders. They can give you very accurate figures on construction costs. Armed with this information, you can determine whether or not construction will come to a standstill in your area just as we have done for the national scene. If you reach the conclusion that the building of suitable apartments in your area will drop off sharply, you can be confident that a buyer of apartment houses in your area will enjoy handsome profits for many years to come, and you will be hard pressed to find a better alternative for your stock market capital.

Remember that, as a general rule, there is no better time to get into any market than in the deceptively quiet days between the ebb of one supercycle and the flood of the next. Depending on local conditions, you may be in just such a period right now. If not, you will be soon. The retreating tide of a supercycle always presents the astute beachcomber with many attractive opportunities.

16

Office Properties

In the spring of 1986, when Senator Packwood made his auspicious announcement about his committee's dedication to press ahead with tax reform, he leveled his harshest barbs at the nation's market in office buildings.

"We have sixty-story office buildings shooting up in virtually every major city in the country," the indomitable senator announced to his television audience. "These are buildings that no one really needs. They are being built only because the tax shelter benefits made it profitable to do so. These tax shelter benefits make it possible for someone making a million dollars a year to pay no taxes, and that's going to stop."

Ironically, the senator mostly was wrong about how much the old tax code had worked to inflate the office property market. The tax benefits of office ownership were never as large for office building owners as they were for apartment owners since, for all practical purposes, accelerated depreciation could not be used for commercial office space. Packwood's statement did reflect accurately the nature of the office market at the peak of one of the largest and most visible construction booms in U.S. history, but the reason for this boom had much less to do with an archaic and loophole-ridden tax code than it had to do with the familiar chemistry of supercycles. As the Senate turned its attention to tax reform, the office market across the country reached the turbulent crest of a nearly two-decade-long supercycle. As the speech making continued in Washington, the crash began in city center after city center across the country. And by the time the legislation reached the president's desk, the party was all but over.

Although the office building boom of the eighties was quite visible from the perspective of altered skylines, it was largely invisible to the average investor. Most of the boom's participants were large institutional investors who were looking for a place to put their money to work as the country began to emerge from the recession of the early eighties. They soon saw that while high interest rates had effectively stalled office construction in most cities, there were steady changes taking place on the demand side that were still putting a torch to the market.

In significant measure this persistent demand for work space was yet another result of the demographic bulge of the baby boom. As the baby boomers aged into young adults and entered the work force in record numbers, the office market was forced to expand to accommodate them. This work space crunch had begun in the seventies, and despite a decade of building, vacancy rates were still quite low when the high interest rates of the early eighties stalled construction temporarily. In 1981, as builder after builder was forced by the high cost of construction loans to pull back from new building plans, the office vacancy rate nationwide fell to 4.27 percent.

By the end of 1982, interest rates had fallen dramatically. Money for construction loans was suddenly cheap and plentiful once again, and it was flowing into the coffers of America's builders. Soon—except in places like Tulsa and Houston where a crash in oil prices had begun to take a heavy toll—the building boom was on again, this time at an even more furious pace than had been seen in the seventies. In 1982, office vacancies jumped nationally to more than 10 percent. By the end of 1983, vacancies had reached 12.4 percent. Still builders and their lenders were undaunted. As the money flowed from banks and syndicates to builders, and more and more office space was constructed, the national office vacancy rate grew, hitting 17.2 percent by the end of 1984.

The building boom did not peak until the middle of 1985. By the end of that year construction starts, which had been steadily increasing, finally began to cool. But as construction starts turned into buildings, vacancies continued rising, topping 20 percent for the first time ever. As vacancies continued to advance, it was becoming clear that the immense building boom of the eighties would have come to a halt, and the looming threat of tax reform assured it in 1986. Today skylines are marked with fewer and fewer of the spindly cranes that mark the site of a new office tower.

Anytime new building comes to a halt in a real estate market, it is important to look closely at developments on the demand side. We know from repeated experience that a widely perceived building glut may be camouflaging the earliest days of a very profitable new supercycle—just the sort of supercycle we are seeking for our stock market capital. So how long will it take before the empty office space is filled and rents start to rise again?

At first glance, national demographic statistics don't reveal much reason for hope. It took more than twenty years for all of the baby boom generation to enter the nation's work force. During the last of those years, from 1975 through 1985, employment in the United States grew at a compounded annual rate of 2.5 percent—a heady degree of growth by any historical measures. The next ten-year period —1986 through 1995—will, however, see the results of the baby bust that followed the baby boom. Over this ten-year period, employment can be expected to grow at only half that rate.[1]

This trend already had begun to show up by the end of 1985 when a study of Fortune 500 companies showed that they were employing 2.2 million fewer people than they had at the end of 1980. And because comparatively few of the leases for office space held by these companies expired during that period, they were left with an estimated 200 million square feet more office space than they needed. It is further estimated that another 100 million square feet of leased but vacant office space is being held currently by other smaller companies.

This vacancy figure of 300 million square feet is for

what is known in the industry as primary office space—space that is fully modern and ready for the arrival of a contemporary corporation needing up-to-date telecommunications facilities. When this 300 million square feet of leased but vacant space is added to the estimated quantity of unleased space, the result is a staggering 950 million square feet of surplus primary office space—nearly a quarter of the total stock of completed primary office buildings. In light of the reduced rate of growth we can expect in the nation's labor force, how long will it take to fill the one office building in four? A long time.

According to a new MIT study of expected job growth and available office space, the United States had enough vacant work space at the end of 1985 to accommodate a full 75 percent of the growth in employment that can be expected through the end of 1995. To put it another way, in the ten-year period that will end in 1995, builders in the country will have to complete only 25 percent of the volume of primary office space that they built in the ten years between 1975 and 1985.

There's no doubt that the demand side of the picture is gloomy and will stay that way for some time to come. But that doesn't mean we should totally ignore the office property market. We are by now quite accustomed to seeing new supercycles starting in just such a climate of despair. Current high vacancy rates coupled with a lack of foreseeable demand has forced prices for office space way down. To a point this decline is both expected and rational. We must remember, however, that prices for office space were responding to more than immediate economic realities; they were riding the whirlwind of a crashing supercycle, which always threatens to take prices much lower than even the gloomiest conditions warrant. Thus, in many markets around the country, genuine bargains are emerging; when these bargains are captured by farsighted investors, they will furnish the fuel for a new supercycle.

Vacancy rates will be high in most cities for years to come, but they won't be high forever, particularly in a climate where builders have been forced out of the game. So if the price is low enough, office properties may be just the place for our capital.

How do we locate the bargains, those distressed properties whose prices have been battered too much by the crashing supercycle? It is important to remember that there are two primary factors that combine to determine the real value of an office property. The first is relatively easy to determine: the amount of vacant office space that's available in the area. The second factor is somewhat more elusive: the number of jobs that a local economy is likely to produce. We all are aware of the fact that no matter how powerful a national trend may be, there are always incidences of local economies that are able to defy it. To find out whether an office property is underpriced, therefore, it is necessary to look beyond the national trend and to try to analyze correctly what is happening in your locality.

Several studies, including the MIT study I referred to earlier, point to some of the hidden factors that affect local economic growth. One important factor is a community's predisposition for or against entrepreneurship. There are many cities in the country in which apparent economic disaster has served to stimulate strong new growth. Seattle, for instance, was rocked by heavy layoffs by its major employer, Boeing Aircraft, in the early seventies; and Dayton, Ohio, suffered a similar shock when NCR ran into trouble in the middle of that decade. Unlike some other cities, both of these communities worked hard to encourage new entrepreneurial activity, which in turn created new jobs. Both of these cities are doing quite well now. In general, the experts say that cities most likely to suffer long-term damage from economic shocks are those with poor educational facilities and a conservative business establishment dominated by a relatively small number of old wealthy families. These factors tend to discourage the vital entrepreneurial energies that cities need in order to recover.

Recent studies also point out that those cities that house a great number of home offices for large corporations—like New York, Chicago, Philadelphia, Pittsburgh, and Detroit—tend to fare much better in economic hard times than cities whose office space is occupied largely by branch offices. These branch office cities—for example, Denver—are volatile. In good times, branch office activity tends to expand as companies look for new markets in previously untapped regions. But during bad times, these branch offices usually are the first to reduce their activities or close.

Beyond looking closely at the prospects for trend-defying economic growth in your region, it is of obvious importance to determine what the vacancy rate actually is in the city you are evaluating. As you might expect, the highest vacancy rates in the country are to be found mainly in the sun belt. Since the mid-1970s, builders were so certain that a major population switch was occurring from the Northeast to the South and West that they built heavily in those regions, often to the benefit of northeastern cities that now have vacancy rates that are much lower than the national average.

In fact, all of the major metropolitan areas of the states of Maine, New Hampshire, Vermont, Massachusetts, Rhode Island, Connecticut, New York, New Jersey, Maryland, Delaware, and Washington, D.C., will begin to need new office space in 1988. The same is true of all major metropolitan areas of Pennsylvania except for Philadelphia, which won't need any new space until 1990. Due to the higher building activities and slower job growth trends in most of the Midwest, those metropolitan areas will not need new office space until 1991, including Chicago, which has good job growth prospects but a high amount of vacant office space to absorb. As we move south and west the situation worsens. It will take another five to ten years of growth in those job markets to absorb all of the empty office space.

Does this mean that as potential investors in commercial office space we should look only at relatively space-tight northeastern cities? It would, except for that most dangerous of wild cards: new construction. Potential investors are not the only people who are looking hard at statistics like those we are pursuing in this chapter. All across the country there are builders who will not be able to afford to wait a full decade before building new buildings. These builders may flock to the Northeast, and one region alone will not be able to withstand their onslaught. If you see this happen, it will be time to move on to another investment market.

A strong case can be made that the best place to buy, as ironic as it may seem, is in the overbuilt sun belt cities where the threat of another construction boom is not even on the horizon. But the price must be right. Remember that, as we saw in the apartment market, profits in commercial real estate result from more than just location. Just as important is the price that is paid for a property and the income that can be generated from it. Even a half empty office tower in a sluggish locality can return immediate profits and have strong potential for eventual upside growth if the purchase price is low enough. What is the right price?

As we saw in chapter 15, in the days before tax reform, apartments usually were selling at a cap rate that was close to 7.5 percent. Even before tax reform, office properties were selling at cap rates near 10 percent. In other words, based on the income these properties provide, investors were paying an average of 25 percent less for office buildings than they were for apartment buildings.

Given that investors in office properties were not paying as dearly for tax benefits as those with apartments, the passage of tax reform has made much less of an impact on the cap rate necessary to achieve profitability. In effect, the passage of tax reform has equalized the cap rate requirements for both types of income property at a level that is roughly equivalent to the prevailing interest rates—at this writing, 10 percent. Of course, the cap rate must be based on the actual income a seller is receiving from his property. In a situation where a building is only 70 percent rented, the cap rate and thus the selling price, must be figured on the basis of the received income, not the income potential of the completely rented building.

Whether you are picking off bargains in a glutted sun belt office market or investing in a relatively tight office market in the Northeast, you must keep your eyes on the horizon for builders. If you are in a market where they are not, you almost are guaranteed to be in a market that eventually will become tighter and see higher rents. That means property values will increase and profits are ahead. And because you'll be dealing with real estate and not stocks, inflation will be on your side; when it heats up again, it will make all tangible assets more valuable, including office properties.

17

Farmland

At first glance, the vast, verdant pastures that make up America's treasury of farmland would seem an unlikely arena for the rumbling machinations of supercycles. However, it takes little more than a quick recollection of the dust bowl landscapes of the thirties to remind us that the prices of arable land in this country always have been subject to highly profitable or potentially ruinous fluctuation. And that lesson is being brought home again today as the evening news broadcasts pictures of the bankruptcy and foreclosure auctions from locations throughout the nation's heartland.

Like an apartment building or a commercial office tower, the value of farmland stems from the income that can be generated from it. If the prices of agricultural commodities go down, so does the value of the land on which those commodities are grown. Of course, whenever there are fluctuating values in a tradable commodity, there will be anticipation. Whenever there is anticipation, there is the potential for supercycle fluctuation and price distortion.

The frequently sad fact for farmers across the country

is that the farmland on which their net worth largely is calculated is not only subject to price distortion based on the supply of and demand for the land itself but also depends on the prices of the commodities produced on it. And, as even the most casual observer of the nation's commodities markets can attest, the price swings for agricultural products can be extremely vicious. Not only are these prices subject to unpredictable and fierce near-term forces like weather and natural disasters but they are influenced strongly by market forces that may originate miles or even half a planet away.

Inflation, for instance, affects the prices of farm commodities just as it does precious metals, and the price of a commodity such as wheat fluctuates in the same inverse relationship to the dollar as the price of gold. Thus, like gold, the price of wheat or other agricultural commodities moves in accord with the upward and downward cycles of inflation within the business cycle.

Farmland has completed two massive supercycles in the twentieth century—supercycles that surpass even those of stocks in terms of the vast amount of wealth that was affected. The period of soaring inflation that accompanied our participation in World War I brought the first supercycle to a boil in 1920, doubling farmland prices nationally over the decade. The downward leg of that supercycle began in 1921, leading to a widespread agricultural depression that preceded and presaged the Great Depression of the 1930s.

It was to be almost twenty years before America's depression-crushed farms began to show a hint of recovery—not until inflation reappeared during World War II. The war kicked off a new supercycle, one that began slowly and ponderously, but that over the next thirty years was to become an economic trend of unprecedented power.

The early price increases were steady but gradual, slow enough to be rendered almost invisible as a trend. Beginning in the early seventies, however, the character of the market began to change. A global food shortage, rising inflation, and a weak dollar combined to fuel a boom that was to triple U.S. commodities prices by the end of the decade. Lashed by these skyrocketing price increases, the market value of U.S. farmland began a meteoric rise.

In 1970, the average price of an acre of farmland in this

country was $196, which was producing a net operating income that averaged 4.5 percent annually after operational expenses were deducted. When commodities experienced their first price explosion, the relatively conservative farmland market was rather slow to respond. At the end of 1973, even with the higher petroleum prices that came with the first Arab oil embargo, operating income had jumped nationally to $12 an acre. Since the average price of farmland had only risen to $246 an acre, this meant that operating income had doubled—to 9 percent annually.

This discrepancy caught the attention of just about everybody in farm country, and land prices began to take off. Ironically, these increases came just as commodity prices began to level off, and as inflation and oil prices pushed operating costs still higher. By the end of 1977, operating income had slid down from the $12 peak to under $6 an acre, but it made no difference to the booming land market. Land prices had been moving up relentlessly, and were to reach $474 an acre by the end of 1977. This reduced operating yields to less than 3 percent, but nobody cared. It was clear by then that inflation was heating up again, and investors were banking on a hunch that higher inflation would produce higher commodity prices, which would in turn justify still higher prices for land.

Their instincts proved to be accurate. Beginning in 1978, commodity prices shot upward again; by the end of 1980, they had nearly doubled. This time farmland price increases more than matched the rise in commodities. By the end of 1980, even with the increases in commodity prices, farmland prices of nearly $730 an acre had driven the annual yield from net operating revenue down to a scant 1.2 percent. But again investors didn't care. Land price increases were sponsoring further land price increases in the familiar boomtime pattern. And many farmers were borrowing heavily from willing banks to continue expanding their holdings while they still could. As the superheated market rolled on into 1982, everyone was convinced that there was no end in sight. This time they were wrong.

In the hysteria surrounding the land boom, several warning signals were going unread. Much of the American agricultural product had gone as exports to underdeveloped countries, and the United States was pleased to call itself the world's breadbasket. But the price of that bread could not go up forever. As the cost of American grain continued to soar, lashed on even further by a strengthening U.S. dollar, many underdeveloped countries began to discover that other strategies for self-sufficiency suddenly had become quite cost effective. This resulted in reduced international demand, which in turn had a mitigating effect on commodity prices. In 1981, commodity prices began to slide even as farmland price increases continued unabated.

Finally, in 1982, the market crested as well as the more than three-decade supercycle that had powered it. At the peak, farmland hit a national average of $823 an acre.

The farmland crash began mildly. In 1983, the average price per acre nationally fell to $788 but this decline so closely matched declines in commodity prices that the net operating income figure remained at a paltry 1.1 percent. But even a slight downturn was sufficient to shake out many highly leveraged farmers, while other investors felt their growth assumptions cooling. By the following year, the crash had begun in earnest.

As was the case in the office property market, the tax reform act administered an unnecessary *coup de grace* to a moribund market in 1986. This was the result of new regulations limiting the tax benefits that could be claimed by "gentlemen farmers"—those doctors, lawyers, and business executives who had invested in a weekend retreat for some nice tax losses. They now would have to personally manage their farming operations on a day-to-day basis in order to save taxes from their farmland investments. Many of these tax-harassed executives decided to simply dump their property back on the crashing market.

By February 1987, the national average price for an acre of farmland had dropped to $548—a 33 percent decline. And when the inflation rate was factored in, the real loss was even worse. Chart 17.1 illustrates that, when adjusted for inflation, national farmland prices by the spring of 1987 already had fallen below their 1970 levels. Moreover, many states saw declines that were far greater. The national average price per acre as determined by the U.S. Department of Agriculture includes the price of farmland devoted to such relatively stable crops as fruits and vegetables, so it tends to gloss over the enormous losses suffered by landowners in the midwestern grain belts. In states like Ohio, Indiana,

Chart 17.1. U.S. Farmland Prices (per Acre) (Adjusted for Inflation)

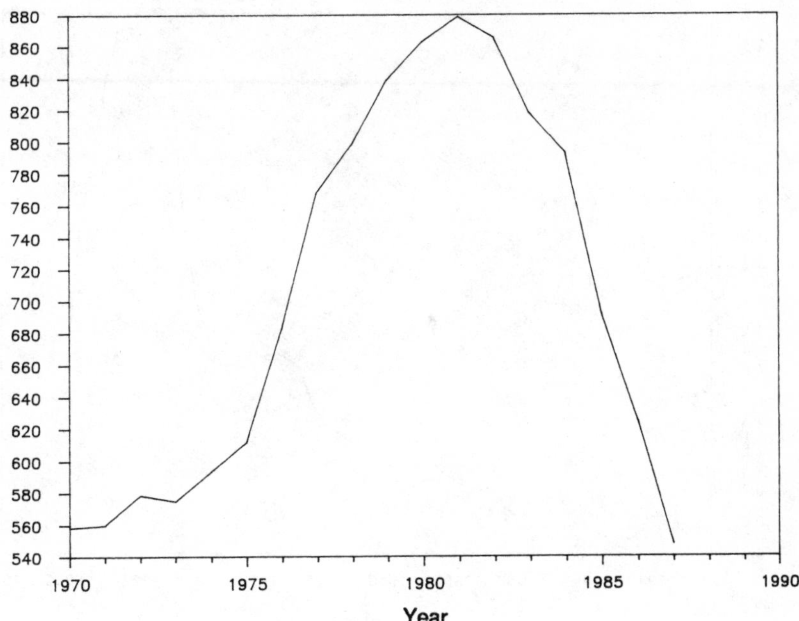

Source: U.S. Department of Agriculture

Illinois, Iowa, and Missouri, prices collapsed more than 50 percent. In those five states, the average price per acre fell from $1,776 in 1981, to $815 in early 1987. And when these prices were adjusted for inflation, they fell to the same levels experienced at the end of the century's other farmland supercycle in the 1930s. Chart 17.2 shows the inflation-adjusted prices experienced in Iowa since 1935. The result traces the pattern of a classic supercycle, which wiped out price increases in a few years that generations of farmers had come to expect.

Has the downward slide of prices finally bottomed out? At this writing, it's difficult to tell for sure, but there are some encouraging signs. For one thing, the supercycle-driven crash in prices has been so severe that it has far outdistanced any declines in commodity prices, and the yield per acre had moved back up to 4.5 percent by the end of 1986. This yield is as high as it was in 1970 before the speculation began, and it comes despite a decline in commodity prices that lasted from 1981 through 1986. Obvi-

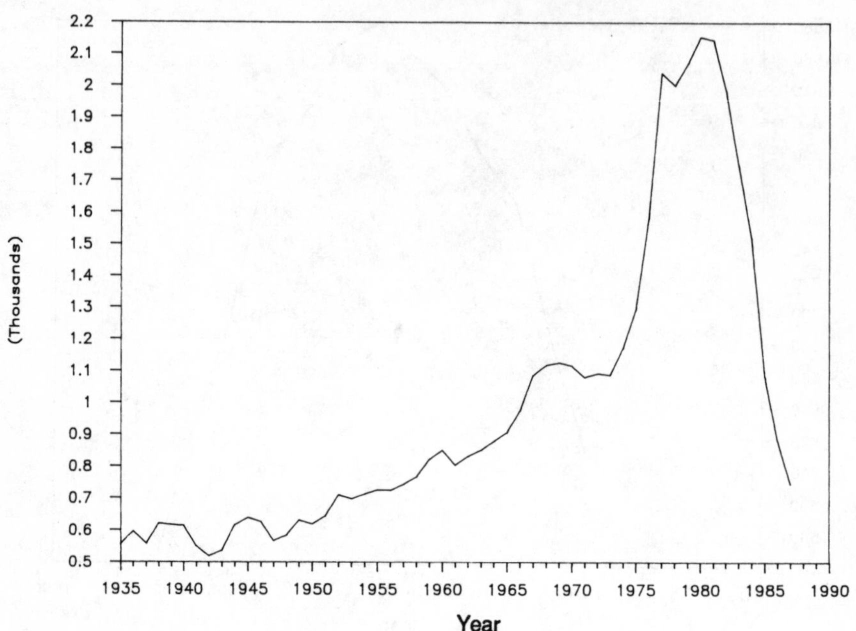

Source: U.S. Department of Agriculture

ously, any reversal of the downward trend in commodities will have a very positive effect on the price of farmland.

Fortunately for investors, there is a convenient way to watch the general trend in commodity prices. In each Monday's *Wall Street Journal,* the Dow Jones Company publishes two commodities indexes: one for current, or spot, prices, and the other for future contracts. In the early months of 1987, the charts on which these indexes were plotted showed a solid gain. It is not coincidental that these gains happened simultaneously with the first signs of renewed inflation in the economy at large, which in turn could be expected to exert a downward pressure on the dollar, making our commodities cheaper abroad.

Perhaps the best early indication of the direction that the value of farmland is taking is the price of farmland itself. Even in the beleaguered Midwest, farmland prices were inching upward through the first half of 1987, and despite depressed commodity prices, net operating incomes were ranging between 6 and 10 percent annually.

Though the readings are still tentative, the weight of evidence seems to indicate that a new supercycle is getting underway in the farmland market. Land prices simply have fallen too low, particularly in view of the almost certain resurgence of inflation that lies ahead. Thus the potential for profit in this market appears to be enormous.

There are several ways that an investor who is not himself a farmer can invest in farmland. Many reputable stock brokerage firms offer limited partnerships formed for the purpose of buying and managing farmland. Land also can be purchased directly, either from brokers or from owners. Remember that whatever the underlying market pressures, the value of any piece of farm acreage directly depends on its ability to produce. Short-sighted land management practices swiftly can deplete the productive value of a piece of land, so it is imperative to have a professional evaluate the condition of the soil before you purchase any land. And when the land is leased to an operator, it is equally imperative that the land be farmed with an eye toward preserving its productivity. A variety of lease, sharecropping, or resident-manager arrangements are available, but whatever form of management is chosen, soil conservation must be a paramount goal. With proper care, American farmland should reap handsome profits for years to come.

18

Single-Family Homes

As more and more investors decide to pull their capital from the stock market, they will find themselves confronted with a plethora of investment opportunities—many of them with tremendous potential for profit. But most investors will not look that far. The vast majority will look no further than the real estate section of the local papers. As we saw clearly in our discussion of the stock market risk indicator, this is not unusual. For more than a century the stock market and the single-family home market have been locked in a titanic struggle for investment dollars; throughout this period, one market's gain has always been the other's loss. We saw that these are evenly matched competitors, and thus one market has never been able to dominate the other indefinitely. Sooner or later one of the two markets becomes overvalued in relation to the other and the pendulum swings again.

To say that one market always fares less well than the other at any given time is not to say that the weaker market actually is declining. It may just mean that the underdog market is advancing at a slower pace. This has been the case with the single-family home market during the recent booming market in stocks. Home prices have been advancing in most parts of the country for more than twenty years. These price increases have created a vast new pool of equity capital that has funded everything from vacation homes to college educations; to millions of Americans, rising housing values and the money they have provided has become a dependable fact of life.

As prices have risen, a swelling tide of buyers has been ushered into the market, being assured all the while by a huge chorus of expert voices that there is nothing to fear and nowhere for prices to go but up. From storefront realtors to bank CEOs, from Wall Street industry analysts to real estate columnists in suburban weeklies, the message has been that housing prices have gone up, will go up again tomorrow, and will continue to go up forever.

These folks have been right for a long time. The single-family home market has survived inflation, stagflation, recession, and interest rates that reached record heights. This record of performance probably will be sufficient to convince most investors that the safest market for their capital is the single-family home. But this time they could be wrong.

In our examination of stocks we introduced the stock market risk indicator to show when stock prices grew to be overvalued when compared to houses, and vice versa. We saw that when this indicator rises over 2.0, it is signifying that houses have come to represent the superior investment value. It is important to remember, however, that while a reading of 2.0 or higher always has presaged a major collapse in stocks, it doesn't necessarily mean that housing prices are about to boom. The signals given in 1929 and 1937, for example, would have pulled investors out of stocks in time to avoid disastrous crashes. And if those investors then had invested in single-family real estate, they would have been in a much safer and more depression-resistant market. But that is not to say that housing prices went up in those years. In fact, housing prices slipped during the crash of supercycle two, though the decline in real estate was much softer than that suffered by stocks, and real estate advanced only moderately during the crash of supercycle three.

Moreover, the fact that housing prices have been increasing for more than twenty years does not mean that this increase has been without incident. Throughout this time there have been periods of rampant speculation in many local markets followed by periods of collapse. There have been other times when sellers were forced to finance buyers into the market because conventional financing had become too expensive. But through a series of setbacks that would have been sufficient to kill most booms, single-family housing prices have continued to rise, because beneath the surface of the market lay a force as powerful as it is familiar: the demographic bulge represented by the baby boom.

Like every generation before them, baby boomers, as they reached young adulthood, moved out of their family homes and into living spaces of their own. In the beginning these living spaces were mostly apartments giving rise to the boom we tracked earlier in this section. But soon, greater and greater numbers of these young adults reached home-buying ages and the family home market came to a rolling boil under the flame of their steady demand.

In a climate dominated by unrelenting demand from potential first-time home buyers, the health of the housing market since 1970 has been relatively easy to predict. It simply has been necessary to examine a matrix of forces that together can be described as affordability.

There are three major components that determine the affordability of houses. The most obvious is the price. But the price of houses can increase and still can become more affordable if the other components are running more favorably. If the second component, the level of the average family's income, is increasing at a faster rate than house prices, it is likely that houses are becoming easier to buy for a growing number of households. And the third major component, mortgage interest rates, is a large factor in determining the size of mortgage payments. When houses suddenly are more affordable they are poised to increase in price, and when they are not they will stagnate or decline.

Chart 18.1 shows the affordability of houses since 1970. Specifically, it shows the ratio of the U.S. median family income to the income necessary to buy the median-price house using a standard 80 percent, thirty-year mortgage at the mortgage interest rates prevailing at the time. From this chart, we can see how far the relative affordability of a house can swing within one supercycle. A ratio of 1.0 or

Chart 18.1. Housing Affordability

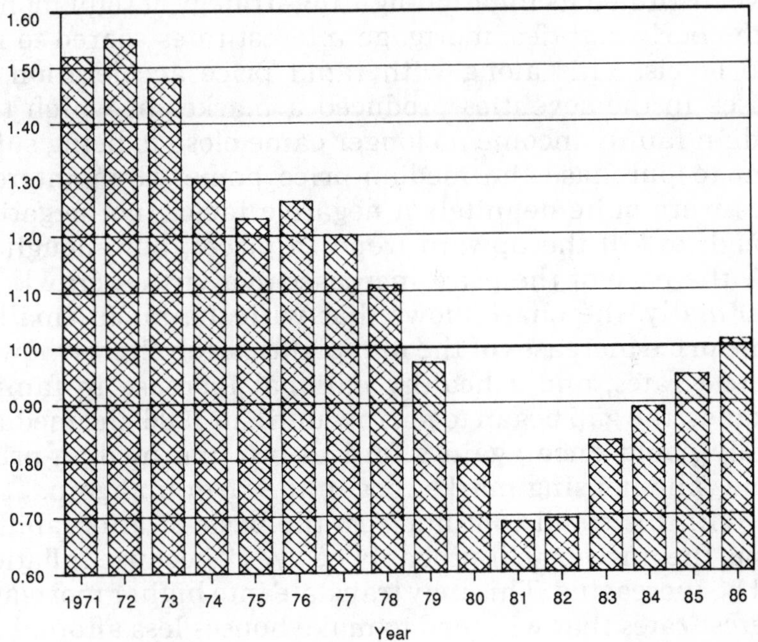

Source: National Association of Realtors

more meant that houses were affordable, that the median family income was sufficient to qualify to buy the median-price home. Conversely, a ratio of less than 1.0 meant that the median family income could not afford the median-price home.

The early years on the chart show the days before the deregulation of banking when there was no expensive competition among banks for savings deposits and when money for mortgages was plentiful. Thus, when the housing boom began in the early seventies, prices skyrocketed in part because the vanguard of the huge new pool of baby boom consumers found a market in which the median family income in America was more than sufficient to buy the median-price home.

The chart also registers the seismic shock that was felt by the entire banking industry in 1978 when President Carter revoked the so-called "Regulation Q" that had mandated the maximum interest rates banks could pay depositors. Suddenly, with these ceilings removed, lending institutions were competing for depositors by offering higher and higher interest rates, and when the Federal Reserve instituted its inflation-fighting strategy of tight money in the early eighties, mortgage interest rates soared to record levels. This along with rapid price acceleration of houses in the seventies produced a market in which the median family income no longer came close to being sufficient to purchase the median-price home. High interest rates were quite definitely a negative factor, not negative enough to kill the upward trend in prices, but enough to slow the pace of the price increases to a virtual crawl.

Finally, the chart shows that with the much smaller home price increases of the mid-eighties, the sharply lower interest rates, and a healthy national increase in family incomes, the gap began to narrow until, in 1986, the median family could once again afford to buy the median-price home. The housing market began to warm up again.

Will this trend continue? On the basis of affordability alone, the answer will probably be "yes," because inflation will be increasing. This may translate into higher mortgage interest rates that will tend to make houses less affordable. Still, it is a fact that throughout this century houses have represented one of the best alternatives to stocks in a rising interest rate environment (such as was present during the crashes of stock market supercycles one and four). This is because inflation influences wages and salaries as directly as it does interest rates, and wages are as powerful a factor in affordability as interest rates. And though high interest rates can tend to have a suppressive tendency on prices, an even more powerful overriding factor will be at work. When inflation heats up and dollars are depreciating, the replacement cost of houses and all of their component parts increases. These increases, in turn, fuel anticipation that leads to further price increases. It is clear therefore that an analysis of affordability will lead to the conclusion that houses will be a good alternative to stocks as long as demand remains constant.

But will demand remain constant? This will be the crucial question to be dealt with by any investor hoping to profit from single-family homes. In this book we have seen how market after market is dominated by the massive supercycles, forces that are frequently so vast and pervasive that they become invisible to all but the most trained and wary eye. The single-family housing market of the seventies and eighties is no exception. In the years since 1970, the housing market has overheated frequently and dangerously. In the early eighties, many localities experienced sharp downturns in prices, and the national housing market was so shot through with speculation that it was primed for a crash. That the local declines didn't turn into a national debacle was due only to the enormous, historically unprecedented demand represented by the baby boom generation. This demand that continues into the present was so immense that factors, which under other circumstances would have been enough to spark the inevitable crash, only resulted in better affordability for an unsatiated mass of potential new buyers.

If this steady demand were to slacken, a new set of conditions would take over and the market would begin its exploration of whether the postwar supercycle in housing simply has pushed housing prices up too far. In all of our market explorations, we have never found a supercycle that went up and didn't come down. Supercycles always drive prices up too far. The supercycle in single-family housing is unlikely to be an exception.

And demand will soften. It doesn't require a very long look at the birth rate chart presented in chapter 15 (chart 15.1) to see that the baby boom eventually will be replaced by a baby bust as the key force within America's single-family home markets.

When will this occur? The Joint Center for Housing Studies of Harvard and MIT has issued studies detailing the rate at which certain age groups form households.[1] They do so by determining what percentage of any given age group functions as a head of household. Using population projections provided by the Census Bureau, they then calculate the number of households that will be formed in future years by simply multiplying the household formation rates for each age group by the number of people who will be in that age group. The sum of all of the household formations in every age group gives us a picture of future housing demand.

The results of these studies show that the strong demand that has bolstered the housing market for more than a decade has begun to slacken, and that there will be an even more pronounced flattening of demand into the early years of the nineties. Beginning in the mid-1990s, and continuing for another ten years, demand will slow markedly by as much as 20 percent over the ten-year period. With the strong bulwark of demand absent for the first time, the housing market suddenly will become vulnerable.

So, for those investors who want to put their stock market capital into the single-family home market, here is the big picture: The supercycle in single-family homes is not over and will not be for as long as it will be responding to baby boom demand, probably until the mid-nineties. Until then prices should respond to the basic affordability factors.

To help you analyze these forces, you can use an affordability index in connection with the stock market risk indicator. This affordability index measures the three primary ingredients that make up the housing affordability equation: home prices, mortgage interest rates, and family incomes. Appendix E explains how to construct and update it.

When the affordability index rises above 1.0, it means that homes are affordable and that the national single-family home market can be expected to be bullish. As long as the affordability index is above 1.0 you can be confident that the single-family housing market will not only outperform stocks but will increase in price in the months to come. When this affordability index is below 1.0 it will be advisable to seek an alternative investment to single-family houses until the 1.0 mark is passed once again.

There is a real danger in basing local real estate investment decisions on national trends. Real estate is far more responsive to local conditions than other capital markets, and a close look at local conditions will give you data that is not available to those who are making nationwide predictions. Is your market tight, and if so, have those conditions attracted builders and developers to your area? Most counties and states publish statistics on housing starts based on applications for building permits in certain localities. This can be a useful predictor of the amount of building activity that you are likely to see in your area.

To get a better sense of your local housing market, you can construct a stock market risk indicator based on local house prices. Of course, it will not generate reliable buy or sell signals for stocks—you need to use national markets for that—but it can tell you about the relative behavior of local house prices to stocks. This information can be valuable because these are the two markets home owners and potential home buyers in your area are actually weighing. Many local real estate boards have home price data going back to the late sixties. It probably is safe to assume that stock prices back then were as inflated in comparison to your local market as they were to the national home market. The test would be to see if they are now. To construct your local risk indicator follow the instructions in appendix E, using your local home prices. It probably won't be perfect but it will give you a better perspective on your area. If your reading today is close to the reading of the late sixties, you can conclude safely that houses in your area are an excellent value relative to stocks.

You also can create a local affordability index by using local figures for income levels, house prices, and mortgage interest rates. This information should be available at your local real estate board, chamber of commerce, apartment association, or libraries. If your local affordability index is above 1.0, you can expect house prices to rise until it reads otherwise. At the same time, if your local risk indicator is close to its readings of the late sixties, you can move money out of stocks and into local houses with impunity.

Your local market is peculiar and idiosyncratic. But remember that it is also part of a vast, complicated, and powerful housing market. It is always important to take national trends and filter them through as much information on your local market as you can gather. The national trend is up and will continue in that direction as long as the affordability index is above 1.0. As long as your local measures are not out of line and builders aren't going crazy in your area, this market will be panic proof.

IV

Conclusions

19

Tactics

On August 13, 1987, the stock market celebrated the fifth anniversary of one of the most astonishing bull markets in its history. Sadly, it was only a few weeks later that the bull market peaked. As extraordinary as the bull market was, it was but a part of an even more extraordinary supercycle—the fifth in the history of twentieth-century American stock trading.

Even in the wake of the Crash of 1987, it was not possible to find many market professionals agreeing about the future. My first piece of tactical advice is by far the most important: Pay attention to the indicators you've acquired from this book and heed their signals immediately no matter what you are reading and hearing from the experts.

Panic-proof investing is not a pursuit for dabblers and hobbyists. It requires a devotion to profit, an ability to look at competing markets dispassionately, and the mental discipline to act with the knowledge that profits are found in that lonely ground that lies ahead of the crowd. The risk indicators and diffusion indexes that I've given you will act as a true compass to this empty plateau where profits lurk. The courage to profit will have to come from you.

The vast convulsion in stock prices that we have labeled supercycle five has had far-reaching economic effects on the lives of all Americans, whether they have personal stock portfolios or not. The boom in securities prices has had a powerful impact on employer-sponsored deferred compensation plans, pension and profit-sharing plans, stock option plans, even IRA or Keogh accounts. As a result, stock market investors frequently have far more financial exposure to the whims of the stock market than they are aware of having. Not only are most of these stock-related assets not under the control of the individual investor but most are managed with exactly the sort of conservative money management philosophy that will cause them to suffer mightily during any major downtrend shift in the market.

If you have been employed by the same company for any length of time, for instance, you will probably be amazed at the amount you personally have riding on the market just from your share of a heavily stock-invested pension plan. Since the stock-related assets over which you don't have control can be expected to perform miserably during a sharp downturn in stock prices, it is all the more imperative for you to manage profitably the stocks and stock-related instruments over which you do have control.

Appendix F contains several questionnaires that will allow you to evaluate your total exposure to the stock market. The questions will help you segregate your assets into those related to stocks, bonds, precious metals, and real estate. The more heavily your total net worth is concentrated in stock and bond-related investments, the more aggressively you will need to act now.

We are experiencing the beginning of a major realignment in America's investment landscape, and you must take part in this vast waltz of capital between markets. Fortunes will be made . . . and lost. Therefore, let's look again at the markets we have examined in this book, and look closely at the alternatives each holds for investors now that the winds of change have started to blow.

Stocks

Just as a sailor will keep a constant watch on his barometer whenever he sails during hurricane season, we must keep a weather eye on any changes in our stock market indicators. As long as the risk indicator is above 1.0 and the diffusion index of leading indicators is above zero, the major trend of the market will be down. In that case, you can hedge your portfolio from the downturn by writing call options against your stocks in the manner we discussed in chapter 8. Since, as we also saw in chapter 8, this options strategy also works when the market is flat or increasing moderately, it will provide you with profits even if your timing is slightly off. The tactics that were discussed in chapter 9 will be appropriate also, including bear spreads in puts on both stocks and bonds.

When the diffusion index of leading indicators approaches zero, it will signal that the bear market will soon end and that a bull market is imminent. If the stock market risk indicator is still above 1.0, the bull market will be relatively brief; it merely will be an interruption in the decline of supercycle five just as the 1971–1973 bull market was in the decline of supercycle four.

When the diffusion index of lagging indicators hits 100, or the Treasury bond–discount rate spread index rises over 3.75 again, there will be no time to waste. Decisive action will need to be taken immediately. If you don't clear out of stocks altogether, implementing the tactics discussed in chapters 8 and 9 will be critical. Bear markets will continue to be more energetic than bull markets until the stock market risk indicator has dropped below 1.0, and only then can you entrust a major portion of your investment capital to stocks again. Meanwhile, you should be moving at least some of your investment capital out of the stock market and into precious metals or real estate.

Precious Metals

There are many different forms that investments in precious metals can take. You can buy gold, silver, platinum, or palladium bullion from a brokerage house, either taking delivery directly or paying a nominal fee for storage. There also are a wide variety of gold coins. Purchase of these have the advantage of liquidity, divisibility, and privacy. The South African Kruggerand was one of the most widely marketed prior to recent anti-apartheid restrictions, but there are numerous other coins including the Austrian one ducat and 100 corona pieces, the British sovereign, the Canadian Maple Leaf, the Mexican 50 peso and Onza pieces, and the U.S. Treasury's own American Eagle. Silver coin investments usually come in the form of bags of the silver nickels, dimes, and quarters that were removed from circulation in the 1960s.

More adventurous investors may be interested in the trading of commodity futures contracts. Like their counterparts in the stock options market, commodity options give an investor the right but not the obligation to buy and sell commodity futures contracts on a variety of precious metals. And like stock options, commodity options offer investors the ability to obtain high leverage in the pursuit of substantial profits with a risk that is limited to the price of the option itself. Millions of dollars will be made in the commodities market as the stock market continues its downward skid, and options will allow investors with the interest and time to share in those profits by exploiting short-term trends. But investors who simply decide to buy bullion and wait on the long-term price increases that surely will be the case for years to come also will profit substantially.

Ironically, it is not even necessary to leave the stock market in order to shift your investment profile from stocks to precious metals. You can simply begin to invest in companies that mine the precious metals. While not immune entirely from a general downturn in stock prices, the prices of mining stocks always have responded much more to the underlying value of the metals being mined. That's because the earnings of those companies are tied firmly to the metals they mine. Since the cost of mining remains relatively stable, a rise in the prices of precious metals boosts the profits of mining companies sharply. This new profit picture should be enough to allow the stock prices to rise during the general market collapse.

There also are several prominent mutual funds invested exclusively in the stocks of companies mining precious metals. Table 19.1 lists some of the major funds of this type. Next to the fund is a phone number that you can call to obtain a prospectus and an annual report. The holdings of each fund as of early 1987 are shown in the table. The last three columns show the sales commission that is charged upon purchase, the redemption fee that is charged when the shares are cashed in, and the amount of money the fund can charge you for the funding of its promotion and advertising efforts (known in the industry as a 12b-1 load). You can see that many of these funds have no fees and others have quite modest charges. Most of these funds can be purchased for between $500 to $1,000, and all can be purchased inside an IRA or Keogh plan.

There is one crucial difference among the funds on this list. This difference has to do with whether there is a fixed limit on the number of shares that the fund can sell. So-called "opened-end" funds have no restriction on the number of shares they can issue. Since the shares have no market value of their own, their value reflects directly the value of the underlying portfolio held by the fund.

"Closed-end" funds are limited in the number of shares they can offer. This means that in addition to the value of the fund's portfolio, the shares have a market value of their own based on the currents of supply and demand. In this way they function very much like any other stock, and like any other stock their prices are subject to wide price swings that can reflect a steep discount or a hefty premium over the value of the funds' portfolios.

All of the closed-end funds I've listed were trading at substantial discounts during the first half of 1987. Even the Central Fund of Canada, which had nearly all its assets in gold and silver bullion, was selling at a 19 percent discount. Goldcorp had 62 percent of its assets in gold bullion and was selling at a 23 percent discount, and the BGR fund was selling at a 30 percent discount. ASA Limited held a portfolio that was made up almost entirely of South African gold stocks. Due to the political situation in South Africa, the shares of ASA were selling at a full 50 percent discount when compared to the value of the fund's portfolio at the end of 1986.

For many years, a growing number of investors have come to regard South Africa's economy as being extremely imperiled by the fight over its apartheid racial policies, and

TABLE 19.1
PRECIOUS METALS MUTUAL FUNDS

OPENED-END PRECIOUS METAL MUTUAL FUNDS

Fund Name	Phone	Total Net Assets	Bullion (%)				Mining Shares (%)					Cash(%)	Loads (%)		
							SOUTH AFRICAN		OTHER COUNTRIES						
		MILL. $	GOLD	SILVER	PLAT.	PALL.	GOLD	PLAT/PALL	GOLD	SILVER	MIXED		SALES LOAD	REDEM. FEE	12b-1 LOAD
Bull-Bear Golconda	800-847-4200	33	28				12	3	33		24				1.0
Colonial Advanced Strategies	800-225-2365	62							97			3	7.2		0.25
Fidelity Select American Gold	800-225-6190	86	6						59	2	25	8	2.0	1.0	
Fidelity Select Precious Metals	800-225-6190	172	2				52	1	23		14	8	2.0	1.0	
Financial Programs—Gold	800-525-8085	76					8		75			17			
Franklin Gold	800-632-2350	91					53		39	2		6	4.2		
Freedom Gold & Government[1]	800-225-6258	70							16	4		12		3.0	0.75
IDS Precious Metals	800-328-8300	59							77			23	5.3		$6.00
Keystone Precious Metals	800-343-2898	98	12				6	3	66		3	10		4.2	1.25
Lexington Gold Fund	800-526-0056	53	13				19		55	4		9			
Midas Gold Shares & Bullion	800-323-1010	16	3						80	3		14	6.4		0.25
Oppenheimer Gold	800-525-7048	43	2		2	2	29	14	40	3	3	5	9.3		
Permanent Portfolio[2]	800-531-5142	89	20	5											0.25

United Services Gold Shares	800-824-4653	467		84	4			4	8			
United Services New Prospector	800-824-4653	117				78	10		12		2.0	
United Gold & Government[3]	816-283-4000	125			5	70			5.	9.3		
USAA Gold	800-531-8000	31				70			30			
Van Eck—Gold Resources	800-221-2220	38				91	3		6	8.1		0.25
Van Eck—Int'l Investors[4]	800-221-2220	820		59		20			8	9.3		
Vanguard VSP Gold	800-662-7447	27	9	29	3	49			11		1.0	0.07

CLOSED-END PRECIOUS METAL MUTUAL FUNDS

			Bullion (%)				Mining Shares (%)					
		Total					SOUTH AFRICAN		OTHER COUNTRIES			
Fund Name (Exchange)	*Market Discount (%)*	*Net Assets* MILL. $	GOLD	SILVER	PLAT.	PALL.	GOLD	PLAT./PALL.	GOLD	SILVER	MIXER	*Cash (%)*
ASA Limited (NYSE)	50	702					95	2				3
BGR (TSE)	30	61	10	4		4	9		68			5
Central Fund of Canada (TSE)	19	85	58	38					2		2	
Goldcorp (TSE)	23	200	62				14		21			3

[1]The remaining 68 percent was in government bonds.

[2]Other holdings: 10% Swiss Francs, 35% U.S. Treasury bonds, 30% nonprecious metal stocks.

[3]The remaining 20 percent was in short-term government bonds.

[4]The remaining 13 percent was in nonprecious metal stocks.

South African investments of all kinds have come to be regarded as increasingly risky. This attitude has been felt particularly by precious metals investors. South Africa has a limited number of mines, all of which are subject to the sort of racially charged labor problems that led to widespread strikes in the late summer of 1987. Moreover, in the case of a political rebellion, they would be quite vulnerable to attack. If production at these mines is stopped or slowed considerably for any length of time, the value of South African mining stocks would be reduced substantially.

As these fears took hold in the market, investors began to dump large numbers of South African mining shares, severely depressing their price. By the end of the second quarter in 1987, the price/earnings ratio of the mining stocks had declined dramatically. At that time the average P/E ratio for South African gold stocks had shrunk to four.

Meanwhile, the threat of a mining slowdown in South Africa has caused a corresponding increase in the value of mining stocks from other countries. By the end of the second quarter of 1987, North American mining stocks were selling at P/E ratios that were topping forty—a P/E ratio that was a staggering ten times higher than South African stocks.

A close look at the complexion of the mutual funds listed in table 18.1 reflects this strong bias against South African stocks. The assets of these funds taken together amount to nearly 4 billion dollars, but only half of that amount was invested in South African stocks. In fact, some funds were advertising openly the fact that their portfolios contained no South African stocks at all.

While it is understandable that investors feel shy about the unstable situation of South African precious metal stocks, there are strong risks attached to a strategy of avoiding them altogether. The fact that South African stocks are selling at a sharp discount means that other mining stocks are selling at a hefty premium. That premium could be justified if political instability curtails or eliminates South African production, but political instability can cut two ways. If South Africa's political situation were to improve suddenly, huge amounts of money would flow into South African stocks from other gold stocks, and an investor who had avoided such stocks totally probably would find himself with huge losses even in the face of an uptrending supercycle in precious metals.

Therefore, I believe that it is prudent for investors in mining stocks to maintain a position in mining companies in South Africa so that it will be impossible to be blind-sided by any political development that might occur in that troubled land. A portfolio that is divided between South African and other mining stocks should be able to weather any major changes in supply or investor sentiment while still being carried upward by the supercycle in gold. (For example, a portfolio that will often represent a good value and a safe balance will include ASA—when it holds cheap South African gold stocks and is selling at a hefty discount to boot—and other heavily discounted Canadian closed-end funds.)

South African gold stocks can be grouped into three categories. Oddly enough, the most speculative are the ones with the highest dividends. These companies own mines with the lowest quality ore (the lowest number of ounces of precious metal per ton of ore) and, consequently, incur the highest mining costs. These mines also have relatively short remaining lives. Examples include Blyvooruitzicht, St. Helena, Free State Geduld, President Brand, and Western Holdings. These stocks will respond to changes in the price of gold and investor sentiment regarding South African investments, but not to the extent of other South African stocks, and are suitable only for short-term holding periods of one to three years.

At the other end of the spectrum are the stocks with the lowest dividends. These companies have the mines with the highest ore quality, which keeps their production costs low, and their mines have the longest remaining lives. These stocks include Kloof and Driefontein Consolidated. These stocks are the blue chips of the group and will respond most sharply to changes in the price of gold and investor sentiment.

Between these two ends lies a group of stocks that offer a balanced potential for high-dividend income and capital growth. These stocks include Vaal Reefs, Buffelsfontein, and Western Deep Levels.

As far as the other precious metals are concerned, there are only two companies that mine platinum as their primary business. They are both South African mining stocks and they are called Rustenburg and Impala. Eighty percent of the world's platinum is produced from mines owned by these two companies. Rustenburg is the world's largest producer. The largest silver mining stocks include Coeur D'Alene Mines, Hecla Mining, Callahan Mining, and Sunshine Mining. There also is a high-yielding bond that can be converted into the common stock shares of Coeur D'Alene Mines. (Standard and Poor's bond guide lists the current features of this bond.) There are no companies that mine palladium exclusively, so bullion, commodities, or commodity options are the only ways to invest in that metal.

While a new supercycle in precious metals is imminent, and long-term gains in precious metals can be expected for years to come, it must be remembered that precious metals respond very strongly to changes in the business cycle. Whenever a rise in interest rates causes the economy to soften, prices of precious metals suffer. Therefore, investors should remain attentive to the diffusion index of lagging indicators. Three or four monthly declines in this index are a reliable signal that the business cycle is weakening significantly, and can serve as a reliable sell signal for investors who want to maximize their profits in the precious metals market. (The diffusion index of lagging indicators began declining six months before the peak of the last supercycle in gold.)

Real Estate

Of the many investors who will want to look into investing their stock market capital in real estate, some will be daunted by the comparative hassle and lack of liquidity that characterizes most real estate investment. Fortunately, however, there are also some very liquid vehicles for real estate investment that will benefit handsomely from the supercycle that lies ahead. One such vehicle is our old friend, the real estate investment trust, dusted off and buffed up for the eighties.

As we saw in the apartment boom of the 1970s, the financial health of a REIT is linked critically to the properties it holds, and its price will swing sharply in accordance with the health of its portfolio. The makeup of that portfolio divides the REIT industry into two distinct groups that can behave quite differently. Some REITs primarily hold mortgages and the value of these so-called mortgage REITs will fluctuate inversely with interest rates like a bond. Equity REITs, in contrast, invest in properties directly and they are the same thing as owning a portion of a portfolio of real estate properties. Depending on the kind of properties and their location, many of these equity REITs will benefit handsomely from the new supercycles ahead in real estate.

Unfortunately, filtering out the promising REITs from the pack of equity REITs often is not an easy job. Some equity REITs are in the process of liquidating and the income they report includes profits from sales. Others may be suddenly setting up reserves for future losses. However, from the annual report or the information in reports from Standard and Poor's, Moody's, or Value Line, you can strip out these extraordinary items and focus on the rental income, operating expenses, and thus the net operating income from the properties in the REIT's portfolio. By using the cap rate method described in chapter 15, you can evaluate the portfolio. For example, if the net operating income from a portfolio of properties held by an equity REIT is $15 million, a 10 percent cap rate would put the overall value of the holdings at $150 million ($15 million divided by 0.10). The next step would be to divide the overall value by the number of shares outstanding of the REIT. The result will be the value per share of the real estate held by the REIT. If there are 10 million shares outstanding, the value per share would be $15. See how this number compares to the market price of the shares. Over the years, I have seen established REITs trade at both substantial premiums and discounts for no apparent reason. The key is to find a solid equity REIT trading at a discount, one with a portfolio of well-located properties and adequate cash reserves for contingencies. This will take some scouting at first, but your effort will be rewarded well in the years ahead.

In recent years, another relatively liquid vehicle for real estate investment has been introduced. It is called a master limited partnership and, like a REIT, it is traded on a public exchange like a stock. Master partnerships actually are conglomerates formed by a syndicator, and made up of a number of smaller real estate limited partnerships.

Frequently, many of these component limited partnerships are in trouble, and are being linked to stronger components by a syndicator, hoping to cut his losses and make some money on up-front fees. As a result, the market is quite skeptical of newly formed master partnerships, and they trade at a substantial discount at first. Once the partnership has been trading for awhile, the dust will settle enough that it is possible to determine the value of the underlying portfolio. If an astute investor can determine this true value before the initial discount disappears, he frequently can find himself possessing a genuine bargain. To make this determination it is necessary to get an annual report or some other catalogue of the partnership's holdings that can be submitted to a cap rate analysis. This analysis will reveal whether the partnership is trading at a discount or a premium.

Both REITs and real estate master partnerships offer investors a way to invest in real estate while remaining quite liquid. What they trade off for this liquidity is control. The most traditional way of making profits is to actually take title to property. Fortunately, there exists at the moment several ways to purchase property and farmland at substantial discounts.

Crashing real estate supercycles have forced thousands of banks and savings and loans to foreclose on apartment properties and office buildings across the country. These lending institutions, saddled with a great deal more real estate than they had ever hoped to own, are in big trouble if more than 2 percent of their assets are tied up in foreclosed real estate. This real estate, which banking circles call "real estate owned" or REO, is not only a financial drain and a source of problems for the industry's governmental regulators but it is a giant headache, because banks and savings and loans are not set up to manage property. With no management skills or supervisory expertise on staff to run these properties, cash flow diminishes, deferred maintenance builds up, and the drain on the lender gets worse.

In the last few years the financial drain on the nations thrift institutions caused by REOs became so severe that savings and loans began failing en masse. The resources of Federal Savings and Loan Insurance Corporation (FSLIC), which insures depositors, became strained. As savings and loans failed, their REOs were dumped in the lap of FSLIC.

Late in 1985, FSLIC set up a subsidiary of its own, called the Federal Asset Disposition Association (FADA), for the express purpose of disposing of all of the REOs from bankrupt savings and loans. FADA now has offices in major cities across the country, and each of these offices is looking for investors to buy the local real estate it is being forced to sell.

FADA is a motivated seller, and so is any bank or savings and loan with 2 percent or more of its assets in REOs. (The percentage of REOs is revealed on a lending institution's "statement of condition" or its balance sheet that can be found in its annual report. Look for the line that reads "real estate owned.") However, like any motivated seller FADA is not going to tell you it is desperate to sell its real estate. It is going to try to sell at top dollar. So don't walk into your local savings and loan, bank, or FADA office and say you have arrived to buy real estate for 75 cents on the dollar with nothing down. This is precisely what you are trying to do, but humiliating the lending officer is not the best first step.

Instead, conduct yourself as a real estate professional even if your experience is limited. Describe the kind of real estate you are looking for and ask if there is any such real estate for sale. Follow up your inquiry with a letter with some references or your qualifications if possible. FADA will be more willing to sell you its real estate at your price and terms if it thinks you know how to manage the property. Don't forget this real estate was obtained through foreclosure and the last thing wanted is another flaky buyer. FADA may send you a "buyer profile questionnaire" asking for your experience record and your areas of interest.

No matter who you're dealing with—your local bank, savings and loan, or FADA—you can be confident that the institution is eager to make a deal. It also can lend you money to purchase the property, frequently at below-market interest rates, and as an added bonus it can be made possible for you to avoid the brokerage commissions that are added to the cost of most real estate transactions.

These tactics also will work when it comes to buying farmland from local banks and savings and loans, and should be used when approaching the largest holders of foreclosed farmland: federal land banks. These banks are arms of the federally chartered Farm Credit System and recently have begun massive sales efforts to rid their balance sheets of foreclosed farmland. And to make it more affordable, these banks will lend you the money to buy their farmland at cut-rate interest rates below 5 percent.

Conclusions

The investment options listed do not constitute a comprehensive list of places where your money can flourish. You will not be interested in mastering the complexities of every market. It is important to remember that panic-proof investing does not require an intimate knowledge of every market that is competing for capital. It does require alertness, the sure understanding that prices in every market always are driven to extremes, and the courage to act prudently in the face of strong emotional winds.

Many of the readers of this book will pick an investment opportunity because they have direct knowledge and experience of a market, or because they have a friend or acquaintance who can guide them into familiarity with an investment path. That's good, but it does not obviate the requirement for you to keep your own counsel. As I've demonstrated in this book, experts often are seduced by the market in which they have dedicated their energies. All experts are human. They want the good times to go on forever. And almost always they are disappointed at some point.

Although we have been examining these investment options one at a time, I should stress that it is always good to have your eggs in more than one basket. Supercycles are perverse, and it is always a good idea to limit your exposure to any one of them.

Finally, it must be acknowledged that panic-proof investing is not for the lazy. The strategies and tactics we have discussed in this book are only the beginning. To make them profitable will require some effort. You must continue to update the market indicators I've presented here, and when the time to move into new investment markets arrives, it will be necessary to make some phone calls and do further reading and thinking. But as you do that work remember that you are working at a distinct advantage: You will be doing your work ahead of the crowd. If you choose carefully and thoughtfully, the decline of supercycle five may well represent your doorway to financial independence.

A Final Note

While I have tried to update the figures in this book as much as possible, the lead time required for publishing a book even with the best and most responsive publisher makes it difficult to give specific and timely advice. Investment conditions can and often do change rapidly. For this reason I publish an investment advisory letter that regularly updates all of the investment indicators presented in this book, and gives timely advice on stocks, bonds, precious metals, and real estate, as well as on the condition of the economy. If you would like information about it, please send your name and address to Sound Advice, P.O. Box 23, Rheem Valley Branch, Moraga, CA 94570. Your questions and comments about this book may be sent to the same address.

Appendix A Updating the Stock Market Risk Indicator

This indicator uses the monthly average of the S&P 500 Stock Index to measure stocks that can be obtained from a publication called *Business Conditions Digest,* published by the Commerce Department. This publication also contains the data you will need to update the diffusion indexes (chapter 6 and appendix B). The current subscription rate is $44 per year and it can be obtained through the Government Printing Office order desk in Washington, DC (202-783-3238). I also update this indicator regularly in my advisory letter (see page 215).

To measure house prices, the national monthly median new house price is used, which is available from another Commerce Department publication called *New One-Family Houses Sold and for Sale.* The subscription rate is $20 per year and you can order it through the Government Printing Office. You will find that the most current house prices available will be for two months earlier, so this risk indicator uses the prices of two months earlier for the current month.

To update this index, the first step is to adjust house

prices so that they are in the same order of magnitude as the S&P 500 Stock Index. This is accomplished by dividing the monthly median new house price by 1,000. This makes the indicator oscillate between 1.0 and 2.0, rather than between 0.001 and 0.002. This step simply produces more convenient numbers.

At this point the formula, which we will refer to as formula 1, looks like this:

$$\frac{\text{S\&P 500 Index}}{(\text{house price}/1{,}000)}$$

Plugging in the stock index values and house prices for each month since 1895 into formula 1, and plotting these results, produces a risk indicator that looks the same as the one shown on chart 4.2, except that it slopes upward. This is because stock prices are in the numerator, and they have risen slightly faster than house prices. This can be corrected by calculating the slope and adjusting each month's results accordingly. The slope is 0.04 percent per month. Mathematically, this slope can be removed by dividing each month's result by 1.0004. Simply following this procedure will reproduce the risk indicator you see in chart 4.2. For updating purposes, however, you need a formula that incorporates this adjustment automatically.

Instead of dividing formula 1 by 1.0004 for each month that has passed since 1895, you first can plug today's values into formula 1. Second, multiply 1.0004 times itself as many times as there are months since 1895, and then divide formula 1 by the result. But you should realize that an easy way of multiplying a quantity times itself a number of times is to simply raise it by an exponent equal to that number. For example, ten squared is the same thing as ten times ten; ten cubed is the same thing as ten times ten times ten; ten to the fourth is ten times ten times ten times ten, and so forth. Thus an equation that multiplies 1.0004 times itself *N* times is as follows:

$$1.0004^N$$

To update our risk indicator, *N* equals the number of months that have passed since 1895. So our full risk indicator formula is:

$$\left[\frac{\text{S\&P 500 Index}}{(\text{House price}/1{,}000)}\right] \div \left[1.0004^{N}\right]$$

To make updating easier, N could be expressed as follows:

$$N = [Y + (M/12) - 1895] \times 12$$

where Y is the current year and M is the current month expressed as a number (i.e., January = 1, February = 2, etc.). The equation for simply dropping in values then is as follows:

$$\left[\frac{\text{S\&P 500 Index}}{(\text{House price}/1{,}000)}\right] \div \left[1.0004^{[Y + (M/12) - 1895] \times 12}\right]$$

For example, if in June 1988 the S&P 500 Stock Index is 275 and the median new house is $100,000 in April 1988, the stock market risk indicator will read 1.63. The calculation will be as follows:

$$\left[\frac{275}{(100{,}000/1{,}000)}\right] \div \left[1.0004^{[1987 + (6/12) - 1895] \times 12}\right] =$$

$$2.75 \div [1.0004^{(1{,}122)}] = 1.63$$

march 1992, Home = $105,000 (IBD 6-11-92)

May S+P = 414.30 ~~median~~ Avg.

$N = (1992 + 5/12 - 1895) \times 12 = 1169$

$$\frac{414.30/105}{1.596} = 2.47$$

Appendix B Business Cycle Indicators

Treasury Bond–Discount Rate Spread Index

The Federal Reserve Bank of St. Louis puts out a weekly publication called *U.S. Financial Data* that tracks various interest rates as well as money supply figures. It is free if you write to P.O. Box 442, St. Louis, MO 63166. This index, as well as the diffusion indexes, also are updated regularly in my advisory letter.

Diffusion Indexes

To update these indexes yourself, you will need to subscribe to *Business Conditions Digest.* The current subscription rate is $44 per year and it can be obtained through the Government Printing Office order desk in Washington, DC (202-783-3238).

Updating the Diffusion Index of Leading Indicators

The eight leading economic indicators used in this index are updated each month in *Business Conditions Digest.* Their names and series numbers are as follows:

Series 1. Average weekly hours of production for nonsupervisory workers in manufacturing (hours)

Series 8. Manufacturers' new orders in 1982 dollars, consumer goods, and materials
Series 12. Index of net business formation
Series 19. Index of stock prices, 500 common stocks
Series 29. Index of new private housing units authorized by local building permits (1967 = 100)
Series 32. Vendor performance, companies receiving slower deliveries
Series 36. Change in manufacturing and trade inventories on hand and on order in 1982 dollars (smoothed)
Series 111. Change in business and consumer credit outstanding

To update this index you will need to write down or input into your computer the readings on these eight indicators for the current month as well as the levels recorded six months earlier. Compare each indicator with the reading of six months earlier. Assign a value of 1.0 for each indicator that is higher, a value of 0.5 for each indicator that is unchanged, and a value of zero for each indicator that is lower, and then add up these numbers. Divide the sum by 8, and multiply by 100. The result is the level of the diffusion index of leading indicators for the latest month for which you have data. For example, if five of the above leading economic indicators are higher than their levels of six months earlier, one is unchanged, and two are lower, your total will be 5.5. This sum divided by 8 and multiplied by 100 will yield a level in the diffusion index of leading indicators of 68.75 percent.

Updating the Diffusion Index of Lagging Indicators

The six lagging economic indicators used in this index are updated each month in *Business Conditions Digest.* Their series numbers and descriptions are as follows:

Series 62. Index of labor cost per unit of manufacturing output (actual data)
Series 77. Ratio of manufacturing and trade inventories to sales in 1982 dollars
Series 91. Average duration of unemployment (weeks)
Series 95. Ratio of consumer installment credit outstanding to personal income
Series 101. Commercial and industrial loans outstanding (constant 1982 dollars)
Series 109. Average prime rate charged by banks

The process is the same for updating this index except that the average duration of unemployment (series 91) is an inverse indicator. Because it measures unemployment rather than employment, a higher reading indicates economic weakness rather that strength. Thus, give yourself 1.0 when this indicator is *lower* than it was six months earlier, and a zero when it is *higher.* Score the rest of the indicators in the same fashion as you do with the diffusion index of leading indicators explained above. Divide the sum by 6 and multiply by 100. For example, suppose that series 91 is lower than six months ago (give yourself one point), two of the other indicators are higher (add another two points), one is unchanged (add one-half point), and the remaining two indicators are lower (add nothing). Your total would be 3.5. When this sum is divided by 6 and multiplied by 100, it yields a reading of 58.33 percent for the diffusion index of lagging indicators.

Appendix C Requirements for Spreads and Uncovered Options

Spreads

For spreads that have a defined loss potential, brokerage firms will only require you to deposit the most you can lose, subject to a $250 minimum per spread. For example, the put bear spread shown in table 9.1 involved the purchase of one OEX 285 put at $1,050 and the sale of one OEX put at $850. The most that could be lost on this spread is the difference between the option prices, or $200. However, this requirement is less than the $250 minimum so you would be required to deposit $250 for one spread. If two spreads were purchased the requirement would be $400 and $200 for each additional spread. Regardless of what happens to the price of the options during the term, no additional requirements will be imposed.

Commission costs are ignored in the above example, but they can be significant. The purchase price of the OEX 285 put would be increased by a brokerage commission while the sales proceeds from the OEX 280 put would be reduced by a brokerage commission. Thus, the requirements for the spread are raised by both commissions. You mostly will find that because brokerage firms have a fixed minimum commission of $25 or $30, commission costs per spread decline sharply from one to two spreads, and moderately with each additional spread. I recommend thinking in terms of at least two spreads.

The requirement can be deposited in cash or by check with your broker. Options settle in one day so the due date will be the day after the trade date. In most instances, the brokerage firm will require that the requirement be in your account before a spread is purchased.

The requirement can be borrowed as long as you have equity in your account. Margin requirements change every now and then, but currently the margin requirement for stocks is 50 percent. That means that you can borrow up to half of the value of the stocks in your brokerage account. You also can borrow against bonds and as much as 95 percent currently can be borrowed against Treasury bills or bonds. The interest rate floats with the general level of interest rates and your broker will quote you the current rate.

Uncovered Options

Uncovered options have no defined loss potential, so the margin requirements are more complicated. First, let's look at an example of one uncovered call.

Suppose that you sold a call option with a strike price of 50 when the underlying stock was 48. The basic requirement is 30 percent of the price of 100 shares of the underlying stock, or \$1,440 (\$4,800 × 0.3). This basic requirement of \$1,440 is reduced by the amount that the stock is below the strike price (out of the money) which in this example is \$200. Thus, the initial requirement is \$1,240.

It is important to note that a minimum requirement must be maintained (called a maintenance requirement) which will change with the price of the underlying stock. For example, if the stock were to increase two points in value, it would no longer be out of the money and the \$200 reduction would not be allowed. The maintenance requirement would be 30 percent of \$5,000, or \$1,500. For each point the stock increases above the strike price (50), another \$100 would be required in addition to 30 percent of the current price of the stock. For example, a rise to 53 would raise the margin requirement to \$1,890 [(\$5,300 × 0.3) + \$300].

The cash that you receive for selling the call can be

used toward the initial margin and maintenance requirements. The equity in your account from other securities also can be used and there are no interest charges. To acquaint you with the mechanics and the jargon, let's take our example a step further. Suppose you had $10,000 of stocks in a margin account. The brokerage firm's computers would create a "special miscellaneous account" and credit that account with one-half of your stock equity, or $5,000. This $5,000 is referred to as SMA (the initials for "special miscellaneous account"). This $5,000 is treated like cash, and you can use it toward your initial margin requirements for writing uncovered options and for maintenance requirements. As long as you have sufficient SMA in your account, you don't need to deposit any money to write uncovered options.

Only when the underlying stock rockets does it become necessary to deposit any money or additional securities while writing two options against 100 shares of stock. One of the options will be considered "covered" by the 100 shares of stock, and the other will be considered "uncovered." If the market value of 100 shares of stock is $4,800, our SMA will be $2,400. Let's say we wrote two calls with a strike price of $50 for $400 apiece. This $800 in cash will add to our SMA dollar for dollar, bringing our SMA to $3,200. The requirement on the uncovered call will be $1,240 as we determined above. Because our SMA exceeds the requirement, there is no need to deposit additional money or securities. As the stock moves up, our account gains equity and our SMA account increases accordingly. With the stock at 50, the requirement on the uncovered call has increased to $1,500 but our SMA has risen by half of the increase in equity to $3,300.

As the stock rises above $50 a share, the value of the stock will be frozen at $5,000 because of the covered option against it, so our SMA will remain at $3,300 regardless of how high the stock goes. The requirements of the uncovered call will continue to increase, however. If the stock continues to rise, at some point our SMA will not exceed the requirement and the brokerage firm will issue a "maintenance call" for more money or securities. That will happen when the stock has advanced 14 points to $64 a share. At that point the requirements on the uncovered call will be $3,320 [($6,400 × 0.3) + $1,400], which exceeds the SMA by $20, so a maintenance call will be issued for $20. If the stock keeps going up, the maintenance call will increase by $130 each time the stock rises one point.

In this example it took a 28 percent increase in the underlying stock to generate a maintenance call. While this is an extraordinary rise in the space of a few months, moves like this happen every now and then, particularly if take-over rumors start. This is why it is important to apply this strategy to a diversified portfolio of stocks. The chance of generating maintenance calls are reduced greatly and the economic rewards are infinitely more reliable.

Appendix D Worksheet for Put Bear Spreads

WORKSHEET FOR PUT BEAR SPREADS

(FOR ONE SPREAD ON 100 SHARES)

(A) Price of put option purchased	$_______	(A)
(B) Price of put option sold	$_______	(B)
(C) Risk: (A) minus (B) equals	$_______	(C)
(D) Strike price of option purchased	$_______	(D)
(E) Strike price of option sold	$_______	(E)
(F) Break-even point: Divide (C) by 100 and subtract the result from (D)	$_______	(F)
(G) Price of underlying index or stock	$_______	(G)
(H) Move needed to break even: Subtract (G) from (F), divide by (G), and multiply the result by 100	%_______	(H)
(I) Maximum profit: Subtract (E) from (D), multiply the result times 100, and subtract (C)	$_______	(I)
(J) Profit-to-risk ratio: (I) divided by (C)	_______	(J)

Appendix E Updating the Affordability Index

Creation and Updating

The data on home prices, mortgage interest rates, and family incomes can be obtained monthly. There also are a couple of newsletters that compile this information in an affordability index. One is compiled each month by the National Association of Realtors (717 Fourteenth Street, N.W., Washington, DC 20005, 202-383-1063) and published in their publication called *Home Sales.* The annual subscription price is $44 for members and $60 for nonmembers. I also update a housing affordability index regularly in my advisory letter. If you would like to compile one yourself, here is how you do it.

Monthly mortgage interest rates are available from the Federal Home Loan Bank Board, and published in the bank's monthly news releases (1700 G Street, N.W., Washington, D.C. 20552, 202-377-6923). Monthly median family income figures are available form the National Association of Realtors (address above) or the U.S. Census Bureau.

Monthly home prices should be based on median prices for existing homes because this is the broadest possible measure. The National Association of Realtors carries these figures for the nation as well as for the Northeast, Midwest, South, and West.

The first step is to obtain the income necessary to qualify to buy the median-price home. The criteria are established by the Federal National Mortgage Association, which requires a 20 percent down payment and that a family's annual income be at least four times the annual mortgage payments. First multiply the median home price by 80 percent to determine the amount of the mortgage. Next look up the mortgage payments in a mortgage amortization table book based on the interest rate for that month obtained from the Federal Home Loan Bank. Then multiply the monthly payment amount by 12 to get the annual figure, and then by 4 to get the qualification income.

The affordability index is the ratio of the median family income to the qualification income. Thus the last step is to divide the median family income by the qualification income you determined in the preceding paragraph. A result of 1.0 or more means that houses are affordable, and a reading below 1.0 means that they are not.

Appendix F Financial Planning Organizer

STOCKS

Long Market Values

Stocks owned in your personal portfolio ______________ (1)

Stock mutual funds you own ______________ (2)

Market value of call options you own ______________ (3)

Market value of put options you wrote ______________ (4)

Stocks in your IRA ______________ (5)

Stocks in your Keogh plan ______________ (6)

Your vested interest in the stocks of your employer's pension plan ______________ (7)

Total long market value (Add lines 1–7) ______________ (8)

Short Market Value

Market value of stocks sold short ______________ (9)

Market value of mutual funds sold short ______________ (10)

Market value of put options you own	______	(11)
Market value of call options you wrote	______	(12)
Total short market value (Add lines 9–12)	______	(13)
Net market value (Line 8 minus line 13)	______	(A)
Stock Market Liabilities		
Margin debit balance*	______	(14)
Personal loans to carry stocks	______	(15)
Total stock market liabilities (Add lines 14 and 15)	______	(16)
Stock market equity (Line A minus line 16)	______	(B)

BONDS AND OTHER DEBT INSTRUMENTS

Government bonds	______	(17)
Corporate bonds	______	(18)
Municipal bonds	______	(19)
Mortgages owned	______	(20)
Other long-term fixed income investments	______	(21)
Total debt instruments (Add lines 17–21)	______	(C)
Debts outstanding to carry these investments	______	(22)
Equity in debt instruments (Line C minus line 22)	______	(D)

PRECIOUS METALS

Current market values of the precious metals you own:

Gold	______	(23)
Silver	______	(24)
Platinum	______	(25)
Palladium	______	(26)
Other	______	(27)
Net market value of mining stocks	______	(28)

*This will be a negative number if you have a credit balance

Total market value in precious metals (Add lines 15–20) ____________ (E)

Debts outstanding to carry these assets ____________ (29)

Equity in precious metals (Line E minus line 29) ____________ (F)

REAL ESTATE

Market value of personal residence ____________ (G)

Mortgage balances ____________ (30)

Equity in personal residence (Line G minus line 30) ____________ (H)

Market value of investment properties ____________ (I)

Outstanding mortgages ____________ (31)

Equity in investment properties (Line I minus line 31) ____________ (J)

OTHER ASSETS

Cash in checking and savings accounts ____________ (32)

Certificates of deposit ____________ (33)

Treasury bills ____________ (34)

Savings bonds ____________ (35)

Insurance policy cash values ____________ (36)

Other liquid assets ____________ (37)

Accounts receivable ____________ (38)

Market value of a business ____________ (39)

Automobiles ____________ (40)

Furniture ____________ (41)

Other personal property ____________ (42)

Other assets ____________ (43)

Total other assets (Add lines 32–43) ____________ (K)

Charge card debt ____________ (44)

Auto loans ____________ (45)

Installment loans ____________ (46)

Other debts	________	(47)
Total debts (Add lines 43–47)	________	(48)
Net assets (Line K minus line 48)	________	(L)

SUMMARY

	Asset Value	*Equity*	*Percent of Net Worth*	*Leverage Factor*
Stocks	____ (A)	____ (B)	____% 100 × (B)/(N)	____ (A)/(B)
Bonds	____ (C)	____ (D)	____% 100 × (D)/(N)	____ (C)/(D)
Precious Metals	____ (E)	____ (F)	____% 100 × (F)/(N)	____ (E)/(F)
Home	____ (G)	____ (H)	____% 100 × (H)/(N)	____ (G)/(H)
Investment Real Estate	____ (I)	____ (J)	____% 100 × (J)/(N)	____ (I)/(J)
Other Assets	____ (K)	____ (L)	____% 100 × (L)/(N)	____ (K)/(L)
Totals	____ (M)	____ (N)	____%	____ (M)/(N)

Chapter Notes

Chapter 2

1. Robert Sobel, *The Big Board* (New York: Free Press, 1965). A great deal of the background information for this chapter was obtained from this source.
2. Sobel, p. 157.
3. Sobel, p. 159.
4. Quoted in John Kenneth Galbraith, *The Great Crash* (Boston: Houghton Mifflin, 1954).
5. Sobel, p. 274.
6. Sobel, p. 276.
7. Galbraith.
8. Information is from *Business Week* (February 2, 1987) and Lawrence H. Summers, the Federal Reserve Board.

Chapter 11

1. Robert Sobel, *The Big Board* (New York: Free Press, 1965).
2. Sobel, p. 74.
3. Sobel, p. 75.
4. Robert Irving Warshow, *The Story of Wall Street* (New York: Greenberg, 1929).
5. Roy W. Jastrom, *The Golden Constant—The English and*

American Experience (New York: John Wiley and Sons, 1977).

Chapter 13

1. Robert C. Reese, Jr., "Silver," in *Mineral Facts and Problems* (Bureau of Mines, U.S. Department of the Interior, 1985). The background information on silver was obtained from this source.
2. J. Roger Loebenstien, Jr., "Platinum Group Metals," in *Mineral Facts and Problems* (Bureau of Mines, U.S. Department of the Interior, 1985). The background information on platinum and palladium was obtained from this source.

Chapter 14

1. A good deal of background information for this chapter was taken from my first book: *The Coming Real Estate Crash,* by Gray Emerson Cardiff and John Wesley English (New Rochelle: Arlington House Publishers, 1979).
2. Charles Clever, *Early Chicago Reminiscences* (Chicago: Fergus Printing Company, 1882).
3. Theodore S. Van Dyke, *Millionaires of a Day* (Fords, Howard, Hulbert, 1890).
4. Walton Bean, *California—An Interpretive History* (New York: McGraw-Hill Book Company, 1968).
5. Van Dyke.

Chapter 16

1. Dr. David Birch, *America's Office Needs: 1985–1995,* Massachusetts Institute of Technology Center for Real Estate Development (Chicago: Arthur Anderson & Company, 1986). This study provided a lot of the background information for this chapter.

Chapter 18

1. William Apgar, Jr., H. James Brown, George Masnic, and John Pitkin, *The Housing Outlook 1980–1990* (New York: Praeger Publishers, 1985).

Index

V

W

X

Y